The Death Penalty

Recent Titles in the

CONTEMPORARY WORLD ISSUES
Series

Books in the **Contemporary World Issues** series address vital issues in today's society such as genetic engineering, pollution, and biodiversity. Written by professional writers, scholars, and nonacademic experts, these books are authoritative, clearly written, up-to-date, and objective. They provide a good starting point for research by high school and college students, scholars, and general readers as well as by legislators, businesspeople, activists, and others.

Each book, carefully organized and easy to use, contains an overview of the subject, a detailed chronology, biographical sketches, facts and data and/or documents and other primary source material, a forum of authoritative perspective essays, annotated lists of print and nonprint resources, and an index.

Readers of books in the Contemporary World Issues series will find the information they need in order to have a better understanding of the social, political, environmental, and economic issues facing the world today.

The Death Penalty

A REFERENCE HANDBOOK

Joseph A. Melusky and Keith A. Pesto

 ABC-CLIO™

An Imprint of ABC-CLIO, LLC

Santa Barbara, California • Denver, Colorado

Library of Congress Cataloging-in-Publication Data

Names: Melusky, Joseph Anthony, author. | Pesto, Keith A., author.
Title: The death penalty : a reference handbook / Joseph A. Melusky and Keith A. Pesto.
Description: Santa Barbara, California : ABC-CLIO, [2017] | Series: Contemporary world issues | Includes bibliographical references and index.
Identifiers: LCCN 2017007384 (print) | LCCN 2017019942 (ebook) | ISBN 9781440845505 (ebook) | ISBN 9781440845499 (alk. paper)
Subjects: LCSH: Capital punishment—United States.
Classification: LCC HV8699.U5 (ebook) | LCC HV8699.U5 M46 2017 (print) | DDC 364.660973—dc23
LC record available at https://lccn.loc.gov/2017007384

ISBN: 978-1-4408-4549-9
EISBN: 978-1-4408-4550-5

21 20 19 18 17   1 2 3 4 5

This book is also available as an eBook.

ABC-CLIO
An Imprint of ABC-CLIO, LLC

ABC-CLIO, LLC
130 Cremona Drive, P.O. Box 1911
Santa Barbara, California 93116–1911
www.abc-clio.com

This book is printed on acid-free paper ∞

Manufactured in the United States of America

To my wife, Marie,
To my children, Mike and Jessica, to my daughter-in-law,
Elizabeth, and to the memory of my dad, George, my
mom, Eleanor, and my mother-in-law, Edith.

—J.A.M.

To the memory of my father, George J. Pesto

—K.A.P.

The use of capital punishment in the United States has long been a source of debate. Many argue that it is a necessary means of carrying out justice and deterring crime, while others argue that it is inhumane. Beyond whether or not we should use capital punishment are questions of *how* we use it. Can we ensure that it is carried out fairly—that only the truly guilty receive the death penalty? What crimes should be eligible for the death penalty? Should juveniles or those with diminished mental capacities be eligible for the death penalty? Which methods of carrying out a death sentence are most humane? How do race and gender affect the death penalty? Does capital punishment really deter crime? If not, is the death penalty justifiable on other grounds? Is life without the possibility of parole a viable alternative to the death penalty? What about the substantial costs associated with death sentences? What about wrongful convictions and the exonerations of numerous death row inhabitants?

The Death Penalty: A Reference Handbook discusses essential questions about the death penalty in the United States and connected issues. The book does not take a side, either "for" or "against" capital punishment. It attempts to provide a balanced, objective discussion of arguments, issues, and controversies. The book is designed to be accessible to high school students, undergraduate students, general readers, and individuals interested in capital punishment, the criminal justice system, and human rights. Does capital punishment deter? Do methods of execution matter? Are executions ever botched? Are innocent people ever really sent to death row? Are there racial biases associated with the death penalty? If you are interested in these kinds of questions, this book is for you.

The book begins with a chapter that examines the background and history of capital punishment, including political and social contexts and key events. In addition, it looks at the "purpose" of the death penalty and how it has been carried out.

The next chapter examines key issues and events that have been both troubling and significant. Controversies like those described above are considered, including methods of execution and the availability of drugs traditionally used when a death sentence is carried out through lethal injection.

The next chapter provides essays written by guest contributors who offer varying viewpoints on the issues at hand. Their voices represent different perspectives on matters of vital importance. The contributors—judges, attorneys, professors, and a governor—draw upon their own experiences and individual vantage points.

A "Profiles" chapter includes descriptions of key ideas, individuals, and organizations in the debate over capital punishment.

The "Data and Documents" chapter analyzes data related to capital punishment. The data describe the number of executions carried out, race of defendants and victims, death penalty and non–death penalty states, death row exonerations of innocent inmates, executions by region, methods used, and more. The chapter also includes, among other things, excerpts from documents like the U.S. Constitution, the Code of Hammurabi, the Roman law of the Twelve Tables, and excerpts from some Supreme Court opinions.

The book also includes a "Resources" chapter that provides an extensive annotated bibliography of relevant print and electronic resources, a "Chronology" chapter that describes key moments in the history of capital punishment in the United States, and a "Glossary" that provides definitions of some key terms.

Acknowledgments

Thanks to all the people at ABC-CLIO/Greenwood who worked to make this project a success. We want to thank Nita Lang, assistant managing editor, and Robin Tutt, development editor, for working so closely with us. We appreciate your guidance, support, encouragement, and—especially—your patience! Thank you for the extensions on our deadlines. Thanks to Erin Ryan, senior coordinator, editorial operations for your help with photo research and Leah Georgina, project manager, for bringing this work across the finish line. We extend our appreciation to those who contributed essays for this project, including former governor Tom Corbett (Pennsylvania), Richard C. Dieter (executive director of the Death Penalty Information Center), retired Judge Rudolph J. Gerber (Arizona Court of Appeals), and professors Kim MacInnis (Bridgewater State University), Brett R. Metzler (University of Central Florida), John Rago (Duquesne University School of Law), and Elizabeth Rapaport (University of New Mexico School of Law). Thanks also to Renee Hoffman, reference librarian at Saint Francis University. Thanks to Anna Baughman (Saint Francis University, Class of 2019) for her proofreading help. We are also grateful to Jessica Melusky (Saint Joseph's University, Class of 2018) for her very able research assistance.

The Death Penalty

Introduction

Benjamin Franklin once jested that the only two certainties are death and taxes. And yet at this point in American history, death in the form of the carrying out of a sentence of capital punishment has become as uncertain and as complicated as the launching of a satellite into orbit. The parallels are numerous: both involve hushed countdowns and media attention; both require massive commitment of personnel and money that opponents contend should be spent elsewhere; both can be canceled for a seemingly endless list of reasons by persons far from the event itself; and after the fact, both can only be debated, not retrieved.

The purpose of this book is to help the reader to understand capital punishment—the imposition of the death penalty for crime—in the United States. This requires knowledge of the history of the death penalty before the origin of the country and also short courses in political science, constitutional law, public opinion polling, statistics, and medical technology.

The Death Penalty before It Was Capital Punishment

Before we can talk intelligently about capital punishment, we have to give a meaningful definition to the term, and we need

British military officer, Major John Andre, is hanged after being convicted of being a spy during the American Revolution. Andre was caught holding the plans to West Point after meeting with American traitor, General Benedict Arnold. (National Archives)

to answer some foundational questions, namely: (1) what are the purposes of a system of punishment for crime? and (2) in what order of importance do we rank those purposes?

In this book, we consider capital punishment to be the infliction of death after fair proceedings by the accepted legal authorities as a proportionate punishment for serious crime as those crimes have been defined since about the founding of the United States. Our definition has so many conditions because for most of history, the infliction of death can hardly be considered part of a system of punishment at all. Traditionally, the primary purpose of inflicting the death penalty was very blunt: to maintain order. Whether we go back almost 4,000 years to the Code of Hammurabi, 3,000 years to the crimes code in the biblical book of Exodus, or 1,500 years to the laws of the Germanic tribes that overran the Western Roman Empire, law in a primitive society treated crime chiefly as a danger to public peace. Today we first think of crime as a personal offense against the victim, and next as a violation of an abstract concept of justice, but in a world where most of the population was engaged in growing enough food to avoid starvation, the individual had little importance except as a member of a family, clan, tribe, or city, and anyone outside these circles of kinship was potentially a threat. Before society could afford courts, lawyers, or police forces, justice was a family affair, and the chief ill that early law was aimed at remedying was the chaos caused by successive rounds of reprisals and vendettas between families of a victim and of a criminal. That the use of public law to control private vengeance persists throughout history, consider not only the medieval Montagues and Capulets in Shakespeare's *Romeo and Juliet*, but also the extension of Congress's criminal jurisdiction to Indian territory in 1885 specifically to quell a cycle of revenge killings within the Dakota Territory over control of a Sioux tribe (Smith 2004, 496–497).

Any system of punishment potentially can serve four goals: stopping the wrongdoer (incapacitation or interdiction), stopping other would-be offenders (deterrence), bringing the offender back into society (rehabilitation), and meeting society's sense of what is just (retribution). In classical society, the community was viewed almost as a single living body, and the death penalty was the drastic but necessary cutting out of a diseased part. Because death was inflicted to preserve order, there was little thought of any goal other than interdiction, and it was not a relevant question whether a particular crime deserved death or whether the punishment would deter other crimes. As in Draco's Code for Athens, every crime threatened public order, so every crime could be punished by death.

A simple goal of maintaining order in a close-knit society where there is little separation between public and private life requires only a simple procedural system. In the Greek city–states, for instance, trials were more oratorical contests than examinations of evidence. The penalties in such a system can be simple too, and there does not even have to be much separation between criminal justice and what we would consider tort law. Surviving records of primitive criminal legislation from second millennium Sumeria to Anglo-Saxon England read like compensation schedules. Even though offenses against the gods, the king, or the person and property of a member of the upper class would usually result in death, sometimes a murderer or rapist could satisfy all the demands of the law by paying money, money that society expected the victim's family to take in full satisfaction of the crime. The Germanic tribes even had a specific word, "weregild," for the financial compensation to the victim's family. That is not because former ages prized money so highly; it is because the individual, apart from family and tribe, was regarded so little.

Criminal trials could be dispensed with because, until modern times, society did not even need to link who paid for the crime and who was guilty. In Anglo-Saxon England, for instance, in cases of murder (and the term "murder" especially meant a killing done in secret) where the guilty party could not be found, the financial burden was placed on his presumed kin by fining the village. From the Bronze Age through the

Middle Ages, it was considered proper to order the execution of a substitute member of the offending clan, as in the execution of grandsons of King Saul of Israel (2 Samuel 21:1–10) to make peace with a rebellious tribe for Saul's offenses. The giving of hostages to secure good conduct in war and peace and the execution of hostages in response for someone else's crimes were acceptable practices throughout Europe, at least through the Hundred Years' War (1337–1453).

That the chief goal of punishment was to prevent society from descending into chaos, and the elimination of a person perceived as a threat to public order, the desired end whether that person was innocent or guilty, explains why banishment—something we think of today as only a forced relocation—was often prescribed as the alternative penalty to death. To be "outlawed" and therefore expelled from the protection of kin and clan was often tantamount to a death sentence to the exiled, but from the vantage point of the punisher, the death or survival of the individual was immaterial to the goal of interdiction.

Moving into the Christian era, there was an increased appreciation for the individual, including both the criminal and would-be criminal, and punishment as a deterrent to others moved to the front rank. This explains the classical and medieval use of bloody and torturous methods of executions, especially for religious dissent and other matters that we deem purely private opinions today. In eras where the sovereign had a quasi-religious role, or even when religious homogeneity was seen as vital to public safety, the spread of a heretical religious view was a greater danger than a random killing. This was slow to fade away; in some of the American colonies, heresy was still a capital crime until the 1700s.

As the feudal era drew to a close and the nation–states emerged in Europe, monarchs saw opposition to their reign or their dynasty as great a threat as heresy. Executions for treason were ordered for what we would consider political disagreements. When you read about gruesome forms of execution, remember that their invention was often specifically for treason, and their cruelty was intended not merely to dispatch the traitor but to appall and cow any potential followers. From the colonial era to today, anyone who suggested that political dissidents be tortured to death would be universally condemned, but that is primarily due to our change of views about political dissent and torture and not to changes in our views about the death penalty itself. When in 1800, President John Adams pardoned John Fries from being hanged for treason after a minor rebellion in Pennsylvania against the collection of federal taxes, that was a statement of confidence that the United States was in no danger, not a statement about capital punishment.

As societies became less preoccupied with the threat of chaos, the focus of thought came to be more about the individual. The "deservingness" of the individual became a focus of crime and punishment, and by the Middle Ages, retribution began to be considered an important goal. There is no doubt that this was influenced by the spread of Christianity in Europe: God was a judge who passed an eternal sentence on the soul, and this consciously and unconsciously influenced thinking about earthly punishments as well. Both the sinner and the criminal "got what he deserved" or "brought the punishment upon himself." Additionally, during the Renaissance, the image of the world as a living organism was replaced by the image of the world as a machine: punishments rebalanced the smooth running of society that crime had disrupted. This idea of balance suggested that punishments need not always be mortal, and meant that increasingly sophisticated justice systems should ask what particular punishment was due to the accused. This also implied increasing concern for the procedure used to try the accused.

The story of due process is as long and winding as the story of scientific discovery, but it is important to note that concern for fair procedures in inflicting death preceded (sometimes by centuries) actual concern for reducing the use of the death penalty in all societies. The biblical book of Daniel contains an account of trial with defense counsel, cross-examination, and the sequestration of witnesses. The Roman Republic (and later the Empire) had a relatively sophisticated process of trial, with evidence obtained by torture of witnesses who were not forthcoming with the evidence desired by the questioner and a right to appeal to the public assembly before any execution. Rhetorical flair, and whether your attorney had it, was also important in Rome: in a famous debate in the Senate in 63 BCE, Julius Caesar opposed the death penalty for suspected revolutionaries supporting Cataline. Caesar proposed that fines and life imprisonment would be adequate, but Cato the Younger argued that this would send the wrong message to other revolutionaries and endanger the public safety. The defendants were executed (Grant 1989, 127–128).

The barbarians who succeeded the Romans held the belief that supernatural means of proof were best, and for those cases when the criminal was not caught in the act, they used procedures such as requiring the accused to proclaim his innocence under oath, sometimes while holding a relic of a saint or touching the body of the victim of homicide. Trials by the ordeals of water, bread, or hot iron were also used on the Continent and in the British Isles. When Norman law followed the Normans to England after the Battle of Hastings in 1066, trial by battle was added to mix. All of these methods reversed what we think of as the natural order by requiring a trial before punishment: with these primitive methods, the trial often *was* the punishment. Even if people were not always sure that God guaranteed the outcome was correct, at least there was a speedy and final verdict.

But the Normans should be credited with bringing England the precursor of modern jury trials. At first, these inquests (or "recognitions" as they were called) were used solely for the issue of determining who had the better claim to land. In 1215, however, the Roman Catholic Church effectively abolished trial by ordeal throughout Western Europe by forbidding clergy to take part in it. The loss of this traditional method and the obvious unsuitability of most persons for trial by combat opened the way for expansion of jury trials into the realm of criminal law. Not every defendant wished to submit to trial by jury, and as late as the end of the 17th century, forcing the accused to enter a plea was a procedural step necessary for the court to hold a jury trial. The efforts used to obtain the consent of the defendant to jury trial, traditionally by pressing the accused between two wooden doors with ever-increasing weights piled on top, were not considered punishment but were often fatal. Other features of due process that we take for granted, like the ability of the accused to have counsel, to testify in his own defense, and the ability to call witnesses in his own defense, took centuries to become accepted. As Chapter 2 will show, unsettled questions of due process continue to influence capital punishment.

How Did This History Affect Capital Punishment in the United States?

At the foundation of American politics is the assertion that government draws its legitimacy from the consent of the governed. This is because the founding of the United States took place during the Enlightenment, the era after the divine right of kings was swept away by the English Civil War (1642–1649) and just before the age of reason was swept away by the French Revolution (1789). In science and in politics, it was an era of a few simple but powerful ideas: the theory of gravity explained the movement of the planets without crystal spheres or angels, and the theory that government was a social contract assumed the possibility of governmental reform with or without the consent of a monarch. Most educated adults in England and in the American colonies in 1776 would have agreed with the Declaration of Independence written to justify rebellion from King George III (and deliberately echoing John Locke's *Second Treatise of Government* [1690] written to justify Parliament's expulsion of King James II) that the consent of the people to a form of government must be judged from its effectiveness in fulfilling the three purposes of government: the protection of life, liberty, and property. The Preamble to the Constitution formally committed the United States to that relatively modest understanding.

The Constitution was written in 1787 as a procedural framework for working out the practical problems of governing that the Articles of Confederation had failed to solve since the end of the Revolutionary War. The original text contained just 4,223 words: its brevity was deliberate, and its lack of specificity is one of the reasons it endures as the oldest written constitution in the world. Even after the Bill of Rights added 10 amendments in 1791, everyone recognized that the Constitution did not give answers to some profound disagreements about the country's policies. Then, that meant disputes over proposed alliances with France or England and conflicts over the slave trade; today, it means divisions over the balance between civil liberties and national security and the dividing line between public initiatives and private responsibilities. Then and now, competing factions claim that their position is required by the Constitution because the Constitution is seen as the country's single unassailable authority.

So it is with the death penalty, as a once minor issue of crime and punishment has evolved into a wide-ranging debate about law and society. But for the first 100 years of U.S. history, that was not so. The lengthy history of death as a punishment for crime was not much on the framers' minds when they met in Philadelphia: retiring the debts incurred in the Revolutionary War and presenting a united front in international trade and foreign affairs preoccupied the framers. Article I, Section 8, gave Congress power to define and set the punishment for crimes such as counterfeiting and piracy, and Article III, Section 2, Clause 3, provided a remedy for the grievance against King George III listed in the Declaration of Independence of transporting criminal defendants "beyond Seas" (to admiralty courts in the West Indies or London, thereby depriving accused smugglers of trial before sympathetic local juries) by requiring the federal government to hold trials of all federal crimes before a jury of the state where the crimes were committed. The only other crime and punishment provisions were aimed at other episodes of abuse of civil liberties in England's history: Article I, Section 9, permits Congress to suspend the writ of habeas corpus only in emergencies and prohibits Congress from passing ex post facto criminal laws, and Article III, Section 3, provides a narrow definition of treason. But there was no debate over capital punishment. If they had been asked, the framers would have expressed a strong belief in punishment as retribution and would have considered themselves to be quite mild in comparison with generations only recently past that hanged witches and burnt heretics and political dissenters. Even in 1790, when the First Congress debated the first federal crime bill, the mandatory death penalty for treason, piracy, counterfeiting, murder, robbery, and rape did not draw much debate; the controversial issue was whether the bodies of executed criminals could be used by medical schools (they could), not whether criminals should be executed (Little 1999, 364). A typical death penalty case of the era is *United States v. Smith* (1820), in which the Supreme Court rejected by a 5–1 vote Daniel Webster's argument for a condemned pirate that the crime of "piracy, as defined by the law of nations" was not sufficiently specific to make robbery on the high seas an offense (it was); the Court unanimously assumed that the Constitution permitted pirates to be hanged.

Crime and punishment had figured in a small way in *opposition* to the Constitution, as opponents of ratification tried to raise fears that the Constitution would permit Congress to create prerogative courts like those used by James I and Charles I to suppress political dissent in the 17th century. During the ratifying convention in Virginia, delegate Patrick Henry pointed out the lack of a provision banning cruel and unusual punishments:

> What has distinguished our ancestors?—That they would not admit of tortures, or cruel and barbarous punishment. But Congress may introduce the practice of the civil law,

in preference to that of the common law. They may introduce the practice of France, Spain, and Germany—of torturing, to extort a confession of the crime. They will say that they might as well draw examples from those countries as from Great Britain, and they will tell you that there is such a necessity of strengthening the arm of government, that they must have a criminal equity, and extort confession by torture, in order to punish with still more relentless severity. We are then lost and undone. (Cogan 1997, 619)

An even more pointed objection was made by Abraham Holmes during the Massachusetts convention:

They are nowhere restrained from inventing the most cruel and unheard-of punishments and annexing them to crimes; and there is no constitutional check on them, but that *racks* and *gibbets* may be amongst the most mild instruments of their discipline. (Cogan 1997, 619)

But the Constitution provided for only a Supreme Court and left it to Congress to create lower federal courts, and few feared the hypothetical punishments of nonexistent courts.

When the amendments that became the Bill of Rights were debated in Congress in 1789, there was much concern over preserving the right to jury trial, but little concern over punishment. Consider the remarks in opposition to the proposed ban on cruel and unusual punishment by Representative Samuel Livermore, himself a former chief justice of the New Hampshire Supreme Court:

The clause seems to express a great deal of humanity, on which account I have no objection to it; but, as it seems to have no meaning in it, I do not think it necessary. What is meant by the terms "excessive bail"? Who are to be the judges? What is understood by "excessive fines"? It lays with the court to determine. No cruel and unusual punishment is to be inflicted; it is sometimes necessary to hang a man, villains often deserve whipping, and perhaps having their ears cut off; but are we, in future, to be prevented from inflicting these punishments because they are cruel? If a more lenient mode of correcting vice and deterring others from the commission of it could be invented, it would be very prudent in the legislature to adopt it; but until we have some security that this will be done, we ought not to be restrained from making necessary laws by any declaration of this kind. (Cogan 1997, 618)

Since the Constitution provided that the people, through their representatives in Congress, would define both crimes and their permissible punishments, it seemed an obvious rejoinder to Livermore that the people would not legislate or permit punishments they considered excessive.

And federal crimes could only be created by Congress. In *United States v. Hudson and Goodwin* (1812), the Supreme Court made this clear: unlike English courts, where the criminal law had been formed over the centuries by judges appointed by the monarch, federal courts had no power to create a common law of crime:

> The legislative authority of the Union must first make an act a crime, affix a punishment to it, and declare the Court that shall have jurisdiction of the offence.
>
> Certain implied powers must necessarily result to our Courts of justice from the nature of their institution. But jurisdiction of crimes against the state is not among those powers. . . . [A]ll exercise of criminal jurisdiction in common law cases we are of opinion is not within their implied powers.

So Why Does the Eighth Amendment Ban Cruel and Unusual Punishment?

To find the era in American history when the death penalty or cruel and unusual punishments—and the two terms were not the same—became a matter of public debate, one must go back a century to the colonial era and examine England, not England's colonies. That is so for two reasons. First, laws were made in England and not in the colonies. Despite the official role played by gentry such as Sir Walter Raleigh, Thomas West (Baron De la Warr), and Cecil Calvert (Lord Baltimore), in the first half of the 17th century, the colonies were settled for the most part by the dissenters, failures, and outcasts of England, hardly persons with whom Parliament and ministers would discuss the laws, much less trust with self-governance. The martial law imposed in 1610 on the struggling Jamestown settlement in Virginia, the Duke of York's laws imposed in 1665 on New York after its acquisition from the Netherlands, and John Locke's 1669 draft of a proposed constitution for South Carolina permitted capital punishment, in some cases, for minor offenses such as blasphemy or unauthorized trading with Indians. No one put the provisions to a vote.

Second, England is the place to look because by the 17th century there was a genuine debate there about crime and punishment, even though the terms of that debate would sound strange in modern ears. After the decision by King Henry VIII in 1534 to create a national church with himself at its head, the power of the state was used in England to enforce religious orthodoxy and political allegiance. Beheading, burning, or the more grisly punishment traditionally prescribed for treason—hanging, drawing, and quartering—were the standard means to carry out the Tudor dynasty's policies. Queen Mary I (reigned 1553–1558), Henry's daughter by Queen Catherine of Aragon, earned the legend "Bloody Mary" by executing Protestants during her short-lived attempt to undo the separation from Rome, and Queen Elizabeth I (reigned 1558–1603), Henry's daughter by Queen Anne Boleyn, resumed the executions of Catholics and other politically unreliable members of the upper class. Monarchs now ruled by divine right, not because the Church approved of them, and anyone who disagreed was a heretic and traitor who deserved death.

On the Continent, the situation was just as bad, as any religious impulse from the Reformation was swamped by the ambitions of kings to consolidate or extend their national borders, and atrocities were excused as zealous pursuit of heretics throughout the 16th century. The 1555 Peace of Augsburg was considered to be a policy of toleration because, after the ruling prince chose the religion of all his subjects, dissenters were permitted to take their possessions with them when they fled. Other measures, such as the 1598 Edict of Nantes that restored civil rights to French Huguenots, were adopted only until the armies were exhausted and were revoked (as was the Edict in 1685) as soon as it was convenient.

In England, Elizabeth I's long reign brought order, and although Calvinist doctrines spreading from the Continent would eventually clash with the Tudor position that monarchs answered only to God, for the most part, the country agreed with the throne or kept silent; Puritan and Presbyterian reformers who pressed too hard tended to join Catholics and other political threats like Queen Mary Stuart (beheaded in 1587) on the scaffold.

When Elizabeth I died in 1603, Mary Stuart's son King James VI of Scotland took the throne as King James I (reigned 1603–1625) of England. King James I made use of Puritan support in the wave of anti-Catholicism that followed the Gunpowder Plot of 1605, but for the most part, the Stuarts maintained Tudor authoritarianism (the last two persons executed for heresy in England were burned by James I in 1612) while failing to maintain the Tudor popularity.

On his coronation in 1625, King Charles I inherited his father's two decades of struggle with the increasingly Puritan and increasingly independent Parliament. The harsh punishments of religious dissenters by his courts contributed to his estrangement from the rising Puritan mercantile class. Parliament particularly hated the Stuart monarchs' use of prerogative courts—specialized executive agencies, like the Court of Star Chamber and the Court of High Commission, begun under the Tudors to root out corruption and enforce political and religious orthodoxy. The three common law courts—Exchequer, Common Pleas, and King's Bench—that had their origins in the 11th century had operated for centuries by writs and by jury trial, but the new pre-rogative courts used the more modern inquisitorial methods that had spread throughout the Continent with the medieval revival of the study of Roman law; as Patrick Henry would later point out, they could force a witness to incriminate himself under oath or after torture. They could also inflict corporal punishment that included cropping of ears and branding with hot irons, punish-ments that were coming to be considered cruel, especially when imposed on members of the upper class. Such punishments were certainly not in use in the common law courts, and so in the language of the day, they were "unusual."

In the early 1640s, Parliament successfully abolished these courts as arbitrary and cruel, but this was not based on a prin-cipled opposition to harsh punishments: Parliament pushed for the equally arbitrary and political beheadings of the Earl of Strafford (1641) and Archbishop Laud (1645). Charles I's inability to use an archaic feudal revenue system to finance a modern national government and unwillingness to exchange reforms for financial support led in 1642 to open war with Par-liament. After the Parliamentary armies led by Oliver Crom-well defeated the Royalist armies, Parliament tried Charles I in its own ad hoc court and condemned him to death by behead-ing in 1649.

England had seen kings killed before, but Charles I's behead-ing posed a new problem in political philosophy. Under feu-dalism, government had been, in theory and often in fact, a contract between the lord and his vassal. The monarch, in per-son, was the embodiment of sovereignty, and when monarchs were overthrown at least in theory, some person still was the rightful sovereign. For almost a thousand years, Englishmen had been used to punishment for crimes because they were an offense against the "King's Peace," but with no king on the throne, what justified the hangman's noose in the countryside?

This could have led to widespread legal reform. There had been calls before and during the English Civil War for an end to religious persecution, for a reduction in the number of capital crimes, and for a general reform of English law to make it more understandable. Some reformers, like Roger Williams, the founder of the Providence, Rhode Island settlement, brought their ideas to America. But in England, despite Cromwell's appointment during the Protectorate (1653–1659) of a committee to study reform, the opposition to change by lawyers of all factions meant that little was done before dissatisfaction with Cromwell's son and successor, Richard, led to the restoration in 1660 of King Charles II (reigned 1660–1685). Certainly capital punishment had not been abolished; the amnesty that accompanied Charles's return to the throne excluded persons directly involved in the death of the king's father, and in 1660, they were duly hanged, drawn, and quartered. According to eyewitnesses like Samuel Pepys, this was done to the general approval of the London mob, which had come to consider executions as entertainment.

Nevertheless, there was change both at the fringes and at the heart of English law. By the end of the 17th century in England, Protestant denominations outside the established Anglican Church were being tolerated, and there was a general end to using the death penalty to punish Catholics and other religious dissenters.

To understand further changes in capital punishment, we have to examine the due process of law. The phrase "due process of law" can be traced to a 1354 statute of King Edward III as the English equivalent of the Latin phrase *per legem terrae* (by the law of the land) in Magna Carta. In chapter 39 of Magna Carta, King John promised that no free man would be killed, imprisoned, outlawed, or exiled except by the law of the land and after the judgment of his peers. As Magna Carta was reconfirmed by succeeding kings, the original concession King John made in 1215 to respect the rights of the barons who had revolted against him evolved into an expectation that royal judges would apply settled law to all persons.

Settled law evolved from century to century by Act of Parliament. For instance, because the idea of a central government with jurisdiction over all crimes grew slowly and alongside much older monastic orders and religious institutions governed by canon law, for centuries, defendants could plead the defense of "benefit of clergy." By proving to be able to read (or at least memorize) a passage of the Bible, a defendant could claim the cleric's right to be tried in a church court and therefore have immunity from secular courts. By separate acts over the centuries, Parliament abolished the benefit of clergy, first for treason, and then in murder cases, but it also extended the defense to women defendants and provided for branding defendants to prevent repeat use of the defense. The haphazard course of statutory reform meant benefit of clergy was still a recognized defense for manslaughter when John Adams used it in defense of British soldiers charged after the Boston Massacre.

Judicial decisions changed the law in significant ways too; in *Bushell's Case* (1670), the practice of coercing jurors by fining and imprisoning them for not reaching the verdict desired by the judge was held to be illegal. This ability of jurors to acquit eventually led to significant changes in capital punishment, since a juror could express opposition to capital punishment only by the all-or-nothing decision to convict or acquit. Due process meant not a particular rule about the number of jurors or days to appeal, but the entire tangle of rules that prevented what Englishmen had feared since Magna Carta: summary procedures that ended with the defendant's life and property being sacrificed to the ambitions of some royal official.

In Parliament's struggles for power with the Stuart kings, the Magna Carta and the concept of due process became rallying cries by parliamentary leaders like Edward Coke (1552–1634), who sought a basis for restraining the power of the monarch. Coke, a lawyer under Queen Elizabeth and subsequently a judge promoted and then dismissed by King James I, was in the third phase of his career in Parliament as a leader of the opposition to Charles I. During this period, he wrote the

Institutes of the Laws of England, the most authoritative treatise on English law from the 1640s until Blackstone's *Commentaries* were published 125 years later. Coke was anxious to
produce as much age and, therefore, prestige as possible for
his arguments, and so in the *Institutes,* he equated due process
as demanded in Parliament in 1628 with the ancient rights of
Englishmen guaranteed by Magna Carta in 1215. American
lawyers from Thomas Jefferson to John Jay, the first chief justice of the Supreme Court, learned their law by reading the
Institutes and were shaped by and accepted Coke's position that
due process was paramount. The Fifth Amendment therefore
guaranteed, but made no attempt to define, "due process"; it
was a piece of history, a rhetorical flourish in tribute to Parliament's struggle with Charles I.

Subsequent parliamentary conflict with King Charles II
produced in 1679 a habeas corpus statute, which gave persons
arrested by the monarch a right not to be held without legal
charges. This in effect was the first effort to compel a speedy trial
in criminal cases, and by 1776, both England and the colonies
considered access to the writ of habeas corpus a fundamental
right. Although the right to habeas corpus could sometimes be
thwarted by the setting of excessive bail, it was part of the due
process that was considered to restrain the king by restraining
the king's judges.

Parliamentary struggle with the last of the Stuart kings, King
James II, highlighted the importance of controlling the judges
who, because they served at the king's pleasure and could be
dismissed for permitting an unsatisfactory judgment, were
often the Crown's most loyal ministers. George Jeffreys was one
of the justices of the King's Bench under Charles II and in that
capacity presided over the 1683 treason trial of Charles's political opponent Algernon Sidney. By law, a conviction for treason
required two witnesses; although only one appeared against
Sidney, Judge Jeffreys ruled that a draft of Sidney's *Discourses
on Government*, opposing the divine right of kings and asserting that God permitted people to create and to alter their form

of government, was itself a sufficient second witness. The punishment for treason remained death by being hanged, drawn, and quartered, but Sidney's sentence was reduced to death by beheading. His *Discourses* were published and avidly read in the colonies, where Sidney was widely considered a martyr (Bailyn 1992, 34–35).

Two years later, with James II having succeeded his older brother as king, Jeffreys tried, convicted, and sentenced Titus Oates for perjury. Oates had been a professional informant and had provided false testimony in the treason trials of Catholic noblemen convicted and executed for allegedly participating in plots to assassinate King Charles II. With the shift in the political winds, Judge Jeffreys, who had presided over some of the treason trials in which Oates had testified, now found Oates guilty of perjury. By common law, felonies were punishable by death, but perjury was a misdemeanor, and the punishment for a misdemeanor could be any punishment short of death ordered by the judges. Jeffreys ordered Oates to be stripped of his clerical status, flogged by the hangman while being walked to prison tied to the hangman's cart, and then imprisoned for life with the condition that he be taken out five times a year and placed in the public pillory, a punishment that sometimes resulted in death from the stones of a hostile mob. Although the House of Lords refused to overturn Oates's conviction, the lords who dissented from that decision wrote that Oates's punishment was "cruel, barbarous, and illegal."

Later in 1685, Judge Jeffreys presided over the treason trials in southwest England known as the Bloody Assizes, after the suppression of an attempted coup by the Duke of Monmouth, Charles II's illegitimate son. Jeffreys drew especial criticism for his conduct in presiding over the trial that convicted Alice Lisle, the widow of one of the members of the Parliament who had executed Charles I. Lisle was found guilty of treason for harboring fugitives from the battlefield. Although King James commuted the legally prescribed sentence of death by being burned at the stake to death to allow Lisle's execution by beheading, Jeffreys's reputation was beyond repair, and he was forever associated in England and the colonies with denying defendants fair trials and with ordering cruel and obsolete punishments.

In November 1688, an almost bloodless coup known as the Glorious Revolution brought James II's daughter Mary and her husband William of Orange to the throne. In 1689, Parliament presented a Declaration of Rights to the new monarchs, complaining that James II had been responsible for inflicting "illegal and cruel" punishments. The Bill of Rights, the statutory form of the Declaration, remedied many of the abuses of Charles II's and James II's judges by providing that "excessive bail should not be required, nor excessive fines imposed, nor cruel and unusual punishments inflicted." This and many other provisions of the English Bill of Rights would be adopted in the American version a century later.

How Did the Ban on Cruel and Unusual Punishment Become Linked to the Death Penalty?

The cruel and unusual punishments that sparked the English Bill of Rights were corporal punishments, not capital punishment, but the 18th century saw movement on capital punishment in two directions. On the one hand, Englishmen were conscious that France, though the center of European culture and learning, was an absolute monarchy. English authors celebrated the relatively wide participation of its upper class in government and the relatively greater procedural defenses persons accused of crime had against arbitrary judicial action. French authors praised English law in part to criticize French law, as in Baron Montesquieu's 1748 treatise *The Spirit of the Laws*. Notice his twin concerns with proportionate retribution and deterrence:

> It is an essential point, that there should be a certain proportion in punishments, because it is essential that a

great crime should be avoided rather than a smaller, and that which is more pernicious to society rather than that which is less.

. . .

It is a great abuse amongst us to condemn to the same punishment a person that only robs on the highway, and another who robs and murders. Surely, for the public security, some difference should be made in the punishment.

In China, those who add murder to robbery are cut in pieces: but not so the others; to this difference it is owing, that, though they rob in that country, they never murder.

In Russia, where the punishment of robbery and murder is the same, they always murder. The dead, say they, tell no tales.

Where there is no difference in the penalty, there should be some in the expectation of pardon. In England they never murder on the highway, because robbers have some hopes of transportation, which is not the case in respect to those that commit murder. (Montesquieu 1748, 116–118)

On the other hand, the English upper classes felt increasingly threatened by the social unrest caused by the enclosure movement and the Industrial Revolution, not to mention their perennial fear of Scottish or Irish rebellions. Parliament passed increasingly draconian laws for the punishment of property crimes, particularly the Waltham Black Act of 1723, and eventually quadrupled the number of capital crimes between 1689 and 1800. The lenity of English punishments was only relative to those of other countries: for crimes that were perceived to threaten the political order such as the Scottish Jacobite risings of 1715 and 1745, English justice could be savage. The Black Act itself was so named because its most famous provision made poachers who blacked their faces to avoid identification eligible for the death penalty, without benefit of clergy. Counterfeiting and forging were harshly punished, and while it was an unlucky thief who drew a hanging jury, close to two-thirds of forgers were executed.

But as Montesquieu noted, there was the hope of transportation to the American colonies as an indentured servant to meliorate the ferocity of statutory penalties, especially for petty theft and crimes by the poor. In 1718, the British government began subsidizing the transportation of criminals to the colonies, and this continued even after the beginning of the Revolutionary War until 1776. (Transportation resumed after the war, this time with Australia as the destination.) In the American colonies, the chronic shortage of labor and the settlement of the frontier reduced the pressure to execute persons for property crime and justified the depiction of English law as less severe than that of other nations. And given the high mortality rates from disease in workhouses and debtors' prisons, and from the rigors of transportation itself, deaths by execution did not seem to take a great proportion of criminals.

Many cultural changes start among outcasts at the margin and end up as orthodoxy, while in other cases, elite opinions filter down to become the slogan of the common man. Both are true of legal reform in the latter half of the 18th century. Legal changes like the increased independence of juries and practices like transportation had a practical impact on the number of persons suffering the death penalty, but in this century, a movement to abolish capital punishment had its intellectual birth. As the British colonies were moving toward independence, they acquired their understanding of crime and punishment from two writers, one a well-known English judge and law lecturer, William Blackstone, and the other, a young Italian political reformer hardly remembered, Cesare Beccaria. One of Beccaria's few memorials is a small town in Pennsylvania named after him in 1807; it is only miles from the prison that for decades housed that state's death row. In 1764, Beccaria's essay "On Crimes and Punishments" condemned the use of torture in judicial proceedings on the Continent and called for the abolition of almost all capital punishment.

It had the same effect on contemporary thinking about crime and punishment that Locke's *Second Treatise on Government* had on limited monarchy and Montesquieu's *Spirit of the Laws* had on separation of powers. The prominence of deterrence in Beccaria's essay appealed to intellectuals of the Enlightenment because deterrence was simple and quasi-mathematical and did not rely on now-unpopular religious notions about what a criminal deserved. Beccaria made the assumptions that the only objects of punishment were incapacitation of the criminal himself and deterrence of other would-be criminals, and that perpetual imprisonment was a more effective deterrent to crime than capital punishment because deterrence was not due to the severity of punishment alone, but the product of the severity of punishment times its duration:

> It is not the intensity of punishment that has the greatest effect on the human spirit, but its duration, for our sensibility is more easily and more permanently affected by slight but repeated impressions than by a powerful but momentary action. The sway of habit is universal over every sentient being; as man speaks and walks and satisfies his needs by its aid, so the ideas of morality come to be stamped upon the mind only by long and repeated impressions. It is not the terrible yet momentary spectacle of the death of a wretch, but the long and painful example of a man deprived of liberty, who, having become a beast of burden, recompenses with his labors the society he has offended, which is the strongest curb against crimes. That efficacious idea—efficacious, because very often repeated to ourselves—"I myself shall be reduced to so long and miserable a condition if I commit a similar misdeed" is far more potent than the idea of death, which men envision always at an obscure distance. (Beccaria 1963, 46–47)

John Adams and Thomas Jefferson both quoted Beccaria approvingly, as did Blackstone.

Beccaria was, like Englishmen Thomas Hobbes and John Locke and Frenchman Jean-Jacques Rousseau, a believer in a social contract, and he thought of crime and punishment in terms of contract rights and duties. Beccaria reasoned that since a man has no right to take his own life and the government was a contract in which all of its members obtained some rights by surrendering others, no one could surrender a right to the state he did not have. The state therefore could not possess a right to take life as a punishment for crime.

Beccaria considered and rejected other justifications for capital punishment, writing that it could not be defended as analogous to the traditional religious concept of a just war because, except in the rare circumstance of unquelled rebellion, it was unnecessary to protect the public. In the long run, it did not deter others from committing crimes:

> The death penalty cannot be useful, because of the example of barbarity it gives men. If the passions or the necessities of war have taught the shedding of human blood, the laws, moderators of the conduct of men, should not extend the beastly example, which becomes more pernicious since the inflicting of legal death is attended with much study and formality. It seems to me absurd that the laws, which are an expression of the public will, which detest and punish homicide, should themselves commit it, and that to deter citizens from murder, they order a public one. (Beccaria 1963, 50)

A generation later, this idea filtered down to the other end of the social scale in Thomas Paine's *The Rights of Man* (1791), attacking the ineffectiveness of the death penalty to eliminate what he considered the root cause of crime:

> When, in countries that are called civilized, we see age going to the work houses and youth to the gallows, something must be wrong in the system of government.

. . .

Civil government does not consist in executions; but in making that provision for the instruction of youth, and the support of age, as to exclude, as much as possible, profligacy from the one, and despair from the other.

. . .

Why is it that scarcely any are executed but the poor? (Paine 1989, 294)

Blackstone, the author of *Commentaries on the Laws of England*, a four-volume treatise on English law published between 1765 and 1769, was the weightiest influence. The next two generations of American lawyers who read Blackstone's *Commentaries on the Laws of England* as their principal legal text would have absorbed Blackstone's assessment of penal systems:

We may further observe that sanguinary laws are a bad symptom of the distemper of any state, or at least a weak constitution . . . [t]he laws of the Roman kings, and the twelve tables of the decemviri, were full of cruel punishments . . . the Porcian law, which exempted all citizens from sentence of death, silently abrogated them all. In this period the republic flourished: under the emperors severe punishments were revived, and then the empire fell. (Blackstone 1979, vol. IV, 590)

Unlike Beccaria or Paine, however, Blackstone was a lawyer immersed in the common-law tradition that made changes slowly and incrementally. Although Blackstone read and cited Beccaria approvingly, like most English critics of the excessive punishments for petty crimes, Blackstone did not abandon retribution or propose to disturb capital punishment for murder. Not only were there centuries of precedent to consider, but also Blackstone believed there was divine support for retribution beginning with the command to Noah in Genesis 9:6 that "whoso sheddeth man's blood, by man shall his blood be shed" (Blackstone 1979, vol. IV, 9).

As Blackstone's quote from the Bible illustrates, not even all those who agreed with Beccaria's recommendations accepted Beccaria's premise that the principal goal of punishment was deterrence. German philosopher Immanuel Kant, for instance, found Beccaria's argument to be immoral because it disregarded retribution—the punishment the criminal himself deserved—in favor of the effect of the punishment on others. But it is safe to observe that Beccaria's ideas were simpler than Kant's and therefore more accessible to society at large.

It is worth noting that as Beccaria's novel emphasis on deterrence was spreading, the older idea of punishment as "just desserts" led England in the early 19th century to abolish capital punishment for minor property crimes. The idea of punishment as rehabilitation was also emerging, and this had its first impact not on punishment but on prison reform. In the late 18th century, many English county jails originally built to briefly detain defendants on their way to trial had become warehouses for debtors and the mentally ill; they were disease-ridden incubators of vice and cruelty. There was an active movement in both England and the United States in the late 1700s to make prison conditions more humane and to promote the rehabilitation of the criminal.

Everyone agreed that it was just to punish the murderer, the rapist, and the burglar. But was Beccaria right that deterrence must govern the severity of *any* criminal penalty, even for murder? Did Blackstone's appeal to the Old Testament support a legitimate argument that murder called for blood in retribution? There would be ebbs and flows in the first hundred years of the new country's history, but essentially, Americans adopted Beccaria's rhetoric and Blackstone's approach.

Capital Punishment in the New Republic

The Constitution provided that the people, through their elected representatives in Congress, would define the elements of crimes and permissible punishments, and it seemed too obvious for discussion that the people would hardly permit cruel punishments for themselves. And the death penalty, carried out by a straightforward hanging as provided for by law, was not seen as either unusual or cruel. The last significant legislation before the Constitution was passed by the Articles of Confederation Congress on July 13, 1787, when the delegates were already meeting in Philadelphia. The "Ordinance for the Government of the Territory of the United States, Northwest of the River Ohio," mapped out the governing of the territory that would become the states of Ohio, Michigan, Indiana, Illinois, Wisconsin, and part of Minnesota. Section 14 of the Northwest Ordinance was a forerunner of the Bill of Rights, and Section 14, Article 2, prohibited "cruel or unusual punishments," only one sentence after providing that criminal defendants could not be held without bail "unless for capital offenses, where the proof shall be evident or the presumption great." Clearly, capital punishment could exist side by side with a ban on cruel or unusual punishment.

The understanding that capital punishment was similarly not affected by the Eighth Amendment was reinforced by the other amendments to the Constitution. The Fifth Amendment provides that no civilian shall be held to answer for a "capital crime" without a grand jury indictment and that no person can be "deprived of life, liberty, or property, without due process of law." The amendment clearly contemplates that Congress can authorize capital crimes and, assuming due process of law is provided, executions.

Although there were public figures who advocated abolition of the death penalty, most notably signer of the Declaration of Independence Dr. Benjamin Rush, and although there was an American Society for the Abolition of Capital Punishment, the death penalty was not a major social issue in the early 19th century. Before the Civil War, slavery dominated public debate. The American criminal justice system, except insofar as it punished slaves or punished attempts to free slaves, was considered lenient by Americans themselves and by Europeans like Alexis de Tocqueville, who wrote his classic analysis of the United States, *Democracy in America*, after coming to study the penal systems of American states. As already noted, the Supreme Court had held that only Congress could make federal law, and representatives in Congress would not remain in office long if they legislated criminal penalties that offended the people they represented. The same movement away from judge-made crimes and toward legislative definition of punishments was going on in the states, especially in the new states being formed on the frontier. The universal opinion of lawyers that the ban on "cruel and unusual punishment" was a footnote from history was expressed by Supreme Court Justice Joseph Story in his 1833 legal textbook, *Commentaries on the Constitution*. Story's assessment of the phrase was that:

> This is an exact transcript of a clause in the bill of rights, framed at the revolution of 1688. The provision would seem to be wholly unnecessary in a free government, since it is scarcely possible, that any department of such a government should authorize, or justify such atrocious conduct. It was, however, adopted, as an admonition to all departments of the national government, to warn them against such violent proceedings, as had taken place in England in the arbitrary reigns of some of the Stuarts. (Story 1987, 710–711)

After the Civil War, Justice Thomas Cooley of the Michigan Supreme Court succeeded Story as the nation's most influential legal treatise writer. Cooley's views on the marginal nature of the Eighth Amendment were similar to those of his predecessor. Cooley's 1868 text, *A Treatise on the Constitutional Limitations Which Rest upon the Legislative Power of the States of the American Union*, remained in print for six decades with little change from Cooley's original assessment:

> It is certainly difficult to determine precisely what is meant by "cruel and unusual punishments." Probably any

punishment declared by statute for an offense which was punishable in the same way at the common law could not be regarded as cruel or unusual in the constitutional sense. And probably any new statutory offense may be punished to the extent and in the mode permitted by the common law for offenses of similar nature. But those degrading punishments which in any state had become obsolete before its existing constitution was adopted, we think may well be forbidden by it as cruel and unusual. (Cooley 1927, vol. 1, 694)

If a punishment was permitted in the tradition of the common law and had not fallen out of common use, in other words, it was neither unusual nor cruel.

The Supreme Court's only significant examination of the meaning of the Bill of Rights before the Civil War came in the unanimous decision in *Barron v. Mayor and City Council of Baltimore* (1833). Barron owned a wharf in the Baltimore harbor that over time was rendered useless by silt that accumulated as a result of road construction projects in Baltimore City from 1815 to 1821. Barron sued the city on the grounds that the city had taken his property without just compensation, something forbidden by the Fifth Amendment. Chief Justice John Marshall wrote that the Bill of Rights had been passed to restrain Congress and provide "security against the apprehended encroachments of the General Government—not against those of the local governments." In other words, the Eighth Amendment did not even apply to state governments.

This was of little significance: most states had constitutions containing the same language as the Eighth Amendment, and inspired by the growing appeal of the rehabilitative ideal, the trend of legislation was toward less severe criminal punishments. This included the abolition in the 1820s and 1830s of imprisonment for debt, and in 1846, Michigan's abolition of the death penalty except for cases of treason. Most states retained the death penalty for murder and the other common law felonies, and left it to the governor to pardon defendants on a case-by-case basis. There were several state abolitionist organizations in the pre–Civil War era that were chiefly aimed at ending the spectacle of public executions—Connecticut moved hangings to inside the state penitentiary in 1830 and Maine enacted a moratorium on executions in 1835 because public hangings had become unruly—but there was no assertion, even by those who sought complete abolition of the death penalty, that a properly conducted death by hanging was unusual.

There were arguments to be made about other modes of execution besides hanging. For example, the Supreme Court considered a case from the Utah Territory in 1878, *Wilkerson v. Utah*. Wilkerson was a convicted murderer who appealed the judgment of the territorial court, where the Eighth Amendment applied, ordering his execution by a firing squad. Wilkerson's attorneys, apparently conceding that he could be hanged, argued that he should not be shot because it was cruel and unusual. An earlier statute providing that he could be beheaded had been repealed. Justice Nathan Clifford delivered the unanimous opinion of the Court affirming the sentence:

> Cruel and unusual punishments are forbidden by the Constitution, but the authorities referred to are quite sufficient to show that the punishment of shooting as a mode of executing the death penalty for the crime of murder in the first degree is not included in that category, within the meaning of the eighth amendment. Soldiers convicted of desertion or other capital military offences are in the great majority of cases sentenced to be shot, and the ceremony for such occasions is given in great fulness by the writers upon the subject of courts-martial.
>
> . . .
>
> Where the conviction is in the civil tribunals, the rule of the common law was that the sentence or judgment must be pronounced or rendered by the court in which

the prisoner was tried or finally condemned, and the rule was universal that it must be such as is annexed to the crime by law. Of these, says Blackstone, some are capital, which extend to the life of the offender, and consist generally in being hanged by the neck till dead.

. . .

Such is the general statement of that commentator, but he admits that in very atrocious crimes other circumstances of terror, pain, or disgrace were sometimes superadded. Cases mentioned by the author are, where the prisoner was drawn or dragged to the place of execution, in treason; or where he was embowelled alive, beheaded, and quartered, in high treason. Mention is also made of public dissection in murder, and burning alive in treason committed by a female. History confirms the truth of these atrocities, but the commentator states that the humanity of the nation by tacit consent allowed the mitigation of such parts of those judgments as savored of torture or cruelty, and he states that they were seldom strictly carried into effect.

. . .

Difficulty would attend the effort to define with exactness the extent of the constitutional provision which provides that cruel and unusual punishments shall not be inflicted; but it is safe to affirm that punishments of torture, such as those mentioned by the commentator referred to, and all others in the same line of unnecessary cruelty, are forbidden by that amendment to the Constitution.

. . .

Had the statute prescribed the mode of executing the sentence, it would have been the duty of the court to follow it, unless the punishment to be inflicted was cruel and unusual, within the meaning of the eighth amendment to the Constitution, which is not pretended by the counsel of the prisoner. Statutory directions being given that the prisoner when duly convicted shall suffer death, without any statutory regulation specifically pointing out the mode of executing the command of the law, it must be that the duty is devolved upon the court authorized to pass the sentence to determine the mode of execution and to impose the sentence prescribed.

As *Wilkerson* shows, the Eighth Amendment was assumed by the Court to preclude only tortures from English history, such as drawing and quartering and burning at the stake.

Modern burning at the stake came to the Court in *In re Kemmler* (1890), a challenge to the new electric chair that New York had adopted as its method for capital punishment. William Kemmler was the first man condemned to die in the electric chair at Auburn State Prison, which had been the state's model progressive reformatory. Accepting without scrutiny the determination made by New York's highest court that, in its turn, had accepted the findings of a legislative committee that had decided that electrocution was a humane way to die, Chief Justice Fuller spoke for a unanimous Supreme Court:

It appears that the first step which led to the enactment of the law was a statement contained in the annual message of the governor of the state of New York, transmitted to the legislature January 6, 1885, as follows: "The present mode of executing criminals by hanging has come down to us from the dark ages, and it may well be questioned whether the science of the present day cannot provide a means for taking the life of such as are condemned to die in a less barbarous manner. I commend this suggestion to the consideration of the legislature." The legislature accordingly appointed a commission to investigate and report "the most humane and practical method known to modern science of carrying into effect the sentence of death in capital cases." This commission reported in favor of execution by electricity.

. . .

It is not contended, as it could not be, that the eighth amendment was intended to apply to the states, but it is urged that the provision of the fourteenth amendment, which forbids a state to make or enforce any law which shall abridge the privileges or immunities of citizens of the United States, is a prohibition on the state from the imposition of cruel and unusual punishments, and that such punishments are also prohibited by inclusion in the term "due process of law."

. . .

So that, if the punishment prescribed for an offense against the laws of the state were manifestly cruel and unusual as burning at the stake, crucifixion, breaking on the wheel, or the like, it would be the duty of the courts to adjudge such penalties to be within the constitutional prohibition.

And we think this equally true of the eighth amendment, in its application to congress.

. . .

The enactment of this statute was, in itself, within the legitimate sphere of the legislative power of the state, and in the observance of those general rules prescribed by our systems of jurisprudence; and the legislature of the state of New York determined that it did not inflict cruel and unusual punishment, and its courts have sustained that determination. We cannot perceive that the state has thereby abridged the privileges or immunities of the petitioner, or deprived him of due process of law.

Note that the Supreme Court did not dispute the accuracy of New York's determination that electrocution was humane.

As for the usual execution by hanging, challenges to that method were limited to the claim that it was illegal for states to move traditional public hangings in the vicinity of city hall or the county courthouse to nonpublic executions within a state's penitentiary, to be observed by only officially invited witnesses. In *Holden v. Minnesota* (1890), the Supreme Court held that Minnesota's choice to avoid sensational accounts of public hanging by using official witnesses, and even by forbidding newspaper accounts of the execution, did "not infringe any right secured by the constitution of the United States."

States also formally created "death rows" in this era, by requiring the solitary confinement of the condemned in the weeks leading up to execution. *Holden v. Minnesota* approved solitary confinement until executions were carried out between one and six months after sentencing. And although the Supreme Court did hold that solitary confinement was a severe additional punishment, the Supreme Court rejected a challenge to the four- to eight-week pre-execution period of solitary confinement prescribed by New York law in *McElvaine v. Brush* (1891), denying McElvaine's petition for a writ of habeas corpus with the observations that the punishment did not deprive him of any due process of law and that "it was not intended by congress that the courts of the United States should by writs of *habeas corpus* obstruct the ordinary administration of the criminal laws of the states."

If the question arises in the reader's mind of how the defendant's appeals could be heard in such a short time, the answer is simple: due process of law did not mean there was a right to an appeal, and where an appeal was permitted, the claims that could be raised were limited. This was perfectly constitutional, according to the Supreme Court in *McKane v. Durston* (1894):

> An appeal from a judgment of conviction is not a matter of absolute right, independently of constitutional or statutory provisions allowing such appeal. A review by an appellate court of the final judgment in a criminal case, however grave the offense of which the accused is convicted, was not at common law, and is not now, a necessary element of due process of law. It is wholly within the discretion of the state to allow or not to allow such a review. A citation of authorities upon the point is unnecessary.

Federal law itself had authorized review of appeals in capital cases by the Supreme Court only in 1889. In 1891, this right of appeal was extended to noncapital cases; that same year, Congress created Circuit Courts of Appeals that could hear appeals from federal trial courts in regional "circuits" that comprised several states each. Since the number of justices on the Supreme Court had been fixed at nine shortly after the Civil War, the more easily expandable Courts of Appeals could provide speedier and more thorough review of criminal trials. The Supreme Court retained its right of review, but by 1911, appeals had to go through the Courts of Appeal before the Supreme Court would consider them. This procedural change effectively gave the Courts of Appeal the final word in most criminal cases, a role they keep today.

The Due Process Clause of the Fourteenth Amendment Changes the Bill of Rights

As you read the excerpts from the opinion in *Kemmler*, you noticed the Court mentioning "due process" and "privileges and immunities." That these phrases are relevant to a discussion of the death penalty requires us to the turn to the Fourteenth Amendment to the Constitution.

Disputes over slavery, the Supreme Court's decision in *Dred Scott v. Sandford* (1857), and the election of Abraham Lincoln in November 1860 led to secession and the American Civil War. When the war ended in 1865, the victorious Union faced the dilemma that the Thirteenth Amendment's abolition of slavery implied that the three-fifths compromise in the original Constitution could no longer be used to apportion representatives in Congress. Slaves no longer counted as three-fifths of a person, but Northern Republicans hardly wanted to give Southern Democrats more seats in the House of Representatives. Their remedy was to draft the Fourteenth Amendment. Ratified after much debate in 1868, Section 2 of the Fourteenth Amendment withheld congressional seats from states that abridged the right of freed slaves to vote.

Section 1 of the Fourteenth Amendment provides:

All persons born or naturalized in the United States, and subject to the jurisdiction thereof, are citizens of the United States and of the State wherein they reside. No State shall make or enforce any law which shall abridge the privileges or immunities of citizens of the United States; nor shall any State deprive any person of life, liberty, or property, without due process of law; nor deny to any person within its jurisdiction the equal protection of the laws.

Section 1 not only undid *Dred Scott*, but it also, perhaps unintentionally, overturned *Barron v. Baltimore*'s holding that the Bill of Rights did not apply to the states, by taking the Privileges and Immunities Clause of Article IV and the Due Process Clause of the Fifth Amendment and directly guaranteeing them against interference by the states.

Or so it seemed. During the congressional debates over the amendment, no one specified what the privileges and immunities of citizenship were, or what due process of law meant. The Supreme Court almost immediately sidetracked any discussion of the Privileges and Immunities Clause by interpreting that phrase very narrowly in *Bradwell v. Illinois* (1873) and *The Slaughter-House Cases* (1873), but for the next hundred years, the content of the Due Process Clause of the Fourteenth Amendment would be the most important issue decided by the Supreme Court.

The Fourth, Fifth, Sixth, Seventh, and Eighth Amendments all regulate procedures in court because in the framers' view of history, judges were dangers to, not protectors of, liberty. Although today most think of the Eighth Amendment as a guide for judges to limit the penalties a legislature can impose, the original ban on cruel and unusual punishments in the English Bill of Rights clearly was aimed at judges. In the colonies, sentencing by juries arose as a reaction to the perception that royal appointees imposed overly harsh penalties, and Thomas Jefferson in his revision of the criminal laws of Virginia likewise provided that juries and not judges should impose some sentences.

That so many amendments regulate courts reflects the obvious truth that procedural fairness is important. It is a not so obvious truth that the procedures we allow dictate the success of criminal prosecutions. For instance, in combating drug trafficking, the problem is not so much apprehending the criminal as discovering the crime, and without undercover informants, wiretaps, and surveillance cameras—all procedural devices—society could hardly have effective drug laws. With the advent of DNA testing and forensic psychiatric examination, we tend to think that only scientific innovations change the outcome of cases, but seemingly minor shifts in procedure have been recognized as crucial since the late 19th century.

In *Hurtado v. California* (1884), the Supreme Court reviewed Hurtado's death sentence for murder. In California, the prosecutor commenced a murder prosecution by filing an "information," a written complaint. The information had begun to be used in England several centuries earlier, but only for misdemeanors. Felony offenses that exposed the defendant to the death penalty had to be commenced by indictment, after a grand jury screened the evidence. One of the many legal struggles between Parliament and the Stuart kings was over the royal attempt to use information in felony cases, thus bypassing the protection from political prosecutions that the grand jury process afforded. The Fifth Amendment therefore naturally specified that the federal government must use the grand jury process to prosecute capital or infamous crimes. Hurtado argued that the Fourteenth Amendment's requirement that states provide due process meant that California must use the indictment procedure too, and that his sentence was invalid.

Justice Stanley Matthews's majority opinion upheld Hurtado's conviction and sentence. In a foreshadowing of the debates of the 20th century, both the majority and the dissent written by Justice John Marshall Harlan looked to the history of

English criminal procedure since Magna Carta. Justice Matthews observed that "due process" historically excluded the use of bills of attainder, bills of pains and penalties, acts of confiscation, acts reversing judgments or directly transferring one man's estate to another, "and other similar special, partial, and arbitrary exertions of power under the form of legislation." There was nothing in the use of an information instead of an indictment that resembled these practices. After declaring that there was nothing in the concept of due process that prohibited either changes in laws or differences in procedure in different jurisdictions, the Court held:

> It follows that any legal proceeding enforced by public authority, whether sanctioned by age and custom or newly devised in the discretion of the legislative power in furtherance of the public good, which regards these principles of liberty and justice, must be held to be due process of law.

In dissent, Justice Harlan drew the opposite conclusion:

> If particular proceedings, conducted under the authority of the general government, and involving life, are prohibited because not constituting that due process of law required by the fifth amendment of the constitution of the United States, similar proceedings, conducted under the authority of a state, must be deemed illegal, as not being due process of law within the meaning of the fourteenth amendment. The words "due process of law," in the latter amendment, must receive the same interpretation they had at the common law from which they were derived and which was given to them at the formation of the general government.

The Court had to choose: either due process meant what it meant in 1791 or it changed with the times and could mean different things in different places. Note that in a 180-degree reversal of today's politics, in *Hurtado* it was the "liberal" position that the Constitution meant in 1884 what it had meant in 1791, and the "conservative" position that the Constitution was an evolving document.

Next, in *Ex Parte Wilson* (1885), the Supreme Court again chose the evolutionary approach, adopting Judge Cooley's suggestion that punishments could be constitutional in one age but unconstitutional in the next. Wilson, sentenced to 15 years at hard labor for counterfeiting government bonds, had also been charged by information and not indictment. Unlike *Hurtado*, there was no question that the Fifth Amendment applied to Wilson's prosecution in federal court, so long as Wilson's crime was capital or "infamous." Responding to the prosecution's argument that Wilson's crime was not infamous because Congress had not declared punishment at hard labor to be so, the Court unanimously held:

> What punishments shall be considered as infamous may be affected by the changes of public opinion from one age to another. In former times, being put in the stocks was not considered as necessarily infamous. And by the first judiciary act of the United States, whipping was classed with moderate fines and short terms of imprisonment in limiting the criminal jurisdiction of the district courts to cases "where no other punishment than whipping, not exceeding thirty stripes, a fine not exceeding one hundred dollars, or a term of imprisonment not exceeding six months, is to be inflicted." Act September 24, 1789, *c.* 20, § 9, (1 St. 77.) But at the present day either stocks or whipping might be thought an infamous punishment.

By declaring punishments such as lengthy imprisonment at hard labor, the stocks, and whipping made a crime "infamous" under the Fifth Amendment, the Court was still a large step from declaring that the punishments were "cruel and unusual," but by requiring an indictment, the Court not only made it more difficult to bring a prosecution in Wilson's case but also created a new legal doctrine that would later extend to the Eighth Amendment.

The Supreme Court is part of the common law tradition, and to the extent that its decisions discuss philosophy, it is only to decide a specific controversy presented by lawyers. Lawyers present whatever arguments they hope will win, so the course of Supreme Court decisions is erratic, and changes in fundamental law are sporadic and even unpredictable. It was not criminal defendants, but rather the growing intercontinental network of railroads that most vigorously sought to expand the reach of the Due Process Clause to protect themselves from state and local government regulations. The Supreme Court first considered whether the due process that the Fourteenth Amendment protected included the Fifth Amendment's prohibition of taking property without just compensation. In *Missouri Pacific Railway Co. v. Nebraska* (1896) and *Chicago, Burlington & Quincy Railroad Co. v. Chicago* (1897), the justices announced that states and municipalities could not take a railroad's property unless the railroad received just compensation, on the reasoning that the Fifth Amendment's Takings Clause was so fundamental as to be "incorporated" into the meaning of due process of law.

Lawyers with other clients, including criminal defendants, were quick to use this concept of "incorporation" to press their client's interests: if the Due Process Clause "incorporated" the Takings Clause, maybe other provisions of the Bill of Rights might also be incorporated into the Fourteenth Amendment and therefore restrain state and local criminal laws. This approach had not been successful for the defendants in *Hurtado* and *Kemmler*, not because the Supreme Court justices were particularly hard on criminal defendants but because crime and punishment were predominantly state and local matters and, with the traditional exception for crimes committed against federal institutions or federal officials or on federal property, not the business of the national government. Local control over criminal justice inevitably meant that the criminal penalties, and even the procedures used in courts, could vary from state to state. The next century would see many legal battles over how much variance the Due Process Clause permitted and how much uniformity the Bill of Rights required. As an example, the Sixth Amendment provides:

> In all criminal prosecutions, the accused shall enjoy the right to a speedy and public trial, by an impartial jury of the state and district wherein the crime shall have been committed, which district shall have been previously ascertained by law, and to be informed of the nature and cause of the accusation; to be confronted with the witnesses against him; to have compulsory process for obtaining witnesses in his favor, and to have the assistance of counsel for his defense.

This sets out at least nine ambitious goals about when, where, how, and before whom a criminal trial should proceed. All nine have been incorporated into the concept of due process and therefore bind states as well as the federal government. As we will explore further in Chapter 2, in the last several decades, some of them have been construed as having special applicability to the question of capital punishment.

So Does Due Process "Incorporate" a Ban on Cruel and Unusual Punishment?

Sometimes the goals of maintaining order and achieving procedural fairness act at cross purposes. A criminal justice system that places effective crime control first runs the risk of imposing order at the cost of freedom. A criminal justice system that places due process ahead of crime control risks being rendered ineffectual by use of the system's own protections and risks being perceived to be more about lawyers' and judges' pet philosophies than the desire of society at large for protection from crime. If the first risks authoritarianism, the second risks vigilantism.

Writing in 1964, law professor Herbert Packer described the dilemma: placing crime control first results in a procedural system heavily oriented toward negotiated guilty pleas and leaves the fighting over the guilt or innocence of the defendant to out-of-court negotiations between the prosecutor and the defense counsel. If controlling crime comes first, justice resembles an assembly line. By comparison, by providing maximum assurance that only the guilty are convicted and that a defendant, guilty or not, has at least a fair portion of the resources that the prosecutor has, a system that puts due process first looks very much like an obstacle course (Packer 1964, 13). Just as in the 18th century, Americans had adopted both Beccaria and Blackstone, in the 20th century, the Supreme Court would adopt both models of the criminal process: the Crime Control Model would govern every crime other than murder, and the Due Process Model would be the special province of capital crimes.

This shift started in the early 20th century with a change in what people expected from government. In addition to Locke's protection of life, liberty, and property, the Progressive Era saw local governments promoting public education, regulating food and drugs, and taking steps to solve economic problems by creating unemployment compensation and workers' compensation, attempting to set maximum hours and minimum wages for some industries, and attempting to ban women and children from some jobs. The federal government lagged behind but took steps to regulate the costs of railroad transportation and to exercise control over monopolies and mergers that affected interstate commerce. The Constitution had been written in a day when the only government employee a citizen was likely to ever see was the postman, and the Bill of Rights for an era in which the only government official that might affect one's life was a judge. The challenge for the Supreme Court in

1900 was to interpret the Constitution for the new era: did it permit anything that was not forbidden, or did it forbid anything not permitted in 1789? Reversing of the politics of our century, liberals urged the Supreme Court to defer to the good judgment of legislatures, while conservatives urged judges to use the Constitution to rein in what they saw as assaults on basic liberties. The most contentious issue was the permissible scope of regulation of the economy by the federal government; the issue would not be settled until the 1930s in the New Deal administration of President Franklin Roosevelt. That battle over how the Constitution should be interpreted would spill over to have a profound impact on capital punishment.

The United States had at the same time acquired an overseas empire of sorts as a result of the Spanish-American War (1898), and the Court repeatedly had to grapple with the arguments from litigants in Puerto Rico and the Philippines about whether a provision of the Bill of Rights applied or whether Congress was free to pass any legislation for them it pleased. The Supreme Court's decisions, known collectively as the *Insular Cases*, appeared to endorse the *Hurtado* rule that due process required fundamental protections of the Bill of Rights, but not all of them. The battle to decide what amendments were fundamental would likewise spill over to have a profound impact on capital punishment.

By the late 1920s, the Court had accepted the claim that the First Amendment's freedom of speech was part of due process of law. The 1930s added freedom of the press, free exercise of religion, and freedom of assembly as fundamental rights part of due process too. The Eighth Amendment's prohibition of cruel and unusual punishment did not make the list. Twenty-five years after *Kemmler*, the Court held in *Malloy v. South Carolina* (1915) that South Carolina's adoption of execution in the electric chair to replace hangings did not violate any right to due process of the condemned because South Carolina's choice "is the consequent of a well grounded belief that electrocution is less painful and more humane than hanging." The same year in *Collins v. Johnston* (1915), the Supreme Court held that a 14-year sentence for perjury was not excessive punishment prohibited by the Due Process Clause, reasoning, "to establish appropriate penalties for the commission of crime . . . are functions peculiarly belonging to the several States."

The Court sometimes faced questions of "pure" procedure, and as in *Hurtado*, criminal defendants could not count on the justices being receptive to arguments that state court trials were regulated by a uniform federal standard. The Court decided in *Maxwell v. Dow* (1900) that due process did not require Utah to provide a twelve-man jury in a noncapital case (eight was enough), and in *Twining v. New Jersey* (1908) that the right against self-incrimination did not protect two criminal defendants from a state court judge reminding a jury that they had not taken the stand to deny evidence of their guilt.

In the 1930s, the Court incorporated the Sixth Amendment's right to counsel in *Powell v. Alabama* (1932), a death penalty case involving black defendants tried in the South. Alabama had provided counsel for the Scottsboro Boys—teenagers accused of raping two white women while hitching rides on a train—but the attorney had appeared for his clients only on the morning of trial and had undertaken no preparation or investigation. The Court announced that since the effective assistance of counsel was "at the base of all our civil and political institutions," it was part of due process and that the defendants' convictions could not stand.

The Court finally announced a general formula for which provisions of the Bill of Rights were fundamental and therefore part of due process in *Palko v. Connecticut* (1937). Connecticut charged Frank Palko with capital murder for killing his wife. After a jury convicted him of second-degree murder, the prosecution successfully appealed the life sentence, and on retrial, the second jury convicted Palko of first-degree murder. Justice Benjamin Cardozo, who had been on New York's highest court, explained that only rights "of the very essence of a scheme of ordered liberty" were incorporated into the Due Process Clause, and protection from double jeopardy was not essential. Palko's death sentence did not offend due process because:

> The state is not attempting to wear the accused out by a multitude of cases with accumulated trials. It asks no more than this, that the case against him shall go on until there shall be a trial free from the corrosion of substantial legal error. . . . This is not cruelty at all, nor even vexation in any immoderate degree.

Palko was executed.

A decade later, Justice Cardozo's successor on the Court, Justice Felix Frankfurter, cast the deciding vote that the Eighth Amendment's Cruel and Unusual Punishment clause was essential in *Louisiana ex rel. Francis v. Resweber* (1947). Willie Francis had been sentenced to die in the electric chair for a murder committed when he was 15. Louisiana's electric chair traveled in a truck with a portable generator from parish jail to parish jail and was wired up on the spot as needed. The first attempt to electrocute Francis had failed because the connection was faulty. After *Palko*, double jeopardy would not prevent a second attempt to kill Francis, but what about cruel and unusual punishment? The Court could not agree: four justices said the first attempt was no more important than if Francis had suffered from an accidental fire in his cell, and four justices said that since Louisiana could not torture a prisoner to death by repeated shocks; it made no difference whether the first failure was an accident. Justice Frankfurter, an opponent of the death penalty, cast the deciding vote: since the first failure was not intentional, a second attempt would not be unconstitutional. Francis was executed at age 17.

The Eighth Amendment was finally incorporated in *Robinson v. California* (1962), an otherwise unimportant case that held that California could not make the mere fact of being a drug addict a criminal offense. By this time, what constitutional historians refer to as the "due process revolution" had been in process for a decade, as the Supreme Court found in case after case that procedural protections already in use by the federal government were so fundamental that they applied to all the states too. Many previous decisions, such as *Twining* and *Palko*, were overturned.

Even before the due process revolution, the Court struck down some state criminal laws under other constitutional provisions. In *United States v. Reynolds* (1914), Alabama's criminal surety laws were held to violate the Thirteenth Amendment. These laws, used since slavery ended, provided that when a "surety" paid a defendant's fines and costs for a petty offense, the defendant had to work off the debt or the breach of the contract would be a new criminal offense. This assured a supply of low-cost seasonal labor, but the laborer caught up in this system was, in the words of the Supreme Court, unconstitutionally "chained to an everturning wheel of servitude."

The Equal Protection Clause was used to invalidate sterilization as a punishment for crime in *Skinner v. Oklahoma* (1942). Adopting a perversion of Darwin's theory, some states had passed laws mandating sterilization after some convictions because the defendant was the "probable potential parent of socially undesirable offspring." The Supreme Court found that Jack Skinner's convictions for stealing chickens and for armed robbery did not subject him to this punishment, not because it was cruel or unusual, but for the unconvincing reasoning that, since other offenses did not include the same penalty, Oklahoma was denying Skinner equal protection of law. Fortunately, there was no push to amend the statute to fix that problem.

That the Court would sometimes use other provisions when there was no majority that would extend the Cruel and Unusual Punishment Clause was on display in *Reid v. Covert* (1957), a far-reaching decision about the relation of executive orders and treaties to the Bill of Rights. Reviewing the convictions of two wives who had been tried in courts-martial for murdering their husbands, one a soldier on a base in Germany and one on Okinawa, the Court held that regardless of executive agreements permitting trials overseas by court-martial, the Bill of Rights guaranteed the defendants indictment by grand jury and trial by petit jury. The Court split four to four on the question of executive power, and Justice John Marshall Harlan II (grandson of the judge in *Hurtado*) cast the deciding vote to overturn the convictions specifically because the defendants were exposed to the death penalty. In his view, that penalty called for the law to be "especially sensitive to demands for procedural fairness."

Procedural rights were at the center of the judicial revolution by the Court under Chief Justice Earl Warren in the 1960s, and the Court's consideration of the death penalty during this decade took a decidedly procedural twist. To understand why, you must consider the three-step process the Court typically used to incorporate a provision of the Bill of Rights. The Court's initial examination of an issue, for instance whether suppression of evidence should be ordered as a remedy for violations of the Fourth Amendment, would come in a federal case where there was no question the Bill of Rights applied. Next, some criminal prosecution from a state would present the same issue and the Court would hold that due process did not require that states adopt the exclusionary rule used in federal court. At the third and final stage, sometimes decades later, the Court would decide that after all the Bill of Rights did require states to use the same procedures used by the federal government, and therefore incorporated the exclusionary rule.

The first step in this process hardly got started with the issue of capital punishment, because although Congress quickly responded to sensational crimes with legislation permitting capital punishment (for example, after the Lindbergh baby kidnapping in 1932 and the first wave of aircraft hijackings in the 1960s), federal capital punishment cases were rare. In the few federal capital cases that the Court chose to review, the Court usually considered issues other than the death penalty. In *Ex Parte Quirin* (1942), the Court considered claims by suspected German saboteurs that their capital trials by a military commission were illegal and unconstitutional; in *Rosenberg v. United States* (1953) the Court considered whether Ethel and Julius Rosenberg could be sentenced to death under the Espionage Act of 1917 or should have been charged under a provision of the Atomic Energy Act of 1946 that required a jury's recommendation for the death penalty. The Court ruled against the defendants each time.

By the 1960s, the federal death penalty was almost extinct because the executive branch rarely sought to charge anyone with a capital offense: there were only 24 federal executions between 1927 and 1963, and there were none between 1963 and 1972 (Little 1999, 370). The federal government, and in particular the Bureau of Prisons that had been formed as a separate agency within the Department of Justice in 1930 to run the expanding system of federal prisons, was strongly committed to a view that much crime was as curable as a disease, and that the chief purpose of punishment should be to rehabilitate the criminal. The first two heads of the Bureau of Prisons, Sanford Bates and James Bennett, were strongly against the death penalty, and the bureau did not even have its own death row; for its rare executions, it used whatever method was employed by the state where the execution was to take place.

The Supreme Court's review of the federal death penalty stuck to procedure, applying the Fifth and Sixth Amendment rulings of the previous decade. The Court held that the moribund federal death penalty for kidnapping was unconstitutional in *United States v. Jackson* (1968), but not on the basis that death was cruel and unusual. Rather, the justices reasoned that the statute violated the Sixth Amendment: since sloppy drafting permitted a jury upon conviction after trial either to recommend life imprisonment or to fix a sentence of death, but allowed a judge accepting a guilty plea to sentence a defendant to a maximum of life imprisonment, this unconstitutionally coerced a defendant to give up the right to trial before a jury.

Reviewing state capital sentences as in *Witherspoon v. Illinois* (1968), the Court likewise examined the procedure, not the punishment itself, holding that a state could not impose capital punishment if it excluded jurors who personally opposed capital punishment, but could vote in an appropriate case for the death penalty. In *Boykin v. Alabama* (1969), the Court reversed the death sentence imposed on a young black man who had pleaded guilty to five armed robberies, on the ground that a valid guilty plea required a knowing and voluntary waiver of the defendant's rights, and there was a doubt whether Boykin knew he was facing the death penalty by pleading guilty. The dissent pointed out that although the defendant had challenged the excessiveness of the sentence, he had not disputed the voluntariness of the guilty plea, and it is a rare case where the Supreme Court rules for a party based on a legal argument he has not made.

As the next chapter will describe, in the 1970s, the Court reached the logical conclusion of its approach to the Eighth Amendment through the Due Process Clause by invalidating existing death penalty laws as inadequate but refusing to hold the death penalty itself unconstitutional. This left a host of questions for the Court and for the other branches of government to address. One is to what extent the Supreme Court should prescribe uniform rules. Another is how much governmental power should be devoted to seeking executions, and what government resources should be devoted to preventing unjust ones? The classic formula as expressed by Blackstone in his *Commentaries* was that it is better that ten guilty go free rather than one innocent suffer. But today, two complaints are that too little effort is spent making sure that a capital case is properly tried the first time and that too much time and money are spent reexamining issues of guilt and innocence long after the trial is over.

A peculiarly American question is: whose role is it to make decisions about crime and punishment? Assuming that we can decide whether the legislature, the executive, or the judiciary should be primary, what role do the other branches of government play in this process? The chief goal of punishment has in turn been interdiction, retribution, rehabilitation, and deterrence. In the United States, the collapse in the 1980s of confidence in the ability of punishment to rehabilitate criminals coupled with increased technical ability to collect and analyze crime data led to a renewed emphasis on the goal of deterrence. The emphasis in generations of philosophical questions about retribution has given way to battles of experts over whether the death penalty deters crime, how much it costs, and whether there are statistically demonstrable biases that affect who ends up on death row.

References

Bailyn, Bernard. 1992. *The Ideological Origins of the American Revolution*, enlarged edition. Cambridge, MA: Belknap Press of the Harvard University Press.

Barron v. Mayor and City Council of Baltimore, 32 U.S. 243 (1833).

Beccaria, Cesare. 1963 [1764]. *On Crimes and Punishments*. Translated by Henry Paolucci. Englewood Cliffs, NJ: Prentice Hall.

Blackstone, William. 1979. *Commentaries on the Laws of England*. 4 vols. Chicago: University of Chicago Press. Facsimile of the first edition of 1765–1769.

Boykin v. Alabama, 395 U.S. 238 (1969).

Bradwell v. Illinois, 83 U.S. 130 (1873).

Bushell's Case, 124 Eng. Rep. 1006 (C.P.1670).

Chicago, Burlington & Quincy Railroad Co. v. Chicago, 166 U.S. 226 (1897).

Cogan, Neil H., ed. 1997. *The Complete Bill of Rights*. New York: Oxford University Press.

Collins v. Johnston, 237 U.S. 502 (1915).

Cooley, Thomas M. 1927. *A Treatise on the Constitutional Limitations Which Rest upon the Legislative Power of the States of the American Union*. 2 vols. Eighth edition, ed. Walter Carrington. Boston: Little, Brown, and Company.

deSecondat, Charles Louis, Baron de Montesquieu. 1777. *The Complete Works of M. de Montesquieu.* 4 vols. Translator unknown. London: T Evans. *The Spirit of the Laws,* originally published in 1748, is vol. 1. It is available at http://oll.libertyfund.org/titles/837 (December 1, 2016).

Dred Scott v. Sandford, 60 U.S. 393 (1857).

Ex Parte Quirin, 317 U.S. 1 (1942).

Ex Parte Wilson, 114 U.S. 417 (1885).

Grant, Michael. 1989. *Selected Political Speeches of Cicero.* London: Penguin Books.

Holden v. Minnesota, 137 U.S. 483 (1890).

Hurtado v. California, 110 U.S. 516 (1884).

In re Kemmler, 136 U.S. 436 (1890).

Little, Rory K. 1999. "The Federal Death Penalty: History and Some Thoughts about the Department of Justice's Role." *Fordham Urban Law Journal* 26: 347–508.

Locke, John. 1980 [1690]. *Second Treatise of Government,* edited by C. B. Macpherson. Indianapolis, IN: Hackett Publishing Co.

Louisiana ex rel. Francis v. Resweber, 329 U.S. 459 (1947).

Malloy v South Carolina, 237 U.S. 180 (1915).

Maxwell v. Dow, 176 U.S. 581 (1900).

McElvaine v. Brush, 142 U.S. 155 (1891).

McKane v. Durston, 153 U.S. 684 (1894).

Missouri Pacific Railway Co. v. Nebraska, 164 U.S. 403 (1896).

Packer, Herbert L. 1964. "Two Models of the Criminal Process." *University of Pennsylvania Law Review* 113: 1–68.

Paine, Thomas. 1989 [1791]. *The Rights of Man,* in *Two Classics of the French Revolution.* New York: Anchor Books.

Palko v. Connecticut, 302 U.S. 319 (1937).

Powell v. Alabama, 287 U.S. 45 (1932).

Robinson v. California, 370 U.S. 660 (1962).

Rosenberg v. United States, 346 U.S. 273 (1953).

Skinner v. Oklahoma, 316 U.S. 535 (1942).

Slaughter-House Cases, 83 U.S. 36 (1873).

Smith, Gregory D. 2004. "Disparate Impact of the Federal Sentencing Guidelines on Indians in Indian Country: Why Congress Should Run the *Erie Railroad* into the Major Crimes Act." *Hamline Law Review* 27: 483–533.

Story, Joseph. 1987. *Commentaries on the Constitution of the United States*. Durham, NC: Carolina Academic Press. Reprint of 1833 edition.

Twining v. New Jersey, 211 U.S. 78 (1908).

United States v. Hudson and Goodwin, 11 U.S. 32 (1812).

United States v. Jackson, 390 U.S. 570 (1968).

United States v. Reynolds, 235 U.S. 133 (1914).

Wilkerson v. Utah, 99 U.S. 130 (1878).

Witherspoon v. Illinois, 391 U.S. 510 (1968).

2 Problems, Controversies, and Solutions

Introduction

In his dissenting opinion in *Northern Securities Co. v. United States* (1904), Supreme Court Justice Oliver Wendell Holmes Jr. famously observed that, "[g]reat cases, like hard cases, make bad law." Such cases are hard because they present exceptional issues upon which it may be difficult to base general legal principles. The Supreme Court has said the Eight Amendment has an "evolving standard of decency," under which some aspects of capital punishment can become constitutionally impermissible, but what evidence of evolution is admissible and to which aspects is it relevant? Do methods of execution matter? What crimes should be eligible for capital punishment? Should juveniles or those with diminished mental capacity be eligible for the death penalty? Is the death penalty fairly and consistently applied, or are there racial and other biases? What about the costs of capital punishment? What is the risk of wrongful conviction? What about botched executions and problems with finding drugs for lethal injections?

What Is the Constitutional Status of Capital Punishment?

The short answer is that the Eighth Amendment prohibits cruel and unusual punishments, but not the death penalty. When

---

Newsmen view the sandbagged chair where Gary Gilmore sat to face a firing squad at the Utah State Prison on January 18, 1976. (AP Photo)

written into the Bill of Rights, the phrase "cruel and unusual" did not refer to the death penalty generally. As *Wilkerson* and *Kemmler* illustrated, the late 19th-century capital punishment controversies established that death is a constitutionally permissible penalty if it is not inflicted with wanton cruelty. At that time, the firing squad and the electric chair were not believed to be wantonly cruel. Execution methods matter. History has seen drowning pits, crucifixions, pressing boards, disembowelment, boiling, stoning, burning at the stake, drawing and quartering, breaking on the wheel, and beheading. For centuries, torture, mutilation, and the infliction of gratuitous pain unnecessary to ending the condemned person's life were a desired part of the punishment. They are now disavowed as cruel, unusual, and unacceptable forms of punishment because of evolving community standards of decency. But consider the problems that methods of execution pose for evolving standards: what allows us to draw, in theory, the line between what is cruel and what is acceptable, and how do we in fact measure where on that line a new punishment falls? Consider that in the 18th century, the guillotine was welcomed as a progressive reform when it was introduced in France, because of numerous historical examples of inept or drunken executioners requiring several blows to sever a head. In the American colonies too, beheading was considered worse than hanging, and reserved for Native Americans (*State v. Santiago*, 88). Yet when St. Paul was executed, the Roman Empire considered his beheading a merciful alternative to crucifixion; 1,500 years later, England considered St. Thomas More's beheading a merciful alternative to drawing and quartering. In the 19th century, the electric chair was hailed as the modern replacement for hanging. Hanging had been widely used for centuries, but an improperly fashioned noose with too short a "drop" could leave the condemned to die a slow death by strangulation. With too long a "drop," as in Vermont's 1905 execution of Mary Rogers, the condemned could reach all the way to the ground and have to be yanked off the ground and swung like a pendulum for 14 minutes (Smith 1996, 105). Or the drop could simply tear the criminal's head from him. In 1994, a federal judge granted an injunction against the state of Washington's use of hanging to execute Mitchell Edward Rupe because in prison his weight had ballooned to 410 pounds; Washington's hanging protocol had only contemplated the use of rope for defendants below 220 pounds and Rupe's decapitation was a real risk (Kirchmeier 2000, 616). Rupe's execution was later permanently overturned on other grounds, and he died in prison in 2006.

Death by electrocution was imagined to be instantaneous, but from Kemmler's execution in 1890 onward, electric chairs occasionally malfunctioned with gruesome results. Witnesses reported smoke rising from the head and the smell of burning flesh. The Supreme Court has not revisited *Kemmler*. In the wake of several claims of botched electrocutions, Florida added lethal injection to its methods of execution just after the Supreme Court granted certiorari in *Bryan v. Moore* (1999) to review Florida's use of the electric chair. In February 2000, the Supreme Court granted a last-minute stay of execution to Robert Lee Tarver because it was considering his petition to have Alabama's use of electrocution declared cruel and unusual, but three weeks later, the Court, over dissents by Justices Stevens, Souter, Breyer, and Ginsburg, declined to review the matter and dissolved the stay. Alabama electrocuted Tarver on April 14, 2000. Alabama subsequently changed its law to make lethal injection its default method of execution, with the electric chair as an option if the defendant chooses. Most states had ceased using electrocution after the introduction of lethal injection, and in states that retained "the chair," state courts applying state law have banned its use. In *State v. Mata* (2008), the Nebraska Supreme Court declared that the electric chair violated Nebraska's state constitutional ban on cruel and unusual punishments.

Early in the 20th century, executioners turned to use of gas chambers to avoid the complications of electrocution, and in 1923, the Nevada Supreme Court declared this method permissible in *State v. Gee Jon* (1923), observing that the legislature had determined the method is humane, and adding that: "it would indeed be not only presumptuous, but boldness on our part, to substitute our judgment for theirs, even if we thought differently upon the matter."

Gee Jon's was the first execution by gas, on February 8, 1924. Death by poison gas will be forever attached to its use by Nazis during the Holocaust, and in *Fierro v. Gomez* (1996), the Ninth Circuit Court of Appeals held that California could not use its gas chamber because death by gas inflicted cruel and unusual punishment. California subsequently amended its law to allow lethal injection. In 1999, brothers Karl LaGrand and Walter LaGrand chose to be executed in Arizona's gas chamber, hoping that the Ninth Circuit would apply *Fierro v. Gomez's* reasoning, but Arizona also amended its law to allow the condemned the choice between gas and lethal injection. Karl LaGrand chose lethal injection and was executed on February 24, 1999. Walter LaGrand gambled that by choosing gas the Ninth Circuit would still stay his execution, but in *Stewart v. LaGrand* (1999), the Supreme Court held that an inmate could not both choose an optional form of execution and then challenge the one he chose. Walter LaGrand was executed by gas on March 3, 1999.

Now debates surround the currently favored method of execution: lethal injection. Botched executions have been reported, and problems have arisen in obtaining the drugs needed for various lethal "cocktails." As a result, some abolitionists assert that "humane execution" is a contradiction in terms: no matter how it is carried out, capital punishment will offend prevailing standards of decency, is *always* cruel and unusual, and therefore is absolutely prohibited by the Eighth Amendment. Period. As our discussion below will indicate, in the case of lethal injection the Supreme Court does not agree.

Retentionists respond that history shows that the Eighth Amendment did not ban and was not intended to ban capital punishment, but only inhumane methods of execution that were already obsolete. They note that the Eighth Amendment, like its model in the English Bill of Rights, refers to cruel and unusual punishment in all cases, not to capital punishment alone. Punishments less than death that once were commonly accepted may have gone out of use and be considered cruel and unusual. As a recent example, consider that in 1994, Michael Fay, an American citizen, confessed to stealing road signs and vandalizing cars in Singapore. He later claimed that he had stolen the signs but only pleaded guilty to vandalism because he had been advised that doing so would allow him to avoid being punished by caning. Nevertheless, he was sentenced to be beaten with a cane. The event took place beyond U.S. jurisdiction but many Americans were outraged and debated whether such forms of punishment are acceptable. Few recalled that in this country, whipping was a lawful penalty under federal law and in many states when the Eighth Amendment was ratified. Fewer knew that flogging had been banned as cruel and unusual punishment in *Jackson v. Bishop* (1968) by Judge (later Justice) Harry Blackmun, then on the Court of Appeals for the Eighth Circuit, because (even though still on the statute books in Delaware) flogging had gone out of use everywhere in the United States except for the Arkansas and Mississippi prison systems.

Although it is beyond the scope of this book, since the mid-1970s, the Eighth Amendment has also been increasingly used to litigate claims that prison conditions not intended as punishment (from the quality of food and medical care to use of solitary confinement) nevertheless are cruel and unusual punishment. One of Congress's few forays into legislation touching on the Eighth Amendment was the 1996 Prison Litigation Reform Act, which attempted with little long-term success to reduce the number of frivolous federal lawsuits attacking conditions in state prisons and local jails.

Two of the more common federal and state legislative responses in the 1980s and 1990s to the increase of crime in the 1960s and 1970s were mandatory sentencing statutes and so-called three strikes laws. Mandatory sentences for the possession of substantial amounts of controlled substances and for firearms offenses contributed to the quintupling between 1979 and 2009 in the number of Americans incarcerated in state and federal prisons, to a peak in the latter year of approximately 1.6 million (Carson 2015, 2). Three strikes laws also drastically scaled up the potential penalties for repeat offenders: a first conviction for a minor crime like shoplifting might bring a fine and probation, but the third conviction for the same offense could result in a mandatory 25 years to life sentence (Melusky and Pesto 2003, 9–11).

The Supreme Court's Eighth Amendment jurisprudence makes law, but does so in a fundamentally different way than these legislative actions do. Legislation states what the law shall be in general society, while the judgment of a court states what the law is in the particular circumstances of a case involving specific litigants. On the other hand, legislatures are not bound to the decisions of the previous session: states freely repeal and reenact criminal statutes, including death penalty laws. Judicial decisions, however, become precedents that apply in subsequent similar cases. Under a principle known as stare decisis (Latin for "to stand as decided"), judges look to the previous decisions of their courts not just for guidance but also as having authority. The written explanation for a judgment is called an opinion. In the Supreme Court, a majority opinion has the support of five or more justices; typically, the closer to unanimous an opinion is, the more prestigious it is. A per curiam opinion is one "by the Court," not signed by any particular judge; this kind of majority opinion is often used to correct an error by a lower court when an issue is deemed settled enough not to require extensive explanation. A plurality opinion is one that receives fewer than five votes but more votes than any other opinion. A concurring opinion may be filed by justices who agree with some of the reasoning of the majority but wish to make additional points that the majority does not accept. An opinion concurring in the judgment agrees with the result reached by the majority but none of its reasons. A dissenting opinion disagrees both with the judgment and with the reasoning of the majority. Due to changes in the court's personnel, or even to a justice's change of mind, what today is a dissenting opinion may be the next term's majority opinion.

The Supreme Court Expands "Cruel and Unusual" to Mean "Excessive"

The history of punishments short of the death penalty is important to the understanding of capital punishment in the United States. The first Eighth Amendment attacks on criminal sentences on the ground that the prohibition of cruel and unusual punishments banned excessive sentences (and not just painful methods of execution) were in non–death penalty cases. The decisions in those cases were later used as precedents in capital cases. In *O'Neil v. Vermont* (1892), the Supreme Court dismissed a challenge to a severe sentence imposed on a New Yorker convicted of distributing liquor in Vermont, a "dry" state. The sentence was a fine of $20 per bottle for a total of $6,140, or, if the fine and costs were not paid, imprisonment at hard labor for each unpaid dollar at the rate of 3 days per dollar, for a total of more than 54 years. By a six-to-three vote, the Supreme Court rejected O'Neil's claim that this violated the Eighth Amendment on the grounds that his attorney failed to present the issue properly. In dissent, Justices Stephen Field and John Marshall Harlan complained that even if O'Neil had not properly raised the issue, the Court should hold that the Fourteenth Amendment barred the states from imposing cruel and unusual punishments, just as the Eighth Amendment barred the federal government from doing so. The dissenters concluded that O'Neil was exposed to a sentence six times as great as Vermont's courts could impose for manslaughter, and this disproportionate severity made the sentence both cruel and unusual.

A generation later, the position of the dissent carried the day. Paul Weems, an official in the American government in the Philippines after the Spanish-American War, had been sentenced to 15 years *cadena temporal* after his conviction for altering a public record to steal 612 pesos. Under Philippine law, *cadena temporal* required Weems to perform hard labor while wearing a chain from wrist to ankle, and the punishment was accompanied by loss of the right to vote and the requirement of registering his place of residence with the authorities for the rest of his life. In *Weems v. United States* (1910), six justices agreed that this punishment was cruel and unusual. Justice Joseph McKenna wrote:

> Legislation, both statutory and constitutional, is enacted, it is true, from an experience of evils but its general language should not, therefore, be necessarily confined to the form that evil had theretofore taken. Time works changes, brings into existence new conditions and purposes. Therefore a principle, to be vital, must be capable of wider application than the mischief which gave it birth. This is peculiarly true of constitutions.

After citing *Wilkerson*, *Kemmler*, and the dissent in *O'Neil*, as well as quoting the treatises of Story and Cooley, Justice McKenna announced that just as recent decisions by the Supreme Court had expanded the scope of Article I's Interstate Commerce Clause and the Due Process Clause of the Fourteenth Amendment, so the meaning of cruel and unusual punishment could evolve:

> The clause of the Constitution, in the opinion of the learned commentators, may be therefore progressive, and is not fastened to the obsolete, but may acquire meaning as public opinion becomes enlightened by a humane justice.

Despite Weems's personal good fortune at having his sentence overturned, the opinion in *Weems v. United States* fell into obscurity. In 1952, for instance, Judge Jerome Frank of the Court of Appeals for the Second Circuit affirmed the death sentences of Julius and Ethel Rosenberg for espionage, observing that in the four decades after *Weems*, he could find no federal decision holding a particular sentence to be cruel and unusual unless the entire statute was also held to be invalid.

Then, in 1958, the Supreme Court decided another non–death penalty case and put *Weems's* philosophy back in the forefront. During World War II, Albert Trop had been a 20-year-old private in the U.S. Army who in 1944 deserted for one day. Trop was court-martialed and dishonorably discharged. Under a federal law passed in 1865 to prevent desertions during the Civil War, Trop was also stripped of his citizenship, something Trop found out only in 1952 when he applied for a passport. Chief Justice Earl Warren, speaking only for a plurality of four justices (Justice William Brennan supplied a fifth vote on different grounds), believed that this automatic denationalization was excessive because "[c]itizenship is not a license that expires upon misbehavior." Describing Trop's loss as cruel and unusual punishment, Chief Justice Warren cited *Weems* in support of the assertion that "cruel and unusual" must draw its meaning from "the evolving standards of decency that mark the progress of a maturing society"—a phrase that itself would figure prominently in later Eighth Amendment cases. The chief justice admitted that since Trop could have been shot by firing squad for desertion in wartime, the punishment Trop received was not excessive, but found that denationalization could nevertheless be cruel:

At the outset, let us put to one side the death penalty as an index of the constitutional limit on punishment. Whatever the arguments may be against capital punishment, both on moral grounds and in terms of accomplishing the purposes of punishment—and they are forceful—the death penalty has been employed throughout our history, and, in a day when it is still widely accepted, it cannot be said to violate the constitutional concept of cruelty. But it is equally plain that the existence of the death penalty is not a license to the Government to devise any punishment short of death within the limit of its imagination.

Anyone following Chief Justice Warren's reasoning about the constitutionality of Trop's punishment could see not only that he believed that "excessive" and "cruel" were synonymous, but also that his stance on the intense public debate at the time in the United States, Canada, and Western Europe over legislation proposing to abolish capital punishment had evolved from his 10 years as the governor of California (1943–1953), during which the gas chamber at San Quentin had been active. The chief justice believed that there were strong moral grounds to oppose capital punishment; was he also signaling that its constitutionality depended on whether it "accomplished the purposes of punishment" and whether it remained "widely accepted?"

Four years after *Trop v. Dulles* (1958), the Supreme Court formally took the step of incorporating the Eighth Amendment. Lawrence Robinson had been convicted in Los Angeles of being "addicted to the use of narcotics" on the testimony of a narcotics officer that Robinson had needle tracks in his arms, with no attempt to produce evidence that he had actually used any drug in the city. In *Robinson v. California* (1962), Justice Potter Stewart wrote that this primitive effort to combat drug trafficking failed to comply with the Constitution:

[A] state law which imprisons a person thus afflicted as a criminal, even though he has never touched any narcotic drug within the State or been guilty of any irregular behavior there, inflicts a cruel and unusual punishment in violation of the Fourteenth Amendment. To be sure, imprisonment for ninety days is not, in the abstract, a punishment which is either cruel or unusual. But the question cannot be considered in the abstract. Even one day in prison would be a cruel and unusual punishment for the "crime" of having a common cold.

The Supreme Court's interpretation of the Eighth Amendment was now part of due process and states were banned from irrational punishments, as in *Robinson*, or excessive ones, as in *Trop*. In *Kemmler* and other early cases, the Supreme Court had been very deferential to the judgment of state legislatures and state courts. That had changed significantly by 1962, and voices on and off the Court would urge even further change.

In 1963, Justice Arthur Goldberg, appointed to the Supreme Court by President John F. Kennedy just the year before, called *Weems* and *Trop* to the attention of the other members of the Supreme Court in a memorandum asking the Court to consider the constitutionality of the death penalty itself in six cases on the Court's docket. The Supreme Court could take this step because it had possessed almost complete control over its choice of cases since the Judiciary Act of 1925. The "Judges Bill," shepherded through Congress by chief justice and former president William H. Taft, provided that the route most appeals would take to the Supreme Court would be by writ of certiorari. Granting a "writ of cert" requires four justices to vote to hear an appeal. The certiorari procedure gave the Court the power to shape an area of law by choosing the cases, or even individual questions from cases, that the justices believed to be the most important or the most unsettled. Since the Supreme Court had time to consider only a fraction of the total number of cases before it, it was unusual for the justices to reach out to consider an argument not raised and fully briefed by counsel. Justice Goldberg nevertheless asked the other justices to examine and overturn the death penalty, making three arguments that continue to be relevant to the Court's decision-making a half century later.

Justice Goldberg first asserted that together *O'Neil, Weems,* and *Trop* had expanded the Eighth Amendment to prohibit excessive punishments, not just cruel methods of execution, and that a punishment was excessive when a less severe sentence would serve equally well, and reasoned that since vengeance was no longer considered an acceptable goal for punishment and there was no evidence that the death penalty deterred capital crime more effectively than imprisonment, capital punishment was excessive and therefore barred. Second, when it came to evolving standards of decency, Goldberg pointed out that not only had most of the civilized nations of the Western world abolished the death penalty, but also that current opinion polls in the United States showed a steady decline in public support for capital punishment. Finally, Justice Goldberg urged the Court to consider that, in its decisions concerning due process in criminal cases, the "Court has traditionally guided rather than followed public opinion" and made the erroneous prediction that a Supreme Court opinion would settle controversy, not create it:

> Can there be any doubt that if this Court condemns the death penalty as cruel and unusual—whatever the initial effect—before too long that penalty will no longer be a mode of punishment about which opinion is fairly divided. (Goldberg 1986, 501)

Justice Goldberg's arguments did not persuade the Court to review any of the six cases, much less to strike down the death penalty. Nevertheless, the death penalty was an increasingly rare phenomenon. The federal government had executed George Krull and Michael Krull in 1957 for kidnaping and raping in a national park in Georgia, and executed Victor Feguer in 1963 for the interstate kidnaping of an Iowa physician murdered in Illinois, but would not pursue another execution for decades. In July 1968, as President Lyndon Johnson's administration was winding down, Attorney General Ramsey

Clark testified before the Senate Judiciary Committee in opposition to the death penalty because it was being discriminatorily applied against black defendants. In 1971, the report to Congress of the National Commission on Reform of Federal Criminal Laws recommended abolition of the federal death penalty (Final Report 1971, 311–312).

States that did continue to attempt to carry out the death penalty were faced with reviewing their convictions and sentences against an increasing number of new constitutional law rules being issued by the Supreme Court. When a defendant wanted to challenge his sentence, rulings such as *Miranda v. Arizona* (1966) and *Gideon v. Wainwright* (1963) affected practically every step of a trial from the investigation through the sentencing and could be raised both in state and federal courts. As a result, executions had halted by 1965 for any defendant who did not waive his appeals, and the total number of executions dropped to zero per year from 1968 to 1972.

The Supreme Court Bans and Restarts Capital Punishment in *Furman v. Georgia* (1972) and *Gregg v. Georgia* (1976)

In 1972, the Supreme Court appeared to strike down the death penalty itself in *Furman v. Georgia*. The judgment of the Court, overturning three death sentences imposed on defendants William Furman for a murder in Georgia, Lucious Jackson for a rape in Georgia, and Elmer Branch for a rape in Texas, was only one paragraph long. Each of the nine justices wrote a separate opinion, however, making *Furman* the lengthiest decision the Court had ever issued at the time. (It currently is in third place.) Two of the concurring justices, William Brennan and Thurgood Marshall, concluded that capital punishment is *always* constitutionally prohibited. The plurality—Justices William Douglas, Potter Stewart, and Byron White—objected to the appearance of racial bias or arbitrariness in the procedures determining whether the death penalty applied. Justice

Stewart, appointed to the Court by President Dwight Eisenhower and typically in the moderate middle, observed that because the death penalty was imposed only on a handful of defendants, the death sentences before the Court were cruel and unusual "in the same way that being struck by lightning is cruel and unusual." Justice White, appointed by President John Kennedy and also in the Court's middle, similarly observed that although capital punishment in the abstract was constitutional, the very desire to make the law less harsh by giving juries discretion about whether or not to impose the death penalty had resulted in the penalty being "so infrequently imposed that the threat of execution is too attenuated to be of substantial service to criminal justice." All four justices appointed by President Richard Nixon—Chief Justice Warren Burger and Justices Lewis Powell, William Rehnquist, and Harry Blackmun—dissented. Chief Justice Burger emphasized that the Court had *not* banned capital punishment and invited state legislatures to reform their capital sentencing procedures to limit jury discretion.

Responding to *Furman*, the states revised their death-penalty laws. Eleven states tried to answer the problem posed by the justices by eliminating jury discretion entirely, making the death penalty mandatory for certain crimes. Twenty-five states tried to provide juries with "guided discretion," requiring two-stage trials in capital cases. In the two-stage states, the traditional trial would determine guilt or innocence, and then a separate penalty phase would determine the punishment in light of aggravating or mitigating circumstances.

Four years after *Furman*, in *Gregg v. Georgia* (1976) and two companion cases, *Proffitt v. Florida* (1976) and *Jurek v. Texas* (1976), the Court upheld two-stage death penalty laws, ruling that they successfully addressed the *Furman* objections. Justice Potter Stewart, writing for the majority in *Gregg*, accepted *Trop*'s premise that the Eighth Amendment draws its meaning from "the evolving standards of decency that mark the progress of a maturing society" and *O'Neil*'s and *Weems*'s rationale that "cruel and unusual" includes "excessive," and punishments that inflict unnecessary pain or that are grossly disproportionate to the severity of the crime are prohibited. But, crucially, the majority held that capital punishment for the crime of murder—an extreme sanction for an extreme crime—is *not* invariably disproportionate. Dissenting, Justices Brennan and Marshall reaffirmed the absolute opposition to capital punishment they had expressed in *Furman*.

Capital punishment was back, officially returning under Utah's revised state death penalty statute when convicted murderer Gary Gilmore was executed on January 17, 1977, by a firing squad. In July 1976, Gilmore murdered an employee while robbing a gas station, and the next day murdered a motel clerk during another robbery. His speedy trial and execution were due to Gilmore's abandonment of any appeals. The Supreme Court did issue a short stay of execution at the request of Bessie Gilmore, Gilmore's mother, but then ruled in *Gilmore v. Utah* (1976) that since Gilmore was competent, had waived any challenge to his execution, and opposed his mother's intervention, she could not challenge the death penalty on his behalf. Interestingly, Justice White dissented on this point: since the Eighth Amendment was a limit on the power of government, and not a right of the defendant that could be waived or abandoned, he believed that some court had to review the validity of each death sentence.

Gilmore was a preview of the post-*Gregg* era: states would enact capital punishment laws, prosecutors would choose or decline to invoke them in particular cases, state supreme courts would review the facts of particular cases, and the Supreme Court would remain at the apex of the process that would result either in the invalidation of a death penalty or in an execution rare enough to be a celebrity event. The justices themselves would combine in sometimes unpredictable voting alignments for a majority or a plurality opinion that would grow increasingly longer but cover the same basic questions posed by the Eighth Amendment and Sixth Amendment. The justices themselves would increasingly be defined in the eyes of the general public by their votes on the death penalty.

Justice Brennan, until his retirement in 1990, and Justice Marshall, until his retirement in 1991, consistently stood by their position in *Furman* of opposition to the death penalty for all defendants and all crimes. Eighteen years after *Gregg* and shortly before his retirement, Justice Blackmun joined them, announcing in *Callins v. Collins* (1994) that "the death penalty experiment has failed" and that he would no longer "tinker with the machinery of death." After their retirement, Justices Powell and Stevens expressed their belief that capital punishment had constitutional deficiencies. In a 1991 interview (Jeffries 1994, 451), Justice Powell said that, if he could, he would change his vote to find the death penalty unconstitutional. Powell stated, "I would vote the other way in any capital case. . . . I have come to think that capital punishment should be abolished." He added that he did not think the death penalty could be fairly administered, and lengthy delays breed cynicism about the law, courts, and judicial processes.

Two decades after his 1994 appointment by President William Clinton, Justice Stephen Breyer came close to following Justice Blackmun as an abolitionist in his dissenting opinion in *Glossip v. Gross* (2015). Describing capital punishment as "unfair, cruel, and unusual," he concluded, "I believe it highly likely that the death penalty violates the Eighth Amendment." Justice Ruth Ginsburg, a 1993 Clinton appointee, joined him. By contrast, until his death in 2016, Justice Antonin Scalia was noted for his insistence that the original meaning of the text of the Constitution settled that the Eighth Amendment did not ban the death penalty. As in *Furman*, the controversy continues uninterrupted over the procedures by which it is applied.

As of the beginning of the Supreme Court's 2016 term, 31 states, the federal government, and the U.S. military authorize capital punishment. Nineteen states and the District of Columbia do not. From 1976 through October 19, 2016, 1,438 executions were performed. The peak year for executions was 1998 when 98 were performed. Executions have declined in number, with 28 taking place in 2015. From 1977 through 2015, 1,422 persons were executed in the United States, an average of 36.5 persons per year. Some states use capital punishment far more frequently than others. Texas leads the nation by a large margin. Three states—Texas, Oklahoma, and Virginia—account for over half (53 percent) of all executions. By region, most executions take place in the South (1,172), followed by the Midwest (178) and the West (85). Executions are rare in the Northeast (only four). Together, Texas and Oklahoma account for 649 of these 1,438 executions. Statistics appear to undermine the argument that capital punishment deters serious crimes. The South leads the nation in executions but it also has the highest murder rate (5.5 per 100,000 in 2014). The Northeast, with the fewest executions, has the lowest murder rate (3.3 per 100,000) ("Facts about the Death Penalty" 2016).

Is the Death Penalty Available for Any Crime Other Than First-Degree Murder?

Because courts decide cases, even if the justices make general philosophical statements they, are not law until they are contained in a majority opinion that applies to an actual death sentence for a specific crime. The quintet of cases that the Supreme Court decided in 1976—*Gregg v. Georgia, Proffitt v. Florida, Jurek v. Texas, Woodson v. North Carolina,* and *Roberts v. Louisiana*—all involved the death penalty for murder: Troy Gregg robbed and murdered two men who had given him a ride while hitchhiking, Charles Proffitt fatally stabbed a sleeping man while burglarizing his home, Jerry Jurek murdered a 10-year-old girl, and the defendants in *Woodson* and *Roberts* had participated in robberies that ended with murder. The revised state laws continued to make crimes other than murder eligible for capital punishment, and the Court would decide their constitutionality one by one.

In *Coker v. Georgia* (1977), the Court reviewed a state law that made rape a capital offense. The Court ruled that although rape is a serious, reprehensible, and violent crime, death is a "disproportionate and excessive punishment" for a rapist who does not take human life. Justice White, joined by Justices Stewart, Blackmun, and Stevens, announced the judgment of the Court. White cited history and objective evidence in support of his conclusion, noting that Georgia was the only state that "authorizes a sentence of death when the rape victim is an adult woman, and only two other jurisdictions provide capital punishment when the victim is a child." Justices Brennan and Marshall concurred based on their view that the death penalty is always cruel and unusual punishment. Justice Powell concurred in part on the grounds that death was an excessive penalty because death did not result *and* the victim was an adult woman. Chief Justice Burger, joined by Justice Rehnquist, dissented. So, counting the votes, Justice Powell's distinction between what an excessive penalty was when the victim was an adult and when the victim was not an adult left it unsettled whether the Eight Amendment forbade the death penalty for the rape of a child.

It was not until three decades later, in *Kennedy v. Louisiana* (2008), that the justices answered that question. A Louisiana jury found Patrick Kennedy guilty of raping his eight-year-old stepdaughter, making him eligible for the death penalty because rape of a child under the age of twelve was a capital offense under state law. The jury imposed a death sentence, but in a 5-4 decision, the Supreme Court held that the Eighth Amendment bars states from imposing the death penalty for the rape of a child where the crime did not and was not intended to result in the child's death. Justice Kennedy delivered the opinion of the Court. Justices Stevens, Souter, Ginsburg, and Breyer concurred. Citing *Coker*, where the Court had, 31 years earlier, struck down a capital sentence for the rape of an adult woman, Kennedy concluded that applying the death penalty in any rape case would violate a national consensus that had developed on the issue. Justice Alito, joined by Chief Justice Roberts and Justices Scalia and Thomas, dissented. Alito argued that

Coker did not govern cases involving the rape of a child, that in a federal system Louisiana could depart from the limits on capital punishment chosen by other states, and that in light of the facts of this case and the heinous nature of the crime, the death penalty was not excessive.

What about treason? The Supreme Court has not had occasion to consider the death penalty for treason or espionage since *Gregg v. Georgia*. Treason has, for a thousand years, been regarded as the highest offense known to law, and while a felon had to face death by hanging, the additional punishment of drawing and quartering that *Wilkerson* and *Kemmler* regarded as the definition of cruel and unusual was applied to traitors precisely because of its cruelty. The Framers inherited from the parliamentary opponents of royal power the fear that royal judges could crush political freedom by coming up with expansive interpretations of treasonous conduct; they also had more recent experience with colonial legislatures confiscating the property of persons declared traitors for backing the losing side in the Revolutionary War. For those reasons, treason is the only crime given a definition in the Constitution itself, and is limited to "levying War" against the United States, or "adhering to their Enemies, giving them Aid and Comfort." Note, however, that this does not require proof of murder, and after World War II, in *Tomoya Kawakita v. United States* (1952), the Supreme Court upheld the death sentence for an American convicted of treason for aiding the Japanese war effort by operating a nickel mine that used prisoner of war labor. During the Cold War, two Americans were executed for a crime less than murder after the Supreme Court in *Rosenberg v. United States* (1952) declined to review their convictions and sentences under the Espionage Act of 1917 for passing secret information about nuclear weapons to Soviet agents.

The current espionage and treason statutes do not require proof that death has resulted from the defendant's actions. Is this constitutional? As the late chief justice William Rehnquist once observed (Rehnquist 1998, 221), in matters of national security the Supreme Court does not have a track record of restraining the federal government, so if the Court chose to review a treason prosecution that resulted in a death sentence, the Court's decision whether capital punishment for treason not resulting in death is permissible would be likely to turn on whether the country was then at war.

Of course, death penalty prosecutions require a prosecutor, so although the judges may have the last word about the death penalty, the first and maybe the most serious component in deciding on capital punishment is the attitude of the prosecutor. This has two implications. On the one hand, Congress has authorized federal prosecutors to seek the death penalty for participants in very large-scale narcotics trafficking under so-called drug kingpin provisions, and for participants in continuing criminal enterprises who attempt to kill witnesses or jurors, even if murder is not proved. The constitutionality of these provisions is extremely doubtful after *Coker v. Georgia* and *Kennedy v. Louisiana*, but regardless of which political appointee heads the Department of Justice, federal prosecutors have not sought the death penalty for crimes not resulting in death, so we may never have a final answer.

From the time of the Roman Empire through William the Conqueror's rule of England, central governments have restricted the use of the death penalty by local governments partly to emphasize that they were sovereign. The United States deliberately chose a federal system of dual sovereignty: some powers were exclusively delegated to Congress, some were reserved to the states, and some, like the power to prosecute crime, were shared. Obviously the Supreme Court's due process and Eighth Amendment rulings have had the effect of erasing much local variance in the use of capital punishment, but this process is subject to some exceptions. Since the 19th century, the Supreme Court has held that because states, like the federal government, are considered separate sovereigns, the Double Jeopardy Clause of the Fifth Amendment does not prevent a person from being prosecuted twice for the same crime if one prosecution is by the United States and another by a state. The federal government ordinarily does not prosecute a person already subject to prosecution by a state under an internal regulation known since 1960 as the *Petite* policy, after *Petite v. United States* (1960). In politically charged cases, federal prosecutors have been quite willing to waive the policy. This has implications in states where murders are committed but there is no death penalty. The prosecution of Dzokhar Tsarnaev for the terrorist bombing of the 2013 Boston Marathon resulted in the death penalty being announced in June 2015 only because the trial was held in federal court as a terrorism case, not in Massachusetts as a murder case. While it is legally possible for Massachusetts to try Tsarnaev for the subsequent murder of an MIT police officer during the flight after the bombing, it is doubtful if that would make any sense to attempt to add life sentences to the pending death sentence.

Zacarias Moussaoui, by contrast, pleaded guilty to charges of conspiring to carry out the September 11, 2001 attacks and proceeded to a jury trial on the penalty only. He was subsequently given life sentences by a federal jury in the Eastern District of Virginia. Because generally there is no statute of limitations for murder, it is possible that Virginia, which has the death penalty, could at some point attempt to try, convict, and execute him for the deaths at the Pentagon, or that Pennsylvania, which has the death penalty, could attempt to try him for the deaths of passengers on Flight 93.

Such a calculation did take place in the trial of Timothy McVeigh for the 1995 truck bombing of the federal building in Oklahoma City. McVeigh was charged with the federal crime of murdering specific federal employees, but Oklahoma could have and probably would have stepped in and tried him for capital murder, if McVeigh had not received the death penalty and essentially waived any challenge to his execution in June 2001. Most recently, South Carolina and the federal government jockeyed over which would be the first to seek the death penalty against Dylann Roof for murdering nine members of a Charleston South Carolina church congregation on June 17, 2015.

The other implication of the question about who prosecutes, applicable to both federal and state prosecutions, is that who makes the decision to charge a capital crime varies not only from state to state but also from county to county and city to city. Two 2016 studies by the Harvard Fair Punishment Project note that although there are more than 3,000 counties nationwide, only 16 counties were responsible for five or more death sentences between 2010 and 2015 (Harvard Fair Punishment Project 2016a, 2); a longer range study indicates that just five individual prosecutors were responsible for about 15% of all defendants on death row (Harvard Fair Punishment Project 2016b, 18).

There are several reasons for such variance. The first and most obvious is the fact that the public prosecutor is almost always an elected officer. It is difficult enough for any politician to campaign for any office on the basis of opposition to the death penalty. Massachusetts governor Michael Dukakis's opposition to the death penalty contributed to his defeat in the presidential election of 1992; George Pataki's successful campaign for governor of New York in 1994 emphasized his pro–death penalty stance during the era of highest public approval for capital punishment. Today, support for capital punishment may no longer be a winning issue in many races. In local races in Florida and Louisiana in 2016, the expense of death penalty prosecutions and the publicity given to exonerations may have contributed to the defeat of aggressive pro–death penalty prosecutors. During the 2016 presidential election campaign, Democratic vice-presidential candidate Tim Kaine was attacked for representing death row inmates on a pro bono basis early in his legal career. The attacks failed to generate even much discussion, possibly because Kaine had, as the governor of Virginia from 2006 to 2010, also presided over the executions of 11 inmates on Virginia's death row.

But it is almost unheard of for a candidate for state's attorney or district attorney to campaign against the death penalty because that translates to the losing message "I'm soft on crime." So in municipalities like Los Angeles and Philadelphia (in states that execute practically no one), voters have elected district attorneys who campaigned as aggressive seekers of the death penalty. Once in office, a prosecutor in a state that has capital punishment has leverage that prosecutors in other states do not have. Due to Supreme Court cases pushing the death penalty in the direction of being reserved for the worst of murderers, most defendants who are prosecuted for capital murder have prior felony convictions. Because they have served sentences of imprisonment, they are familiar with life as an inmate. A prosecutor who can offer a choice between a life sentence to be served in the general population of a prison (where there is a certain pecking order that places murderers far above child molesters) and a lengthy stay on death row (that is far more uncomfortable even if it does not ultimately result in execution) has a real bargaining chip. Second, seeking the death sentence permits a prosecutor to "death qualify" the jury. Recall that in 1968, the Supreme Court held in *Witherspoon* that it was permissible to exclude jurors who could never vote for the death penalty, but not to exclude jurors merely because they opposed the death penalty in general. That was necessary to get a fair cross section of the community in an era when the jury had unlimited discretion. After *Gregg*, the Court clarified in *Wainwright v. Witt* (1985) that a juror could be excluded for cause if opposition to the death penalty would either prevent or "substantially impair" the performance of the sentencing task, a more prosecutor-friendly standard. Although juries are unique assemblies of citizens brought together to hear evidence that cannot be exactly duplicated, there are some statistical studies that indicate that death-qualified juries are more likely to convict. This is not due to some deception on the part of prosecutors, but probably the result of a recognizable phenomenon called anchoring: when presented with three alternatives of guilty with the death penalty, guilty with a life sentence, and not guilty, convicting a defendant but "sparing" him the death penalty can be a much less stressful choice for the juror than choosing between just two alternatives.

In *Lockhart v. McCree* (1986), the Supreme Court rejected Ardia McCree's claim that statistical studies showed that a death-qualified jury was unfairly tilted toward a guilty verdict, and practically held that such evidence was irrelevant as long as the jurors could lay aside their opinions and be impartial. Impartiality applies to jurors who favor the death penalty too: in *Morgan v. Illinois* (1992), the Court held that a defendant could "life qualify" the jury too. That is, a defendant must be allowed to question a prospective juror about whether the juror would automatically vote for the death penalty upon being convinced of the defendant's guilt, and to exclude for cause any such juror.

Judges, even when jurors make the life or death decision, are subject to the same psychological pressures that the choice of life or death has on the finding of guilt or innocence. And it is the choice of judges that gives a third motivation to prosecutors to charge capital murder: the court system in a large city or county almost always has a separate division exclusively for criminal cases, and within the criminal division, there are often special panels of judges to handle more serious cases. Because the expense of retrying a capital murder case is a significant budget item even for large cities, the judges (often former prosecutors) chosen for capital cases tend to be much more experienced in criminal matters. They are therefore more likely to keep prosecutions moving toward disposition by a guilty plea or a trial that will withstand appellate review, whether the jury imposes death or some lesser sentence.

Is a Mandatory Death Penalty Ever Permissible?

In two of the five death penalty cases decided in 1976, the Supreme Court began signaling that mandatory death penalty provisions are no longer constitutionally valid. From the Middle Ages forward, the punishment for all felonies was in theory a mandatory sentence of death, with any lesser sentence to be granted by a process of royal pardon. The penalty for misdemeanors was such punishment short of death as the judges decided. As Blackstone and other observers noted, opposition to these harsh penalties often caused juries to acquit obviously guilty persons. Even when the verdict was guilty, the inconsistency of punishment and the precarious nature of executive clemency were two well-known flaws in English law that the founders of the United States intended to correct by providing that the legislature and not judges should define crimes and punishments. In 1794, Pennsylvania divided murder into degrees and retained the mandatory death penalty only for premeditated murder, or murder of the first degree. Elsewhere, legislatures retained mandatory death penalties for treason and the more severe felonies of murder, robbery, piracy, and rape. At the end of the 18th century, punishments fixed by the legislature were considered protection against the historical danger of cruel and unusual punishments by judges.

By the end of the 19th century, the growing affluence of society and the birth of academic disciplines such as sociology and psychology gave rise to a new emphasis on punishment for crime as an opportunity for rehabilitation of the criminal. This led to a reduction in capital offenses: in 1897, Congress limited the death penalty to convictions for treason, murder, and rape. Rehabilitation also spurred increased use of indeterminate sentencing: the legislature still fixed the penalties, but judges sentenced defendants to a range between a minimum and maximum, with a professional parole board to determine when it was safe to release a convict back into society. The Supreme Court in *Williams v. New York* (1949) delivered a near-unanimous endorsement of this model:

> The belief no longer prevails that every offense in a like legal category calls for an identical punishment without regard to the past life and habits of a particular offender.

This whole country has traveled far from the period in which the death sentence was an automatic and commonplace result of convictions—even for offenses today deemed trivial. Today's philosophy of individualizing sentences makes sharp distinctions for example between first and repeated offenders. Indeterminate sentences, the ultimate termination of which are sometimes decided by nonjudicial agencies have to a large extent taken the place of the old rigidly fixed punishments. The practice of probation which relies heavily on non-judicial implementation has been accepted as a wise policy. Execution of the United States parole system rests on the discretion of an administrative parole board. Retribution is no longer the dominant objective of the criminal law. Reformation and rehabilitation of offenders have become important goals of criminal jurisprudence.

This embrace of rehabilitation sounded as tone-deaf as *Kemmler's* confidence in the humane use of electrocution: Samuel Williams had been convicted in New York of murder during a burglary and the jury had recommended life imprisonment. The judge nevertheless sentenced Williams to death after receiving out-of-court evidence that Williams had been reputedly involved in—not convicted of—other burglaries and had a "morbid sexuality." Only Justice Murphy protested that due process should forbid a judge to sentence a man to death on evidence not heard by the jury and not subject to examination by the defendant.

But even in the run-of-the-mill case, the indeterminate sentencing system had its flaws, and by the 1960s, American parole boards were criticized for lenient parole decisions, inconsistent parole decisions, and statistical discrepancies in parole decisions for white and black inmates. By the 1980s, mandatory sentences were back in vogue, and in the 1984 Sentencing Reform Act, Congress abolished parole entirely for federal sentencing. The Sentencing Reform Act also signaled Congress's rejection of the rehabilitative ideal. The new statute expressly stated that courts must recognize "that imprisonment is not an appropriate means of promoting correction and rehabilitation" (18 U.S.C. § 3582). Congress also attempted to reduce disparity between federal judges' sentences by creating a sentencing commission that prescribed sentencing guidelines that would attempt to take the many pieces of data particular to a crime and compute a score that would confine a judge to a fairly narrow sentencing range. Federal judges chafed at this diminution of their power, and in 2005, the Supreme Court held the whole process to have severe constitutional flaws that required the guideline process to be advisory only, instead of mandatory.

But the Supreme Court generally does not find any constitutional difficulty in mandatory sentences, just excessive ones. The Court in *Solem v. Helm* (1983) had adopted *Weems*'s principle that as a general rule, the Eighth Amendment prohibits *all* sentences that are disproportionate to the crime. Jerry Helm was convicted of writing a bad check for $100—his *seventh* nonviolent felony. Under a South Dakota recidivist statute, he was sentenced to life imprisonment without the possibility of parole. Was this sentence excessive? The Court found that it was. Writing for a bare majority, Justice Powell noted that "a criminal sentence must be proportionate to the crime for which the defendant has been convicted." Although a state may be justified in punishing repeat offenders more severely, Helm's individual offenses were all "relatively minor," and sentence of life without parole was the most severe punishment authorized by South Dakota law for *any* crime, including murder. As such, the sentence was "significantly disproportionate" to this crime.

Solem was a rare exception to the Court's refusal to second-guess sentences not involving the death penalty. For instance, in *Harmelin v. Michigan* (1991), the Court upheld a Michigan law imposing a mandatory life sentence for possession of 650 or more grams of cocaine (Harmelin had possessed 672 grams), and in *Ewing v. California* (2003) and *Lockyer v. Andrade* (2003), the Court upheld California's three-strikes law

power of the parole board to reduce the maximum length of imprisonment came to be considered the arbitrary power to prolong the minimum length of a sentence.

One year before *Furman*, the Court considered whether this sweeping power the jury had been given over life or death had evolved into a deprivation of due process. Dennis McGautha and a codefendant were convicted by a California jury of armed robbery and first-degree murder; in a separate sentencing proceeding that left the decision to the complete discretion to the jury, the codefendant received life and McGautha a death sentence. James Crampton was sentenced to death by an Ohio jury for shooting his wife. Ohio law did not provide for a separate penalty phase; the jury verdict fixed the punishment at death unless the jury recommended mercy, and Crampton's jury did not so recommend. In *McGautha v. California* (1971), the Supreme Court upheld the challenged laws. Justice John Marshall Harlan wrote for the majority, with Justice Hugo Black concurring separately to emphasize that history showed that the Eighth Amendment did not ban the death penalty. Justices Brennan, Marshall, and Douglas dissented. Justice Douglas wrote separately to stress how Ohio's unitary trial procedure stacked the deck in favor of death: a defendant who avoided taking the stand to bolster a defense that he was not guilty had no chance to address the jury before sentencing, and ran the risk of having the jury conclude he was not only guilty, but also lacked remorse. One year later, following Justices Harlan's and Black's retirements and Justices White and Stewart's consideration of the matter in *Furman*, the holding in *McGautha* was effectively nullified.

North Carolina was one of the states that attempted to meet Justice Byron White's criticism of the death penalty in *Furman* as flawed because it fell on such a small subset of criminals as to be arbitrary: its revised statute made death the mandatory penalty for first-degree murder. James Woodson and Luby Waxton were convicted of first-degree murder during an armed robbery, and automatically sentenced to death; the other two participants in the robbery testified for the prosecution and escaped death by pleading guilty to lesser charges. In *Woodson v. North Carolina* (1976), and the companion case, *Roberts v. Louisiana* (1976), a splintered Court struck down mandatory death sentences. In *Woodson*, Justice Stewart wrote for a plurality of three justices—Stewart, Powell, and President Ford's sole appointee John Paul Stevens—that the character of the defendant and the circumstances of the crime had to be taken into account. Noting that the historical trend had been away from mandatory sentences, the plurality considered enactment of mandatory sentences to be an attempt to retain the death penalty in a form consistent with the Constitution rather than a genuine sign that society had returned to acceptance of mandatory death sentences.

In *Roberts*, Stanislaus Roberts was convicted of first-degree murder in the robbery of a gas station and automatically sentenced to death. His accomplices testified for the prosecution. Louisiana's post-*Furman* law limited capital murder to first-degree murder in the commission of a felony, killing police officers or firefighters on duty, murder for hire, multiple murders, and second or subsequent convictions of murders, and permitted the jury to avoid the death penalty by returning a verdict of second-degree murder, manslaughter, or not guilty. Speaking through Justice Stevens, the plurality found this latter feature to be nothing more than unchecked discretion in new guise: the defendant could avoid the death penalty by inviting the jury to disregard the evidence and choose a verdict for a lesser offense. Justices Brennan and Marshall provided their uniform vote to overturn the death penalty. Chief Justice Burger and Justices Blackmun, White, and Rehnquist dissented.

A year later the Court considered a different Roberts sentenced to death: Harry Roberts, condemned to death for murder of a police officer. In a *per curiam* decision, *Roberts v. Louisiana* (1977) overturned this mandatory sentence too, summing up its decisions of the previous year as "it is essential that the capital-sentencing decision allow for consideration of whatever mitigating circumstances may be relevant to either the particular offender or the particular offense." A decade later, in *Sumner v. Shuman* (1987), the Court considered a question expressly left open in *Roberts*: what about murderers who are already serving a life sentence for murder? Raymond Shuman had been given a life sentence in 1958 for murder and was convicted in 1975 for murdering another inmate. Under Nevada law, Shuman had to be sentenced to death. Justice Blackmun, writing for a majority of six, noted that every state, including Nevada, had since the 1970s repealed mandatory death sentences or had state courts strike them down under state laws. The Court concluded that any departure from an individualized capital sentencing process "cannot be reconciled with the demands of the Eighth and Fourteenth Amendments." It is as settled as any Supreme Court holding can be that mandatory death penalties are forbidden no matter how grave the crime.

Guiding the Jury's Discretion

With the rejection in *Woodson* and *Roberts* of Justice White's suggestion in *Furman* that mandatory sentences could solve the problem of unguided jury discretion, guiding the jury's discretion was left as the only permissible option for a state that wished to retain capital punishment. How was this to be done?

The answer had already been offered by the American Law Institute's (ALI) Model Penal Code. Founded in 1923, the ALI was a permanent organization to study and recommend improvements in the law. As already noted, the end of the 19th century was a time of great debate over the extent of government regulation of economic activity, and more generally a time of flux in what the majority of Americans believed the purpose of government should be. Part of the results of this introspection was an effort spearheaded by the American Bar Association (ABA) to update laws and make them more uniform across state lines. The National Conference of Commissioners on Uniform State Laws, established in 1892, had already begun drafting uniform laws that state legislatures could adopt in virtually every legal field from marriage to consumer credit. The ALI, whose founders included Chief Justice William Howard Taft and future chief justice Charles Evans Hughes, then began an even more ambitious project of publishing Restatements, or analyses, of all judicial decisions on civil law topics like torts and contracts. With the success of that effort, the ALI began a similar project for criminal law, compiling a Model Penal Code that incorporated many recommended due process protections the Supreme Court would later find to be constitutionally required. In 1962, the ALI's official draft of the code recommended a two-stage trial for those states that wished to retain capital punishment: first a trial on guilt or innocence and second a hearing before a judge or the same or a different jury in order to determine the penalty. The presumptive sentence was life: the jury or judge was to impose the death sentence only if the defendant were 18 or older and jury were to find one or more specified aggravating factors (the murder was committed while the defendant was already an inmate; the murder was a second or subsequent conviction for murder; the murder risked death of many other victims; the murder was committed during a robbery, rape, arson, burglary, or kidnapping; the murder was in aid of flight or escape from custody; the murder was for pecuniary gain; or the murder was especially heinous, atrocious, cruel, or depraved) and that these factors were not outweighed by mitigating factors such as the defendant's youth or mental or emotional impairment or lack of a prior record.

Just as England adopted trial by jury as the best available option after the ordeal was abolished, most states adopted some form of the Model Penal Code after *Furman* abolished unguided jury discretion. As *Jurek* held, adopting the code as drafted was not the only possibility: Texas, for instance, limited capital murder at the charging stage to murders with aggravating features such as those found in the Model Penal Code. If the defendant were found guilty of one of these murders, the separate penalty phase asked the jury to answer three questions:

(1) Did the defendant kill deliberately and with the expectation that death would occur? (2) Is it probable that the defendant would commit future crimes of violence that constitute a continuing threat to society? and (3) Was the conduct of the defendant an unreasonable response to any provocation by the victim? This also permitted the defendant to introduce any evidence of mitigating factors because such evidence would be relevant to the question of future dangerousness.

In *McGautha*, Justice Harlan had expressed the opinion of the majority of the Court that unchecked jury discretion was permissible because the alternative was impossible:

> To identify before the fact those characteristics of criminal homicides and their perpetrators which call for the death penalty, and to express these characteristics in language which can be fairly understood and applied by the sentencing authority, appear to be tasks which are beyond present human ability.

For most of the next three decades, the Supreme Court would embark on precisely that task, by examining on a case-by-case basis whether the various forms of the Model Penal Code enacted by states after *Gregg* gave juries adequate guidance.

Mitigation

The Court considered mitigating factors first, beginning with *Lockett v. Ohio* (1978) and *Bell v. Ohio* (1978). Sandra Lockett was convicted of aggravated murder in the armed robbery of a pawnbroker, based in part on the testimony of Al Parker, who negotiated a plea that spared him exposure to capital punishment. Lockett was sitting in the car outside when the robbery took place and Parker shot the victim. At the sentencing hearing before the judge, Ohio law limited the mitigating factors that the judge could consider to three: whether the victim had provoked the offense; the defendant was under duress, coercion, or provocation; or the crime was the product of mental illness or deficiency. The Supreme Court ruled that Ohio's death penalty law was unconstitutional because it did not permit consideration of evidence on a wide range of relevant mitigating factors, such as Lockett's minor role in the offense, her young age, or her lack of serious criminal record.

Willie Lee Bell, at age 16, had participated in a kidnapping that ended in his codefendant shooting the victim with a shotgun. Bell, who had given a confession admitting his participation but denying that he had any idea his codefendant intended to kill anyone, waived a jury trial and chose to be tried by a three-judge panel. Defense counsel often refer to this tactic as a "slow guilty plea" in which the defendant or defense counsel gambles that the waiver of jury trial will be regarded as an acceptance of responsibility that deserves a lesser sentence. That did not work in this case: the judges held that none of the three mitigating factors permitted had been shown, and sentenced Bell to death. Chief Justice Burger, announcing the judgment of the Court in *Bell*, repeated that a trial judge must not be prevented by a state law "from considering as a mitigating factor, any aspect of the defendant's character or record and any of the circumstances of the offense that the defendant proffers." Justice White cautioned that this attempt to require that the sentencing judge or jury consider a wider range of information would invite a return to the pre-*Furman* days of unchecked jury discretion, but agreed that Bell's sentence should be overturned because Ohio permitted the death penalty even when there was no evidence that Bell intended the victim's death.

The plurality of the Supreme Court grew into a majority in only a few years, in *Eddings v. Oklahoma* (1982). Monty Lee Eddings ran away from home in Missouri and at age 16 shot and killed an Oklahoma Highway Patrol officer who stopped him for erratic driving. After he was ordered to stand trial as an adult, Eddings pleaded *nolo contendere* (no contest) to a first-degree murder charge. At the sentencing, the judge considered Eddings's age as a relevant factor, but he refused to consider Eddings's turbulent family history, beatings by his father, and emotional disturbance as mitigating factors, and sentenced Eddings to death. The Oklahoma courts affirmed, observing that Eddings's family history "is useful in explaining why he behaved the way he did, but it does not excuse his behavior." The Supreme Court, per Justice Powell, struck down the death sentence, emphasizing that the Eighth and Fourteenth Amendments require consideration of any aspect of the defendant's character, and any circumstance of the offense that the defendant proffered as a mitigating factor could not be excluded from consideration by the sentencing judge. The author of *Lockett*, Chief Justice Burger, joined by Justices White, Blackmun, and Rehnquist, dissented in *Eddings* on the grounds that the Court had granted certiorari only on the different question of the constitutionality of the death penalty for juveniles.

The Supreme Court's final position on mitigation, announced by Justice Scalia in *Hitchcock v. Dugger* (1987), a rare unanimous capital punishment opinion, is that any evidence that the defendant wants to present in mitigation must be considered and that any attempt by statute or otherwise to limit what can be considered mitigating will render a death sentence invalid. Furthermore, in *Mills v. Maryland* (1988) and *McKoy v. North Carolina* (1990), the Court held that a state cannot require that the jury be unanimous before it accepts a mitigating factor, because that would allow a single holdout juror to tip the penalty in favor of death.

The presentation of mitigation evidence has assumed primary importance as a result of *Oregon v. Guzek* (2006). A jury convicted Randy Lee Guzek of murder committed during a home burglary, rejecting the testimony of his alibi witnesses. The Model Penal Code had advised that states should allow any remaining doubt about the defendant's guilt to be a mitigating factor, and Guzek contended that *Lockett* and the Eighth Amendment gave him the right to introduce additional alibi testimony at the sentencing phase. Without dissent, the Supreme Court said not so. As Justice Breyer explained, sentencing is concerned with how, not whether, Guzek committed the crime: because the jury already decided that question, evidence to convince the jury that they should have a lingering doubt about Guzek's guilt was not mitigating evidence.

After *Oregon v. Guzek*, counsel for defendants present mitigation evidence to convince the jury of one of three things: (1) that because of youth or other circumstance the defendant is redeemable, or at least can live in prison without danger of future violence; (2) that the crime, though intentional, stemmed in part from factors beyond the defendant's control like mental illness or drug use; and (3) that the defendant's life was so troubled as a result of low intelligence, child abuse, neglect, and poverty, that he deserves sympathy despite his crime.

A principal concern of the Supreme Court for the last two decades has been how much effort counsel must put into presenting mitigation evidence. In *Williams v. Taylor* (2000), a Virginia jury sentenced Terry Williams to death after convicting Williams of robbery and murder of an intoxicated man for a couple of dollars. At the penalty hearing, the jury heard about Williams's prior record and his subsequent two assaults on elderly victims. The mitigating evidence from Williams's mother and two neighbors was that Williams was a "nice boy." The jury did not hear about what the Court described as Williams's "nightmarish" childhood of abuse and neglect, about his borderline mental retardation, or about the positive evaluation of him by corrections officers. The Court held that a jury deserved to hear this other side before returning a death sentence and counsel had failed by failing to develop it. In *Wiggins v. Smith* (2003), a Maryland jury heard nothing about Kevin Wiggins's life before he committed murder during a robbery of an elderly woman. A majority of the Court believed that if counsel had made the jury aware of the physical and sexual abuse Wiggins had suffered before and after being placed in foster care, they would likely not have voted for his execution. In *Rompilla v. Beard* (2005), a Pennsylvania jury voted for death after convicting Ronald Rompilla of the murder of a bar owner and hearing about Rompilla's lengthy prior record. The jury had not heard that Rompilla had been born with mental impairments stemming from fetal alcohol syndrome and was raised in an excrement-filled dog pen by parents who beat him.

In each case, the mitigating evidence considered by the Supreme Court had been found by counsel who had entered the case after the direct appeals were over. In each case, the Supreme Court held that trial counsel's failure to dig for available mitigating evidence deprived the defendant of a reliable result. In each case, postconviction counsel and the prosecutor reached an agreement to a noncapital sentence for the defendant.

So what evidence does a capital defendant's counsel have to present to be competent? According to the widely cited ABA guidelines, counsel must conduct an ongoing, exhaustive, and independent investigation of the defendant, beginning at least two generations before the defendant was born, and develop evidence of the effect on the defendant of exposure to toxins in utero, genetic disorders, family history of maltreatment, and illness and trauma. This is all in addition to the usual evidence of school records, work, and criminal history. To be effective, counsel should also interview and be prepared to present witnesses familiar with the impact of race, religion, community environment, and economic status on the defendant's actions (ABA 2008, 689–692).

Given the universe of information that the Supreme Court's mitigation jurisprudence makes relevant, it might sound like any overlooked story from a defendant's life might lead to counsel being held ineffective and a new sentencing proceeding being ordered. This is not the case. In *Bell v. Cone* (2002), the Court held by a vote of 8–1, with only Justice Stevens dissenting, that it was not ineffective for a Tennessee attorney to call no witnesses and make no closing argument at the penalty phase of the trial of Gary Cone, who admitted to the brutal murders of an elderly couple while he was on the run after an armed robbery. The penalty phase added only Cone's criminal record to the evidence the jury had already heard in the guilt phase. Cone's attorney, knowing that under state law the defense could by waiving its closing keep the prosecution from addressing the jury further, gambled that the prosecutor's low-key argument would not be persuasive. The Court held that this gamble, even if unsuccessful, did not deprive Cone of a fair hearing. In *Smith v. Spisak* (2010), the Court unanimously upheld an Ohio death sentence after Frank Spisak's attorney admitted to the jury that Spisak was "sick," "twisted," and was "never going to be any different" but asked that the jury still spare his life. Spisak, who was executed in 2011, had taken the stand in an attempt to convince the jury he was insane, admitting to three murders and other attempted murders in a performance that caused Justice Stevens to concur that after Spisak's testimony not even Clarence Darrow could have obtained a different result.

In short, the justices will defer to counsel's reasonable decisions about what evidence to put on and what arguments to make, but are increasingly demanding proof that the decisions by counsel were made after a thorough investigation of potential mitigating evidence.

Age as a Mitigating Factor? Juveniles at the Supreme Court

The Court took up specific questions about juveniles and the death penalty repeatedly after *Eddings*. In 1983, William Wayne Thompson was 15 when he participated in the murder of his former brother-in-law. Tried as an adult, Thompson was sentenced to death by a jury. As Justice Stevens tersely stated, the three adult codefendants were all tried separately and received a death sentence for a murder that was so brutal that "there is no claim that the punishment would be excessive" for the adults. In *Thompson v. Oklahoma* (1988), Justice Stevens wrote for a plurality of four that Thompson could not be executed for a crime committed when he was below the age of 16. Justice Stevens observed that the last execution of a 15-year-old in America had been in 1948, and that respected professional organizations such as the ABA and ALI, other nations sharing our Anglo-American legal heritage, and the countries of Western Europe find that "it would offend civilized standards of decency to execute a person who was less than 16 years old at the time of his or her offense." Punishment should be "directly related to the personal culpability of the criminal defendant." There is broad agreement that adolescents as a class are "less mature and responsible than adults." For this reason, "less culpability [attaches] to a crime committed by a juvenile than to a comparable crime committed by an adult." Inexperience, less education, and less intelligence makes teenagers "less able to evaluate the consequences" of their conduct. They are "more apt to be motivated by mere emotion or peer pressure" than are adults. Given the lesser culpability of juvenile offenders and their capacity for rehabilitation and growth, the retributive and deterrent purposes of capital punishment are not served by executing a 15-year-old offender, and execution of such juvenile offenders is constitutionally impermissible. Justice O'Connor provided the fifth vote, noting that every state that set a minimum execution age had set it at 16 or older, and that Oklahoma and the states that had set no minimum age may never have considered that certifying juveniles for trial as adults might expose them to capital punishment.

Justice Scalia, joined by Chief Justice Rehnquist and Justice White, dissented, objecting that there was no consensus about the death penalty for 15-year-olds. As he stated, if the issue were whether an *automatic* death penalty for conviction of certain crimes could be extended to individuals younger than 16 when they commit their crimes, without individualized consideration of their maturity and moral responsibility, he would agree that mandatory sentences were opposed by a national consensus regarding it as "cruel and unusual punishment within the meaning of the Eighth Amendment." But the question posed here was "radically different." Was there a national consensus that *no* criminal so much as *one day* under 16, after consideration of his individual circumstances, could *ever* be deemed mature and responsible enough to be punished with death for any crime? Oklahoma gave careful consideration to Thompson's age. A jury, nevertheless, found that his maturity and moral responsibility were sufficiently developed to justify the death sentence. *Some* young offenders in rare circumstances are sufficiently culpable to deserve the death penalty, Scalia concluded.

The next year, the Court considered *Stanford v. Kentucky* (1989): Kevin Stanford was 17 years old when he committed robbery, rape, and murder in Kentucky. Heath Wilkins was 16 years old when he committed a murder during a robbery in Missouri. Both were tried as adults and sentenced to death. Their cases required the Court to decide whether the imposition of capital punishment on an individual for a crime committed at 16 or 17 years of age constitutes cruel and unusual punishment. Unlike *Thompson*, here the Court *upheld* death sentences that had been imposed on both juvenile defendants. Justice Scalia delivered the Court's opinion, joined by Chief Justice Rehnquist and Justice White, who dissented in *Thompson*, and Justice Kennedy, who did not participate in *Thompson*. Justice Scalia pointed out that "a majority of the States that permit capital punishment authorize it for crimes committed at age 16 or above." Death sentences are *rarely* imposed on juvenile offenders, but rare does not mean that it is *never* deserved. In a significant passage, Justice Scalia accepted that it was the Court's duty to identify what society's evolving standards of decency are, but rejected the assertion that it was the within the Court's power to impose the justices' own views. Kentucky and Missouri had made the permissible judgment that *some* juvenile capital offenders commit such heinous crimes that the death penalty is warranted, Scalia maintained.

Concurring, Justice O'Connor provided the fifth vote for the Court's five-to-four decision. Applying the same standard of national consensus she had relied on in *Thompson* to invalidate the execution for murder by a 15-year-old, she found no national consensus forbidding death sentences for murders by 16- or 17-year-olds.

Justice Brennan, joined by Justices Marshall, Blackmun, and Stevens, dissented. They pointed to the rejection of the death penalty for juveniles by most states, the rarity of that sentence for juveniles, the opinions of respected organizations in relevant fields that this punishment is unacceptable, and its general rejection throughout the world to conclude that it is not constitutionally tolerable to execute adolescent offenders. Like Stevens in *Thompson*, Justice Brennan concluded that juveniles under the age of 18 generally lack the degree of responsibility and blameworthiness for their crimes that is necessary for constitutional imposition of the death penalty. As of 1989, *no* 15-year-old capital offender could be sentenced to death, but *some* 16- and 17-year-old capital offenders could be sentenced to death.

Sixteen years later, in *Roper v. Simmons* (2005), the Court again considered the constitutionality of the death penalty for juveniles. Christopher Simmons was 17 when he committed murder. The Missouri Supreme Court set aside Simmons's death sentence in favor of life imprisonment without eligibility for parole, and the Supreme Court granted review to reconsider *Stanford v. Kentucky*. By a 5–4 vote, the Supreme Court affirmed the Missouri Supreme Court, ruling that the Eighth and Fourteenth Amendments forbid imposition of the death penalty on offenders who were under the age of 18 when they committed their crimes. Justice Kennedy switched sides from *Stanford* and wrote the majority opinion, joined by Justices Souter, Ginsburg, Breyer, and Stevens. Kennedy cited the rejection of a juvenile death penalty in most states, the infrequency of its use, the trend toward its abolition, the immaturity and reduced culpability of juvenile criminals, and overwhelming international opinion on the subject in support of the decision. Acknowledging that objections are always raised against categorical rules, Justice Kennedy wrote that in the intervening years, a national consensus had developed that extended the logic of *Thompson* to those who are under 18. Eighteen is the point where society draws the line for many purposes between childhood and adulthood and the *Roper* Court concluded that 18 is the age at which the line for death eligibility should rest.

Justice Scalia dissented, joined by Chief Justice Rehnquist and Justice Thomas, criticizing the majority for failing to give proper respect to precedent when it announced that the meaning of our Constitution has changed over the past 15 years. Scalia criticized the Court for its application of "the evolving standards of decency" of our national society and its conclusion that a national consensus that could not be perceived barely 15 years ago now solidly exists. He also rejected the relevance of international standards to the case at hand.

Justice O'Connor issued a separate dissenting opinion. She agreed that foreign law and international treaties have relevance to the Court's assessment of evolving standards of decency, but she objected to a categorical rule forbidding execution for any crime, no matter how deliberate, wanton, or cruel the offense, committed before age 18. Justice O'Connor conceded that "adolescents as a class are undoubtedly less mature, and therefore less culpable for their misconduct, than adults," but she agreed with many state legislatures that at least *some* 17-year-old murderers are sufficiently mature to deserve the death penalty in appropriate cases. In her view, capital sentencing juries are capable of accurately assessing a youthful defendant's maturity and giving due weight to the mitigating characteristics of youth. Justice O'Connor, the only justice who had been a legislator before her appointment to the Court, wrote that if she were a legislator rather than a judge, she too might be inclined to support legislation setting a minimum age of 18, but some states, including Missouri, had decided to make the death penalty an option for 17-year-old capital murderers, and without a clearer showing that a genuine national consensus forbids the execution of such offenders, Justice O'Connor believed the Supreme Court should not substitute its own subjective judgment on this difficult moral question for the judgments of the nation's democratically elected legislatures.

Juveniles and Other Crimes: Are They a Guide to Future Cases?

In *Roper v. Simmons*, the Court said the Eighth Amendment mandated the position on executions that the ALI had suggested four decades earlier in the Model Penal Code, but the Court was not done with juveniles and the Eighth Amendment. After 2005, the Court's standards of decency regarding juvenile sentencing evolved relatively quickly. Terrance Graham was 34 days short of his 18th birthday when he committed an armed home invasion and robbery. A repeat offender, he was sentenced to life in prison without parole. Joe Sullivan was 13 when he committed two counts of burglary and two counts of sexual battery. After hearing oral argument in both cases, the Supreme Court dismissed its writ of certiorari as improvidently granted in *Sullivan v. Florida* (2010), meaning it would not address the merits of Sullivan's claim, but did decide the merits of Graham's claim in *Graham v. Florida* (2010) that the Eighth Amendment does not permit a juvenile offender to be sentenced to life in prison without parole for a non-homicide crime. Justice Kennedy, joined by Justices Stevens, Ginsburg, Breyer, and Sotomayor, delivered the opinion of the Court. Chief Justice Roberts concurred separately. Citing *Kennedy v. Louisiana* (capital punishment is impermissible for non-homicide crimes), *Atkins v. Virginia* (capital punishment is impermissible for criminals with low-range intellectual functioning), and *Roper v. Simmons* (capital punishment is impermissible for juveniles), Justice Kennedy found the challenged Florida sentence to be unconstitutional. He concluded that the fact that life sentences are rarely imposed on non-homicide juvenile offenders demonstrated that a national consensus had developed opposing such sentences. In addition, Justice Kennedy stressed that juvenile offenders have lessened culpability, non-homicide crimes are less deserving of the most severe sentences than premeditated murders, and such sentences have been widely rejected throughout the world. Justices Thomas, Scalia, and Alito dissented.

Concurring, Chief Justice Roberts agreed that juveniles are generally less culpable than adults and that Graham's sentence was excessive. A defendant's age is relevant to sentencing. But Roberts objected that the majority went too far in establishing an unnecessary and unwise categorical rule that "a sentence of life without parole imposed on *any* juvenile for *any* non-homicide offense is unconstitutional" and suggested that the Court should limit its holding to the offenses that Graham committed *in this case*, because some juvenile defendants may commit more "heinous or grotesque" non-homicide crimes and may deserve more severe punishment. In dissent, Justice Thomas argued that sentences of life without parole for juvenile offenders would not have offended the Framers of the Constitution. The fact that so many states permit such sentences indicates that no national consensus stands in opposition. Thomas criticized the majority for rejecting the judgments of legislators, judges, and juries who have decided that such sentences fit the crime in particular cases. Thomas was unwilling to assume that he and his fellow justices "are any more capable of making such moral judgments than our fellow citizens" and asserted that the Florida legislature, not the Court, should determine whether or not such sentences should be available. For Justice Thomas, in the face of overwhelming legislative support for life without parole sentences for juvenile non-homicide offenders, the majority imposed a categorical prohibition on them and in so doing substituted "its own sense of morality . . . for that of the people and their representatives."

What about Joe Sullivan? Although the Court had dismissed his case, he too was entitled to resentencing as a result of *Graham v. Florida*. He received two consecutive 40-year sentences for the sexual assaults, and with various credits against his sentence for good conduct that the Florida Department of Corrections (like other state and federal prison systems) uses as an incentive for good conduct, Sullivan will be eligible for release in 2019, some 30 years after his conviction.

Just two years after *Graham v. Florida*, in *Miller v. Alabama* (2012) and *Jackson v. Hobbs* (2012), the Court concluded 5–4 that a mandatory sentence of life without parole for a juvenile, even one who committed murder, was cruel and unusual punishment. In July 2003, when he was 14 years old, Evan Miller had taken part in the killing of Cole Cannon. Miller and was convicted and sentenced to a mandatory term of life imprisonment without the possibility of parole. In the companion case, 14-year-old Kuntrell Jackson and two 14-year-old accomplices robbed a local movie rental store in Blytheville, Arkansas. During the robbery, one of the other boys shot and killed the store clerk. Jackson, convicted of capital murder and aggravated robbery, was sentenced to a mandatory term of life imprisonment without the possibility of parole.

Justice Elena Kagan, President Barack Obama's second appointee to the Court, wrote that constitutional prohibition against cruel and unusual punishment forbids mandatory sentences of life without the possibility of parole for juvenile homicide offenders. Justice Breyer, joined by Justice Sotomayor, issued a separate concurring opinion. Chief Justice Roberts Jr., joined by Justices Scalia, Thomas, and Alito, filed a dissenting opinion.

Justice Kagan pointed out that in neither Miller's nor Jackson's case did sentencing authorities have discretion to impose a different punishment on the 14-year-old offenders. State law mandated that the juveniles be sentenced to die in prison even if a judge or jury thought that the nature of the crime or a defendant's youth, lessened culpability, or greater capacity for change made a lesser sentence more appropriate. Such mandatory sentences conflict with the requirement of individualized sentences for juveniles facing "serious" penalties because "children are constitutionally different from adults for purposes of sentencing." A lack of maturity, undeveloped sense of responsibility, recklessness, impetuosity, failure to appreciate risks and consequences, vulnerability to outside pressures from family and peers, and limited control over their own environment on the part of juveniles make their criminal actions less likely to be signs of "irretrievable depravity."

The majority did not claim that life without parole was categorically banned for juvenile homicide offenders. *Mandatory* sentences, however, were another matter. A judge or jury must be able to consider relevant mitigating circumstances before imposing the harshest possible penalty for juveniles. Laws that require that *all* juveniles convicted of homicide receive life sentences without possibility of parole, regardless of their age and the nature of their crimes, violate "th[e] principle of proportionality, and so the Eighth Amendment's ban on cruel and unusual punishment."

Chief Justice Roberts disagreed, joined by Justices Scalia, Thomas, and Alito. Roberts agreed that determining the appropriate sentence for a teenaged murderer presents "grave and challenging questions of morality and social policy," but emphasized that it is not the Court's role to answer such questions, but rather to apply the law. Because the text of the Constitution does not preclude mandatory life without parole sentences for juveniles, and because, in fact, such sentences are not "unusual," legislatures should be able to authorize such sentences. It is too early to tell whether the Court's hostility to mandatory life without parole will remain confined to juvenile murderers or be the springboard from which the justices will reexamine *Harmelin* and mandatory life without parole sentences for adult offenders too.

The ruling in *Graham v. Florida* had resulted in the resentencing of Joe Sullivan even though his case had been dismissed. What effect did *Miller v. Alabama* have on the dozens of juveniles who had been sentenced in state and federal courts who had already exhausted all their appeals? The Court considered that matter in *Montgomery v. Louisiana* (2016). Henry Montgomery was 17 years old in 1963 when he murdered a deputy sheriff. At his first trial, he had received the death penalty; after he successfully appealed he was again convicted, this time receiving a mandatory life sentence. Was he entitled to be resentenced at age 69, after more than five decades in prison? Six members of the Court, in an opinion by Justice Kennedy, said yes: they held that *Miller v. Alabama* had limited the power of the state and federal governments to impose mandatory sentences, and that as a result Louisiana had either to resentence Montgomery or make him eligible for parole. Writing for three dissenters, Justice Scalia protested that under the Court's settled precedents, Montgomery was not *constitutionally* entitled to any relief and that what the Court had in effect done was to rewrite *Miller v. Alabama* to abolish all life sentences for juveniles, not just mandatory life sentences.

Is First-Degree Murder Enough to Warrant the Death Penalty or Must There Be Aggravating Circumstances?

The Model Penal Code suggested in the 1960s that a murder was not a capital murder unless there were aggravating circumstances and the aggravating circumstances outweighed any mitigating ones. In the 1970s, many but not all states followed the Code's lead, and in the 1980s, the Supreme Court turned to the question whether this formula was constitutionally required. There were two parts to the question: how bad was the crime itself and, especially when there was more than one participant, how bad was the defendant?

Justice White had concurred in the overturning of death sentences for accomplices in the 1978 *Lockett* and *Bell* decisions. Four years later, he returned to the issue of a proportionate sentence for persons who are convicted as aiders and abettors to murder, in *Enmund v. Florida* (1982). Earl Enmund served as the driver of a getaway car during a bungled robbery of a farmhouse, which ended with his codefendants shooting and killing the elderly homeowners. Enmund neither killed anyone nor witnessed the killings. By aiding and abetting the murderers, Enmund himself could be found guilty of first-degree murder, according to Florida law. For purposes of punishment under the Eighth Amendment, however, Justice White wrote that the focus must be on "[Enmund's] culpability, not on that of those who committed the robbery and shot the victims." Because Enmund's culpability was plainly different from that of those who actually killed, his death sentence was invalid. Justice Brennan concurred, repeating his unconditional rejection of capital punishment. Justice O'Connor, joined by Chief Justice Burger and Justices Powell and Rehnquist, dissented.

The Supreme Court narrowed *Enmund* five years later in *Tison v. Arizona* (1987), holding the death penalty constitutionally permissible for accomplices if their participation in a crime was "major" and if they displayed "reckless indifference to human life." Writing for the majority made up of the *Enmund* dissenters and Justice White, Justice O'Connor found that Ricky and Raymond Tison had "actively participated" in events leading up to and following four murders. In *Enmund*, the defendant had not himself actively participated in the killing and was not present when it occurred. Here, the Tison brothers' level of personal culpability was much greater: they smuggled a cooler full of guns into prison to help their father escape from a life sentence, then helped flag down and abduct a passing motorist and family members that their father and another escaped inmate shot to death. Because Ricky and Raymond Tison were "actively involved in every element of the kidnapping-robbery and [were] physically present during the entire sequence of criminal activity culminating in the murder of the Lyons family and the subsequent flight," their own personal involvement in the crimes was "substantial" and "sufficient to satisfy the *Enmund* culpability requirement" and they could be executed.

What Aggravating Factors Are Permissible?

Clearly, some murders are more gruesome than others and some murderers are more dangerous than others. In the four decades after *Gregg*, the Court has attempted to express how the Eighth Amendment draws the distinction between murders and capital murders. The Court has accepted the Model Penal Code's position that even premeditated murder is not enough for the death penalty: there must be proof of some aggravating factor, and that aggravating factor must be defined properly in a statute, and notice of what aggravating factors the prosecution intends to prove must be given to the defendant. Unlike the case of mitigating factors, the jury must be unanimous in agreeing on each aggravating factor.

The Court took up the question in *Godfrey v. Georgia* (1980). The Model Penal Code had contained a catch-all aggravating factor that permitted death for murders that were "especially heinous, atrocious or cruel, manifesting exceptional depravity." Georgia's formulation of this principle was that a killing was capital murder if it "was outrageously or wantonly vile, horrible, and inhuman." Robert Godfrey believed that his mother-in-law was behind his estranged wife's refusal to reconcile with him; he went to his mother-in-law's residence and shot the two of them to death as they played cards with his 11-year-old daughter. He then called the sheriff's office, admitted his guilt, and directed officers to the shotgun he used. The Georgia Supreme Court found the crime to fall within Georgia's statutory aggravating factor, but Justice Stewart wrote for a plurality that noted that Georgia's courts had previously restricted application of this section to murders involving torture or similar physical abuse, and reversed because there was "no principled way" to distinguish this case from many other murders in which the death sentence was not imposed.

So was the problem the language of the Model Penal Code or the Court's belief that the Georgia courts had applied it incorrectly? The Court suggested the former in *Maynard v.*

Cartwright (1988). William Cartwright went to the residence of his former employer and shot him to death; Cartwright also shot and stabbed his employer's wife, but she lived to testify against him. The jury imposed the death penalty after it found two of the Model Penal Code's aggravating factors adopted in Oklahoma: that Cartwright had created a risk of death to more than one person and that his murder of his former employer was "especially heinous, atrocious, or cruel." There was no question Cartwright had attempted multiple murders, but was the one he committed "especially" bad? Justice White wrote for a unanimous Court that the language of the provision was just too vague to guide the jury and that subsequent review by a court was insufficient to cure the problem. The fact that the other aggravating factor was undisputed did not save the sentence, either, since there was no way of determining what weight the jury had put on the invalid factor.

Although subsequent review by a court was held inadequate, the Court accepts that prior review and a narrowing interpretation by a court of aggravating factors can make otherwise vague language constitutionally sufficient. The Court considered that problem in a case from Arizona, *Walton v. Arizona* (1990), and in one from Idaho, *Arave v. Creech* (1993). Jeffrey Walton and his codefendants robbed a man at gunpoint, kidnapped him, and drove him in his stolen car into the desert where Walton shot him in the head. The blinded victim died of dehydration after a week of being stranded in the desert. Thomas Creech was already serving life sentences at the Idaho State Penitentiary for some of the 26 murders that he had confessed to committing when he provoked a fight that resulted in Creech beating and kicking to death a fellow inmate who was serving a term of imprisonment for stealing a car. A jury convicted Walton; the sentencing judge imposed the death penalty based on the finding of Arizona's aggravating factors that the murder had been committed for money and in an "especially heinous, cruel, or depraved manner." Creech pleaded guilty; the sentencing judge imposed the death penalty based on the finding of Idaho's aggravating factor that "the defendant exhibited utter disregard for human life."

In both cases, the Court upheld the death sentences because previous decisions by Arizona and Idaho courts had limited the seemingly vague language to mean the infliction of torture, mental anguish, or physical abuse. These decisions served to adequately narrow the class of crimes eligible for the death penalty. The Court noted that the chief problem in *Godfrey* and *Maynard* was that the jury had not been not given limiting instructions; in Arizona and Idaho, the sentencing was done by a judge, who was presumed to know the law.

Although the jury must find an aggravating factor to make a defendant eligible for the death penalty, the jury can use the same factor that they have already found at the trial on guilt or innocence. In *Lowenfield v. Phelps* (1988), Leslie Lowenfield was sentenced to death by a Louisiana jury based only one aggravating factor: that he intended to harm more than one person. This was something the jury had already found by convicting him of killing the woman he lived with, three members of her family, and a friend. Lowenfield contended that there was nothing new to narrow the class of murderers to those deserving of death, but the Supreme Court held that was not necessary: Louisiana's definition of capital murder sufficiently narrowed the class of persons at the guilt or innocence stage by requiring a permissible aggravating factor.

And in the end, it is the narrowing of the set of all murderers to those especially deserving of the ultimate penalty that the Court's precedent requires. This does not have to be done exactly as the Model Penal Code prescribes. In *Zant v. Stephens* (1983), the Court considered whether a defendant's prior criminal record could be considered in making the decision whether to impose the death penalty. Alpha Stephens escaped from a county jail and embarked on a three-day long course of burglaries, car thefts, and robberies. Stephens and an accomplice murdered a man who had come upon them in mid-burglary. The jury found that Stephens's commission of the murder while an escapee and his lengthy criminal prior record were both aggravating factors, and imposed a sentence of death. Georgia Supreme Court held that having a substantial prior criminal record was an insufficient aggravating circumstance but that Stephens's sentence could be upheld because under Georgia law the jury's correct finding of the other aggravating circumstance made Stephens eligible for the death penalty. Unlike other states that required juries to weigh aggravating factors against mitigating factors, in Georgia the only significance of an aggravating factor was to narrow the class of murderers. The Supreme Court, noting that Georgia protected defendants by requiring the Georgia Supreme Court to review every death sentence to ensure consistency, agreed that Georgia did not have to use a weighing system, that one valid aggravating circumstance was enough, and that Stephens could be executed.

Who Can Decide on the Death Penalty?

As you noticed, in *Walton v. Arizona* and *Arave v. Creech*, the Court approved almost the same language it had found too vague in *Godfrey v. Georgia* and *Maynard v. Cartwright* based on the fact that in Arizona and Idaho judges did the sentencing and were presumed to know the narrower definition of the state's aggravating factors. Was judge sentencing preferable? Was it even permissible? The Sixth Amendment provides for a trial by jury, and the Supreme Court increasingly came to view the sentencing stage of a capital trial as a trial in itself. Its rulings on sentencing by judges and by juries have therefore evolved over the last several decades. Among the issues considered by the Supreme Court in restoring the death penalty was the question, who can impose the death penalty? Historically, the sentence imposed by a judge for any felony was death; the infliction of any lesser punishment was at the discretion of the king, not the judge, and certainly not the jury. The traditional role of the jury was to find the facts, and its choices were to acquit or convict. The jury became involved in sentencing when capital statutes were amended in the 19th century to allow a jury to impose a sentence less than death, an amendment aimed at getting a hesitant jury to convict. As Justice White noted in his concurrence in *Furman*, this policy of bringing community judgment to bear on the sentence as well as guilt or innocence "so effectively achieved its aims" that capital sentences became so rare as to be arbitrary. Justice White implied that one solution was to return to mandatory sentences; the Court rejected this in 1976. Justice White's other solution to jury discretion was to permit sentencing by judges alone. The Court accepted this for the next four decades.

Twenty-nine of the states reenacting their death penalties after *Furman* gave the capital sentencing decision to the jury, with Nevada allowing a panel of three judges to impose sentence if the jury could not agree. Arizona, Idaho, Montana, and Nebraska gave the sentencing responsibility to the judge alone. Florida, Alabama, and Indiana allowed a judge to override a jury recommendation of life

In *Proffitt v. Florida* (1976), the Supreme Court approved Florida's capital sentencing statute that gave the jury the duty of rendering an advisory verdict and then required the trial judge to undertake a "specific and detailed" review before imposing the sentence. The plurality opinion expressed its confidence that this was not only permitted, but probably the better procedure:

> And it would appear that judicial sentencing should lead, if anything, to even greater consistency in the imposition at the trial court level of capital punishment, since a trial judge is more experienced in sentencing than a jury, and therefore is better able to impose sentences similar to those imposed in analogous cases.

The Court expressed similar confidence in judge only sentencing in *Walton v. Arizona* (1990) and *Arave v. Creech* (1993), observing that because a trial judge was presumed to be familiar with the definition in previous case of terms that might be too vague for a jury to construe, judicial sentencing might even be more consistent than jury sentencing.

The Court considered the obvious problem that arises when a jury recommends life imprisonment and the judge decides to impose the death penalty in *Barclay v. Florida* (1983) and *Spaziano v. Florida* (1984). In *Barclay*, the judge rejected the jury's 7–5 recommendation of life for Elwood Barclay, a black man convicted of the racist murder of a white hitchhiker; the sentencing judge had served in World War II and Barclay's professed desire to start a race war seemed to the judge to call for just, swift, and permanent removal of Barclay, whom he regarded as a would-be Nazi. In *Spaziano*, the judge sentenced Robert Spaziano to death for killing and disposing of the bodies of two girls in the Altamonte city dump. In both cases, the Supreme Court considered the arguments that jury sentencing was constitutionally required, and in *Spaziano*, the majority conceded that the argument that the jury was the constitutionally required voice of the community's conscience had "some appeal" but held that the Constitution did not prescribe only one way of sentencing.

Most sentences are not capital decisions. In 2000, the Court considered a controversy that had gone on in state and federal courts since the proliferation of sentencing guidelines in the 1980s: the problem that, in many felonies, the evidence the judge used to sentence a defendant was different from the evidence that the jury considered believable in finding the defendant guilty. To illustrate, consider a jury verdict that a defendant is guilty of conspiracy to distribute cocaine based on testimony about two one-ounce transactions. The jury typically did not make any finding of the amount involved, but at sentencing the judge could hear testimony about other alleged drug sales, determine that the defendant was responsible for 10 ounces, and impose a more severe sentence. Was the amount of cocaine an element of the offense the jury must find, or just a sentencing consideration like the defendant's prior record? Recall that during the heyday of the rehabilitation era, *Williams v. New York* (1949) had approved the capital sentence of a judge overriding a jury's recommendation of life on the basis of inadmissible evidence contained in a presentence report.

In the modern era, the Court took up the issue in *Apprendi v. New Jersey* (2000). Charles Apprendi had pleaded guilty to firing several bullets into the house of a black family that recently moved into an all-white neighborhood, but explained that he did so because he was drunk, not a racist. After a sentencing hearing, the judge found that Apprendi had committed a hate crime and imposed a sentence of imprisonment beyond the maximum allowed for the firearms offense alone. The Court reversed, holding that the Sixth Amendment requires that any fact that exposes a defendant to a greater punishment than the one authorized by a jury verdict must be proved beyond a reasonable doubt to a jury.

Two years later, the Court held that *Apprendi* applied to capital cases in *Ring v. Arizona* (2002). Seven justices struck down Arizona's judge-only procedure, with only Chief Justice Rehnquist and Justice O'Connor (the two justices from Arizona) dissenting. A jury found Timothy Ring guilty of felony murder in an armored car hijacking; this earned Ring a life sentence, but exposed him to capital punishment under Arizona law only if a judge found aggravating factors and no sufficient mitigating factors. The trial judge sentenced Ring to death for his major role in planning the robbery and other aggravating circumstances, after testimony by a codefendant at the sentencing hearing. The Court concluded that the finding of an aggravating circumstance exposed Ring to greater punishment than the jury verdict alone, and therefore under *Apprendi* a jury had to find the aggravating circumstance.

In the decade after *Ring*, the Court decided that *Apprendi* applied to sentences based on plea bargains, on the federal sentencing guidelines, to sentences involving fines, and to sentences imposing mandatory minimums. It seemed only a matter of time before the Court would consider a capital case involving Florida's advisory jury. In 1998, Timothy Hurst stabbed a coworker to death and robbed the restaurant where they both worked, leaving her body in the freezer. The jury recommended death 7–5, and the trial judge agreed, sentencing Hurst based on the jury's recommendation and on her own findings of fact. In *Hurst v. Florida* (2016), eight justices held this to be prohibited: because the role of a Florida jury's recommendation was advisory only, and it was the judge's findings of aggravating circumstances that were indispensable to the death sentence. Under *Apprendi* and the Eighth Amendment, in a death penalty case it was the jury who had to find those circumstances.

The few states that still retained judge-sentencing procedures have begun to examine what is left after *Hurst*. In August 2016, the Delaware Supreme Court held in *Rauf v. State* (2016) that Delaware's capital sentencing statute was unconstitutional, too. Delaware required the jury to determine whether an aggravating factor was proved; if so, that made the defendant eligible for the death penalty. At the ultimate sentencing phase, however, it was the judge who determined whether the aggravating factors outweigh the mitigating factors. That decision now must be made by a jury, and unanimously too, said the Delaware court.

In September 2016, the Alabama Supreme Court held, in *In re Bohannon v. State* (2016) that *Hurst* did not invalidate its capital punishment statute. Reading *Hurst* more narrowly than Delaware had, the Alabama court observed that under Alabama law the jury already was required to find the aggravating factors necessary for capital punishment, and that *Hurst* did not involve and therefore did not invalidate Alabama's assignment to the judge of the weighing of aggravating and mitigating circumstances to determine if death was an appropriate sentence.

There is no way to predict whether a jury or a judge in a particular case will be more likely to evaluate the evidence more favorably to the defendant. For that reason, some defense counsel, knowing that a judge is more opposed to the death penalty than are jurors in the community, would rather preserve judge sentencing. Whether they will be able to depends on the Supreme Court's eventual decision about which interpretation of *Hurst* is the correct one.

What Defendants Are Incapable of Deserving the Death Penalty?

It has always been considered that an insane person lacks the mental capacity to commit a crime. In *Ford v. Wainwright* (1986), the Court considered the question whether it is constitutionally permissible to execute a person who has become insane while awaiting execution. No state actually sought to execute an inmate it believed to be incompetent, but the Court identified shortcomings in Florida's procedure that permitted the governor to determine competency without an evidentiary hearing, and ordered further hearings on the question of Ford's competence to be executed. Writing for a plurality of four plus Justice Powell, Justice Marshall pointed to the tradition in common law barring as "savage and inhuman" the execution of a prisoner who is insane and concluded that the Constitution also prohibits the execution of a prisoner "whose mental illness prevents him from comprehending the reasons for the penalty or its implications." The Court stopped short of explaining how elaborate the procedure for finding competency must be.

In *Panetti v. Quarterman* (2007), a majority expanded *Ford* to suggest that to be competent to be executed, an inmate must have a "rational understanding" that he is going to be executed and that the reason for the execution is his commission of murder. The majority held that Texas incorrectly failed to consider Scott Panetti's delusions that Texas wanted to execute him to stop him from preaching and was using his conviction for two murders as a pretext. More importantly, the majority held that a finding that a defendant was competent did not prevent a subsequent claim that the defendant had become incompetent. The implications are obvious: since *Ford* requires some kind of judicial review, and by implication appellate review of the inmate's competency, by the time one appeal is over the inmate's circumstances may have changed enough that a new hearing is necessary.

Does *Ford's* rule against executing the insane apply to mentally retarded individuals? The Supreme Court initially held, in *Penry v. Lynaugh* (1989), that executing mentally retarded individuals who are convicted of capital crimes does not necessarily violate the Eighth Amendment. In this case, however, the Court struck down Johnny Paul Penry's death sentence because the jury had not been properly instructed about how to take into account mental retardation and other mitigating factors. Justice O'Connor, delivering the opinion of the Court, noted that in *Ford*, a clear national consensus supported the conclusion that "the Eighth Amendment prohibits execution of the insane." But here there was "insufficient evidence of a national consensus against executing mentally retarded people convicted of capital offenses for us to conclude that it is categorically prohibited by the Eighth Amendment." Mental retardation is one factor that may "lessen a defendant's culpability for a capital offense" and such mitigating circumstances must be considered in determining appropriate punishment for individual offenders. In *some* such cases, a capital sentence may be constitutionally permissible. Justices Brennan, Marshall, Stevens, Blackmun, Scalia, Rehnquist, White, and Kennedy concurred in part and dissented in part.

Thirteen years later, the Court reexamined *Penry* in *Atkins v. Virginia* (2002): Was it still constitutionally permissible to execute mentally retarded individuals, or had standards of decency evolved? Should the death penalty *ever* be imposed on a mentally retarded criminal? Here the Supreme Court reversed its position from *Penry* and ruled that it is *always* cruel and unusual to execute mentally retarded individuals. Justice Stevens, joined by Justices O'Connor, Kennedy, Souter, Ginsburg, and Breyer, delivered the opinion of the Court. Noting that mentally retarded persons have "disabilities in areas of reasoning, judgment, and control of their impulses," Stevens said that they "do not act with the level of moral culpability that characterizes the most serious adult criminal conduct." Citing an increase in the number of states banning such executions since *Penry* was decided in 1989, the Court concluded that a national consensus had developed that capital punishment is "excessive" for mentally retarded offenders.

In 2014, the Court weighed in on the definition of "mentally retarded" in *Hall v. Florida* (2014), with Justice Kennedy writing for a 5–4 majority that Florida's rule that a person was not retarded if his IQ score was higher than 70 was too limiting and risked the execution of a disabled person solely on the basis of a test score. The same 5–4 majority, with Justice Sonia Sotomayor writing, similarly invalidated Louisiana's 75-point threshold in *Brumfield v. Cain* (2015). In 2017, the Court agreed with the claim of Bobby Moore in *Moore v. Texas* that Texas erred in applying its 1992 definition of mental retardation, instead of current medical guidelines, in considering Moore's claim that he cannot be executed for a robbery murder he committed in 1980. Moore, now 56, had been on death row since he was 20.

Meanwhile, in both Florida and Kentucky, state courts held in 2016 that *Hall v. Florida* applies retroactively to persons on death row, thus opening the door to reexamine the eligibility of death row inmates for execution.

How Can the Jury Be Selected?

If you asked most Americans which lasted longer before being declared unconstitutional, mandatory death sentences or all-male juries, most would not guess that it was not until *Taylor v. Louisiana* (1975) that the Supreme Court struck down Louisiana's law that required women who wanted to serve on a criminal jury to specially apply to do so, and only in *Duren v. Missouri* (1979) that the Court invalidated the rule followed by Missouri and several other states that allowed women an automatic exemption from jury service. This practice violated the principle implicit in the Sixth Amendment right to a jury trial that the Court had been formulating since the 1940s that a "jury" meant a panel drawn from a fair cross section of the community.

What is a fair cross section of the community in a capital case? In *Witherspoon v. Illinois* (1968), the Supreme Court held that states could not exclude from juries all persons opposed to the death penalty: doing so would produce juries that were not fairly representative of the community. A juror *could* be excluded if it could be shown that he (or, a decade later, she) had personal opposition to the death penalty so strong that they could not be trusted to abide by the existing law and conscientiously follow the judge's instructions. Justice Stewart delivered the opinion of the Court, writing that a jury "[c]ulled of all who harbor doubts about the wisdom of capital punishment" falls "woefully short" of the impartiality to which defendants are entitled under the Sixth and Fourteenth Amendments. Stewart found that Illinois had "stacked the deck" against Witherspoon: "In its quest for a jury capable of imposing the death penalty, the State produced a jury uncommonly willing to condemn a man to die." It is often the case that in declaring a particular practice unconstitutional, the Supreme Court provides a road map to achieving the same result: *Witherspoon* is remembered today as the legal authority for prosecutors to exclude excessively pro-defendant jurors, not establishing the right of opponents of capital punishment to serve.

The Role of Statistics

In *McCleskey v. Kemp* (1987), Warren McCleskey argued that Georgia's death penalty system was racially biased. He cited a study by Professor David Baldus, showing that blacks who murdered white victims were the most likely defendants to receive death sentences. The Supreme Court ruled that the *general* data contained in the Baldus study were not sufficient to sustain McCleskey's challenge. Instead, he would have to demonstrate that decision makers in this *particular* case acted with a racially discriminatory intent. Writing for the majority, Justice Powell concluded that "the Baldus study does not demonstrate a constitutionally significant risk of racial bias affecting the Georgia capital sentencing process" and that McCleskey's arguments would be "best presented to the legislative bodies." Justices Brennan, Marshall, Blackmun, and Stevens dissented.

Although the Court has not been welcoming to complex statistical studies that have been offered to prove discrimination, jury bias, or the deterrent effects of sentences, the Court is not insensitive to simple arithmetic. That is, although the Supreme Court has held since the 19th century that a defendant has no right to a jury composed of a particular number of men or women, or meeting some racial profile, the fundamental right to equal protection of law means that both litigants and jurors in civil trials and criminal trials have a right to selection of a jury that is free from the impact of stereotypes. In *Batson v. Kentucky* (1986), the Court held that a prosecutor cannot use peremptory challenges to remove black jurors from the trial of a black defendant. Subsequently, *Georgia v. McCollum* (1992) held that even a defendant could not use challenges deliberately to exclude jurors on the basis of race. As an indication of how seriously the Court takes this doctrine, consider *Ford v. Georgia* (1991). James Ford, a black man, was convicted of murder and sentenced to death, after the prosecution used 9 of its 10 peremptory challenges to remove black prospective jurors. Despite Ford's failure to raise his challenge properly under state law the Court, in an opinion by Justice Souter, reversed the dismissal of his claim and returned it to the Georgia Supreme Court, which found that the evidence of discrimination was overwhelming. Fourteen years later, Justice Souter again found a *Batson* violation in *Miller-el v. Dretke* (2005): it "blinks reality" he wrote, to claim that there could be a race-neutral explanation for the behavior of the prosecutor, who used peremptory challenges to remove 10 of 11 black

Four years later, in *Payne v. Tennessee* (1991), after the retirement of two of the majority from *Booth*, the Court reversed that rule by a 6–3 vote, with Chief Justice Rehnquist writing that holding that the state has a legitimate interest in presenting evidence of the harm done by Pervis Payne, who had stabbed a young mother and her infant daughter to death. The jury returned a death sentence after hearing the grandmother's account of how the surviving son cried because he missed his mother and sister. This evidence was just as proper as Payne's evidence that he had no criminal record and was polite and hardworking. As of 2016, Payne remained on death row while litigating other challenges to his sentence.

In 2016, the Supreme Court returned to the subject in a *per curiam* opinion to clarify the effect of *Booth* and *Payne*. Shaun Bosse was sentenced to death for stabbing a mother to death and killing her two children by stabbing and arson, and part of the evidence the jury heard was the testimony of three relatives of the victims who recommended that Bosse receive the death penalty. In *Bosse v. Oklahoma* (2016), the Supreme Court unanimously held that *Payne* did not overrule *Booth*'s prohibition of victim impact opinions about the crime, the defendant, or the appropriateness of capital punishment. The rule therefore remains that witnesses can give evidence about the crime, but not opinions. That responsibility remains the jury's alone.

In the End, How Can Executions Be Carried Out?

After all the other problems considered by the Court from *Gregg v. Georgia* onward, the most controversial part of the death penalty debate has come full circle to the issue that gave rise to the Eighth Amendment: how may executions be carried out? As we have noted, the Supreme Court has allowed other methods of execution, but lethal injection is the current standard method. From 1976 to 2016, 1,265 executions were performed by lethal injection, 158 by electrocution, 11 by gas chamber, 3 by hanging, and 3 by firing squad ("Facts about the

Death Penalty" 2016). In 1977, Oklahoma was the first state to adopt lethal injection. In 1982, Texas was the first state to use this method when it executed Charles Brooks. All death penalty states and the federal government now use lethal injection as their primary execution method. Typically, an inmate is strapped to a gurney. Heart monitors are attached. Two needles (one serves as a backup) are inserted into usable veins. Tubes connect the needle to several intravenous drips. The first contains a saline solution to prevent clogging of the lines. At the warden's signal, a curtain is raised and witnesses in an adjoining room observe as lethal drugs are administered ("Methods of Execution" 2016).

In *Baze v. Rees* (2008), two inmates challenged Kentucky's three-drug lethal injection process, contending that incorrect administration of the drugs would inflict severe pain and therefore constitute "cruel and unusual punishment." The Court voted 7–2 to reject the claim but could not agree on a majority opinion. Chief Justice Roberts joined by Justices Kennedy and Alito reasoned that capital punishment is constitutional so "there must be a means for carrying it out." Some risk of pain is inherent in any execution method. The Constitution does not require the elimination of any and all such risks, and the risks of an inadequate dose of the first drug used by Kentucky (sodium thiopental, a sedative), the improper mixing of chemicals, or the improper setting of IVs are not "objectively intolerable." In fact, lethal injection is widely tolerated as the preferred method of execution across the nation. Roberts concluded that Kentucky's procedures did not violate the Eighth Amendment. Concurring, Justice Stevens found that his respect for the Court's precedents outweighed his personal conviction that the death penalty was useless, writing "I assumed that our decision would bring the debate about lethal injection as a method of execution to a close. It now seems clear that it will not." He added that the case would also generate debate "about the justification for the death penalty itself." He was right.

Justice Thomas, in a concurring opinion joined by Justice Scalia, said that "a method of execution violates the Eighth Amendment only if it is deliberately designed to inflict pain." The Framers were trying to prevent what Blackstone had described as measures designed "to ensure that death would be slow and painful, and thus all the more frightening to contemplate." Embellishments designed to "inflict pain for pain's sake" would be impermissible, but Kentucky was trying to make capital punishment "more humane, not to add elements of terror, pain, or disgrace to the death penalty."

Justice Ginsburg, joined by Justice Souter, dissented. Kentucky's use of the lethal drugs, pancuronium bromide and potassium chloride, on a conscious inmate would produce "agony" and "searing pain." Therefore, the constitutionality of Kentucky's protocol "turns on whether inmates are adequately anesthetized by the first drug . . ., sodium thiopental." But, Justice Ginsburg wrote, Kentucky "lacks basic safeguards . . . to confirm that an inmate is unconscious." Kentucky "does little" to make sure that the inmate has received an adequate dose of the sedative. The only two people who remain in the execution chamber with the inmate, the warden and deputy warden, lack medical training. "Rare though errors may be," Ginsburg stated, "the consequences of a mistake about the condemned inmate's consciousness are horrendous." The omission of "available safeguards to confirm that the inmate is unconscious" creates an avoidable risk of inflicting "severe and unnecessary pain."

After *Baze v. Rees*, death penalty opponents pressured pharmaceutical companies to prevent sodium thiopental (and, later, another barbiturate called pentobarbital) from being supplied for executions. American manufacturers stopped making the drug and European companies would not allow exported drugs to be used in executions. As a result, Oklahoma decided to use midazolam, a sedative, as the first drug in its three-drug protocol. Clayton Lockett's execution on April 29, 2014, using this method was prolonged and painful, with Lockett dying of a heart attack almost an hour into the execution. After the Lockett execution,

Oklahoma revised its procedures by increasing the midazolam dosage. Four death row inmates—Charles Warner, Richard Glossip, John Grant, and Benjamin Cole—challenged the Oklahoma protocol. They argued that midazolam cannot sustain the level of unconsciousness needed for surgery, so it is unsuitable for use in executions. Warner was executed on January 15, 2015, after the Court declined to stay his execution. Dissenting, Justice Sotomayor wrote she was "deeply troubled by evidence suggesting that midazolam cannot be constitutionally used as the first drug in a three-drug lethal injection protocol." After his execution began, Warner exclaimed, "My body is on fire!" (Murphy 2015). Lockett's family later unsuccessfully sued Oklahoma over the execution. A panel of the Tenth Circuit Court of Appeals found Lockett's prolonged death to be an "isolated mishap" unlikely to happen in future cases, and affirmed the dismissal of the suit in November 2016. One of the three judges on the panel, Neil Gorsuch, was named to the Supreme Court in early 2017.

Having repeatedly faced botched execution claims in Oklahoma and Arizona, the Court granted review to consider Glossip's challenge. In *Glossip v. Gross* (2015), the Supreme Court delivered a 5–4 opinion adopting Chief Justice Roberts's reasoning in *Baze v. Rees* as the law of the land. Justice Alito observed that federal courts had limited competency to make judgments on the medical issues involved and described changes in execution methods as states have sought more humane ways of carrying out death sentences. Citing *Baze v. Rees*, the majority held that the burden is on the inmate to prove that his method of execution is "sure or very likely" to cause needless suffering and must identify a feasible and available alternative that presents significantly less risk of pain, because holding that the Eighth Amendment demands the elimination of essentially all risk of pain "would effectively outlaw the death penalty altogether."

There were two dissents. Justice Sotomayor wrote for four dissenters that it was legally improper to impose on an inmate the burden of identifying an available means for his own execution. Citing Oklahoma's difficulties with Calvin Lockett's execution, she observed that Glossip faced "what may well be the chemical equivalent of being burned at the stake." Justice Breyer, joined by Justice Ginsburg, argued that the Court should reconsider the death penalty entirely.

Heatedly responding to Justice Breyer, Justice Scalia's concurring opinion opened with the words, "Welcome to Groundhog Day. The scene is familiar. . . . A vocal minority of the Court, waving over their heads a ream of the most recent abolitionist studies . . . as though they have discovered the lost folios of Shakespeare, insist that *now*, at long last the death penalty must be abolished for good." Justice Scalia dismissed the dissent as "full of internal contradictions and . . . gobbledy-gook." Justice Thomas wrote a separate concurrence responding to Justice Breyer, reiterating his position in *Baze v. Rees* that the Eighth Amendment prohibits only those methods of execution that are "deliberately designed to inflict pain" and Glossip did not make such a claim. Thomas also criticized Breyer's reliance on a study concluding that Connecticut death sentences do not appear to depend on the "egregiousness" of the crimes, but instead reflect "arbitrary" factors, such as the locality in which the crime was committed (Donohue 2014). In the study, law students reviewed written summaries of murders and assigned "egregiousness" scores based on a rubric. "Depravity points" were assigned to different killings. For example, killing a prison guard earned a defendant three depravity points and killing a police officer merited two. Killing a child under the age of 12 earned two depravity points but killing someone over the age of 70 earned only one point. Thomas maintained that victims deserve more than a "pseudoscientific assessment of their lives." Unlike actual jurors, the law students based their decisions on written summaries. They did not view detailed evidence of the crime, assess the credibility of witnesses, see the remorse of the defendant, or feel the impact of the crime on the victim's family. There are good reasons why these sentencing decisions must be "left to the jurors and judges who sit through the trial, and not to legal elites (or law students)."

Life without Parole?

If a state can't execute a person, must there be some prospect of release or parole? For adults sentenced for murder, life without parole sentences are unquestionably permitted in 2017, but many death penalty opponents make the same arguments against life without parole they make against the death penalty, and opponents of life without parole make the arguments for adults that the Supreme Court has found persuasive for juveniles. Many death penalty advocates defend the death penalty on the grounds that an end to capital punishment will only change the battleground in the war on crime. The Supreme Court's approach to the issue may be foreshadowed by *Harmelin v. Michigan* (1991), discussed earlier, and by *Kansas v. Hendricks* (1997). Kansas's Sexually Violent Predator Act provided for the civil commitment of persons who were likely to engage in predatory sexual violence. Leroy Hendricks, a convicted pedophile who was scheduled to be released from prison, admitted that he continued to harbor sexual desires for children. Hendricks was committed indefinitely to prevent him from endangering others. The Supreme Court upheld this "pre-commitment" or commitment prior to committing an actual crime. Writing for the Court, Justice Thomas stressed that states "may take measures to restrict the freedom of the dangerously mentally ill. This is a legitimate non-punitive governmental objective and has been historically so regarded."

Conclusion and "Last" Words

What will come next? Justice Stevens wrote in *Baze v. Rees* (2008), "I assumed that our decision would bring the debate about lethal injection as a method of execution to a close. It now seems clear that it will not." The number of death penalty states is declining. Annual executions are decreasing. States are finding it increasingly difficult to obtain lethal injection drugs. Some states are exploring alternate means of execution and some, like Arizona, are in 2016 contemplating a return to earlier methods like firing squads. Justice Breyer seems close to joining several earlier justices in the belief that the death penalty is flatly prohibited by the Constitution, and Justice Ginsburg has practically agreed to join him if he takes that step. Justice Scalia has passed away and appointment of his eventual successor was a major campaign issue in 2016. In light of all of this, consider Justice Scalia's final words on the subject. He said that the Court has imposed, under color of the Constitution, "procedural and substantive limitations that did not exist when the Eighth Amendment was adopted," when in his view, the Constitution does not mean what the Court thinks it ought to mean, but "what it meant when it was adopted." For Justice Scalia, the constitutionality of the death penalty was therefore "not a difficult, soul-wrenching question"; it was permitted when the Eighth Amendment was adopted, and so it is clearly permitted today. In later speeches, however, Justice Scalia said he "wouldn't be surprised" if the Supreme Court again found the death penalty unconstitutional (Death Penalty Information Center 2016). His successor, Justice Gorsuch, may provide the answer to that speculation.

References

ABA. 2008. "Supplementary Guidelines for the Mitigating Function of Defense Teams in Death Penalty Cases." *Hofstra Law Review* 36: 677–692.

Andres v. United States, 333 U.S. 740 (1948).

Apprendi v. New Jersey, 530 U.S. 466 (2000).

Arave v. Creech, 507 U.S. 463 (1993).

Atkins v. Virginia, 536 U.S. 304 (2002).

Barclay v. Florida, 463 U.S. 939 (1983).

Batson v. Kentucky, 476 U.S. 79 (1986).

Baze v. Rees, 553 U.S. 35 (2008).

Bell v. Cone, 535 U.S. 685 (2002).

Bell v. Ohio, 438 U.S. 637 (1978).

Booth v. Maryland, 482 U.S. 496 (1987).

Bosse v. Oklahoma, 137 S.Ct. 1 (2016).

Brumfield v. Cain, 135 S.Ct. 2269 (2015).

Bryan v. Moore, 528 U.S. 960 (1999).

Callins v. Collins, 510 U.S. 1141 (1994).

Carson, E. Ann. 2015. "Prisoners in 2014." *Bureau of Justice Statistics Bulletin*. http://www.bjs.gov/content/pub/pdf/p14.pdf.

Coker v. Georgia, 433 U.S. 584 (1977).

Death Penalty Information Center. 2016. "Justice Scalia (Deceased) on the Death Penalty." http://www.deathpenaltyinfo.org/statements-death-penalty-supreme-court-justices#scalia.

Donohue, John. 2014. "An Empirical Evaluation of the Connecticut Death Penalty System since 1973: Are There Unlawful Racial, Gender, and Geographic Disparities?" *Journal of Empirical Legal Studies* 11: 637.

Duren v. Missouri, 439 U.S. 357 (1979).

Eddings v. Oklahoma, 455 U.S. 104 (1982).

Enmund v. Florida, 458 U.S. 782 (1982).

Ewing v. California, 538 U.S. 11 (2003).

"Facts about the Death Penalty." November 17, 2016. Death Penalty Information Center. http://www.deathpenaltyinfo.org/documents/FactSheet.pdf (November 20, 2016).

Fair Punishment Project. 2016a. "Too Broken to Fix: Part I: An In-depth Look at America's Outlier Death Penalty Counties." http://fairpunishment.org/wp-content/uploads/2016/08/FPP-TooBroken.pdf.

Fair Punishment Project. 2016b. "America's Top Five Deadliest Prosecutors: How Overzealous Personalities

Drive the Death Penalty." http://fairpunishment.org/wp-content/uploads/2016/06/FPP-Top5Report_FINAL.pdf.

Fierro v. Gomez, 77 F.3d 301 (9th Cir.), vacated, 519 U.S. 918 (1996).

Final Report of the National Commission on Reform of Federal Criminal Laws. 1971. Washington, DC: Government Printing Office.

Ford v. Georgia, 498 U.S. 411 (1991).

Ford v. Wainwright, 477 U.S. 399 (1986).

Foster v. Chatman, 136 S.Ct. 1737 (2016).

Furman v. Georgia, 408 U.S. 238 (1972).

Georgia v. McCollum, 505 U.S. 42 (1992).

Gideon v. Wainwright, 372 U.S. 335 (1963).

Gilmore v. Utah, 429 U.S. 1012 (1976).

Glossip v. Gross, 135 S.Ct. 2726 (2015).

Godfrey v. Georgia, 446 U.S. 420 (1980).

Goldberg, Arthur J. 1986. "Memorandum to the Conference Re: Capital Punishment." *South Texas Law Review* 27: 493–506.

Graham v. Florida, 560 U.S. 48 (2010).

Gregg v. Georgia, 428 U.S. 153 (1976).

Hall v. Florida, 134 S.Ct. 1986 (2014).

Harmelin v. Michigan, 501 U.S. 957 (1991).

Hitchcock v. Dugger, 481 U.S. 393 (1987).

Hurst v. Florida, 136 S.Ct. 616 (2016).

In re Bohannon v. State, __ So.3d.__, 2016 WL 5817692 (2016).

Jackson v. Bishop, 404 F.2d 571 (8th Cir.1968).

Jeffries, John C. 1994. *Justice Lewis F. Powell, Jr.* Bronx, NY: Fordham University Press.

Jurek v. Texas, 428 U.S. 262 (1976).

Kansas v. Hendricks, 521 U.S. 346 (1997).

Kennedy v. Louisiana, 554 U.S. 407 (2008).

Kirchmeier, Jeffrey L. 2000. "Let's Make a Deal: Waiving the Eighth Amendment by Selecting a Cruel and Unusual Punishment." *Connecticut Law Review* 32: 615–652.

Lockett v. Ohio, 438 U.S. 586 (1978).

Lockhart v. McCree, 476 U.S. 162 (1986).

Lockyer v. Andrade, 538 U.S. 63 (2003).

Lowenfield v. Phelps, 484 U.S. 231 (1988).

Maynard v. Cartwright, 486 U.S. 356 (1988).

McCleskey v. Kemp, 481 U.S. 279 (1987).

McGautha v. California, 402 U.S. 183 (1971).

McKoy v. North Carolina, 494 U.S. 433 (1990).

Melusky, Joseph A., and Keith A. Pesto. 2003. *Capital Punishment: Rights and Liberties under the Law*. Santa Barbara, CA: ABC-CLIO.

"Methods of Execution." 2016. Death Penalty Information Center. http://www.deathpenaltyinfo.org/methods-execution (November 20, 2016).

Miller v. Alabama and *Jackson v. Hobbs*, 132 S.Ct. 2455 (2012).

Miller-el v. Dretke, 545 U.S. 231 (2005).

Mills v. Maryland, 486 U.S. 367 (1988).

Miranda v. Arizona, 384 U.S. 436 (1966).

Montgomery v. Louisiana, 136 S.Ct. 718 (2016).

Morgan v. Illinois, 504 U.S. 719 (1992).

Murphy, Sean. 2015. "Charles Warner Executed." *Huffington Post*, January 15. http://www.huffingtonpost.com/2015/01/15/charles-frederick-warner-executed_n_6483040.html (November 20, 2016).

Northern Securities Co. v United States, 193 U.S. 197 (1904).

O'Neil v. Vermont, 144 U.S. 323 (1892).

Oregon v. Guzek, 546 U.S. 517 (2006).

Panetti v. Quarterman, 551 U.S. 930 (2007).

Payne v. Tennessee, 501 U.S. 808 (1991).

Penry v. Lynaugh, 492 U.S. 302 (1989).

Petite v. United States, 361 U.S. 529 (1960).

Proffitt v. Florida, 428 U.S. 242 (1976).

Rauf v. State, 145 A.3d 430 (Delaware 2016).

Rehnquist, William H. 1998. *All the Laws but One: Civil Liberties in Wartime.* New York: Alfred A. Knopf.

Ring v. Arizona, 536 U.S. 584 (2002).

Roberts v. Louisiana, 428 U.S. 325 (1976).

Roberts v. Louisiana, 431 U.S. 633 (1977).

Robinson v. California, 370 U.S. 660 (1962).

Rompilla v. Beard, 545 U.S. 374 (2005).

Roper v. Simmons, 543 U.S. 551 (2005).

Rosenberg v. United States, 344 U.S. 838 (1952).

Smith, Gene. 1996. "In Windsor Prison." *American Heritage* 47 (May/June): 100–109.

Smith v. Spisak, 558 U.S. 139 (2010).

Solem v. Helm, 463 U.S. 277 (1983).

Spaziano v. Florida, 468 U.S. 447 (1984).

Stanford v. Kentucky, 492 U.S. 361 (1989).

State v. Gee Jon, 46 Nev. 418, 211 P.676 (1923).

State v. Mata, 275 Nebr. 1, 745 N.W.2d 229 (2008).

State v. Santiago, 318 Conn. 1, 122 A.3d 1 (2015).

Stewart v. LaGrand, 526 U.S. 115 (1999).

Sullivan v. Florida, 560 U.S. 181 (2010).

Sumner v. Shuman, 483 U.S. 66 (1987).

Taylor v. Louisiana, 419 U.S. 522 (1975).

Thompson v. Oklahoma, 487 U.S. 815 (1988).

Tison v. Arizona, 481 U.S. 137 (1987).

Tomoya Kawakita v. United States, 343 U.S. 717 (1952).

Trop v. Dulles, 356 U.S. 86 (1958).

Wainwright v. Witt, 469 U.S. 412 (1985).

Walton v. Arizona, 497 U.S. 639 (1990).

Weems v. United States, 217 U.S. 349 (1910).

Wiggins v. Smith, 539 U.S. 510 (2003).

Williams v. New York, 337 U.S. 241 (1949).

Williams v. Taylor, 529 U.S. 362 (2000).

Winston v. United States, 172 U.S. 303 (1899).

Witherspoon v. Illinois, 391 U.S. 510 (1968).

Woodson v. North Carolina, 428 U.S. 280 (1976).

Zant v. Stephens, 462 U.S. 862 (1983).

Introduction

In this chapter, guest contributors share their viewpoints on various topics related to the death penalty. Rudolph J. Gerber considers the deterrent effects of the death penalty. He observes that executions are not speedy, they are carried out infrequently, they do not seek to inflict pain, and they are conducted privately so they do not convey a warning message to the general public. For these reasons, he concludes that deterrence is now a "near impossibility."

Richard C. Dieter argues that there are practical reasons to abolish the death penalty. It risks innocent lives unnecessarily. It is more expensive than alternatives like sentences of life without parole. It is unfair and arbitrary in its application. Social benefits are negligible. Its use is in decline at home and abroad.

Brett R. Meltzer maintains that the death penalty should be retained. It is constitutionally permissible. It is the punishment that proportionally fits certain crimes. It deters at least some potential offenders from committing murders.

Kim MacInnis provides a sociopolitical argument for retaining the death penalty. She examines utilitarian, retributive, and egalitarian arguments in favor of the death penalty. Ultimately, she relies on social and political considerations. Both

---

Protesters against the death penalty gather to talk at the Florida State Prison near Starke, Florida, before the 2014 execution of Paul Howell. In 1992, Howell killed Florida Highway Patrol Trooper James Fulford. (AP Photo/ Phil Sandlin)

U.S. history and culture reflect acceptance of the death penalty. Given the centrality of the concept of majority rule to American democracy and given majority acceptance of the death penalty, she concludes that the punishment must be retained.

Does gender bias affect the application of the death penalty? Proportionally speaking, relatively few women are executed. Is this disparity attributable to cultural inhibitions? Elizabeth Rapaport finds that female execution rates are low because women commit fewer heinous, death-penalty echelon offenses, and they are less likely to have violent criminal histories.

Innocent people have occasionally been sentenced to death. DNA evidence has revealed a number of wrongful convictions. John Rago discusses some of the reasons for such serious mistakes and society's obligation to recognize and rectify such errors at a hastened pace.

Governor Tom Corbett observes that a majority of Americans continue to support the death penalty but that support has been declining. He is concerned that this statistical decline may reflect diminished confidence in the criminal justice system itself.

Does the Death Penalty Deter Homicide?
Rudolph J. Gerber

At the center of the death penalty debate lies the question of "deterrence," a term meaning whether the government's executing a murderer discourages other potential murderers from crime. A necessary prerequisite for deterrence is that potential criminals be able to weigh the advantages and disadvantages of their actions before committing a crime. In the case of a potential murder, they must have an awareness of the realistic risk of execution.

Three areas of research bear on the deterrence question. These blocks consist of:

1. nearly a hundred major studies by criminologists and sociologists over the past half century;

2. about 20 major "multiple regression" analyses done by economists in recent decades; and

3. a definitional approach that considers whether death penalty practices satisfy the conceptual requirements needed for deterrence.

We will look at each of these blocks of material in the following sections in a general fashion. Readers wishing more detail may consult the Justice for All website, a pro–death penalty site supporting the deterrence hypothesis, and, alternatively, the Death Penalty Information Center website, an anti–death penalty site that regularly collects studies against the deterrence effect. (See the Doing More section.)

Major Social Science Studies Finding No Deterrent Effect

The first material to consider involves non-economic social science research. Well over a half century ago Professor Thorsten Sellin conducted some of the most famous of the studies on deterrence by comparing homicide rates in contiguous states with and without the death penalty from 1920 through 1963. As an example of his method, Michigan without capital punishment and Ohio and Indiana, both having capital punishment, each had aggregate recurring homicide rates of 3.5 per 100,000 population. This finding suggests that the death penalty had neither reduced the homicide rates of Ohio and Indiana nor had its absence increased homicides in Michigan. He found similar results from considering states' prison murders and from comparing homicide rates during times when a single state was using or not using the death penalty.

Comparative studies such as Sellin's have some shortcomings as well as built-in controls. To draw compelling conclusions from a comparison of homicide rates, a researcher would need to control for variations in economic and cultural conditions as well as racial demographics. States abutting one another presumably share roughly similar characteristics, making comparison of death-penalty and non-death-penalty states meaningful. However, comparative studies by Sellin and others consistently find no deterrent effect from executions.

More recent studies have been conducted by major social science researchers such as Michael Radelet, James Marquardt, William Bailey and William Bowers. These and other sociological-style studies look at the homicide rates before and after executions to find any changes as a result of carrying out the death penalty. These studies also consistently find no deterrent effect.

Econometric Studies

Coexisting with these social science studies, but appearing more recently, some major economic studies reflect economists' interest in the deterrence issue. Their interest in the topic as well as their methodology reflects an acceptance of the "rational calculator" assumption grounding much modern economic theory. The rational calculator model is a theory about human nature. This model assumes that before taking any action a person will compare the costs and benefits of that action, and then choose the behaviors that secure the greatest benefits with fewest costs.

In 1975 Professor Isaac Ehrlich, an economist, published the first of a series of highly statistical studies of homicide rates between 1933 and 1969. He concluded that each execution resulted, on average, in seven or eight fewer murders. His conclusion generated a spate of scientific analyses using similar statistical methods. Other scholars could not replicate his findings when they used his data. In more recent years, major studies by academic economists Paul Rubin, Naci Mocan and Joanna Shepherd have asserted similar deterrence claims ranging from 8 to 18 lives saved by each execution.

Professors Jeffrey Fagan at Columbia University, John Donohue at Yale University, and Justin Wolfers at the Wharton School have written articles in economic journals critical of the approaches and conclusions of these econometric studies. Their critiques, while differing in detail, focus on the lack of relevant crime data from some states; the insufficient frequency of executions for a reliable data base; and the inability of other researchers to reach the same results from the same data.

In 2011 a government-sponsored research arm of the Department of Justice, the National Research Council, assembled a group of criminology experts to evaluate the existing scholarly research on deterrence. The National Research Council looked in detail at all the major deterrence studies of all kinds and concluded, in April 2012, that none of these studies provided compelling evidence of deterrence. In its final report the council argued that the deterrence hypothesis should not be a basis for any policy decisions.

Conceptual Analyses of the Deterrence Requirements

The deterrence hypothesis can be explored in a third way by looking at how today's U.S. execution practices satisfy the four theoretical prerequisites needed for any deterrent effect. Most if not all criminologists adopt the central factors posited by Cesare Beccaria in his *On Crimes and Punishments* (1764), which set forth four requirements for punishment to deter crime.

- Punishment must appear to a potential offender to result from the crime *quickly*. This is known as "celerity."
- Punishment must be perceived as highly or absolutely *certain* to follow the crime.
- Punishment must appear roughly *proportionate in severity* to the original crime, under a "like deserves like" or "eye for an eye" theory.
- Punishment must occur *in public* to communicate to a large population these three messages.

As to the first requirement of celerity, or how quickly punishment follows the crime, while colonial executions usually occurred within a few days of a finding of guilt, in 2012 the average delay nationally between crime and execution was 12 years. In states like Arizona and California, the delay is roughly two decades. Even the "quickest" states such as Texas and Virginia have delays averaging around 10 years. These data suggest that the celerity requirement is nonexistent.

As to the requirement of certainty, the likelihood of an execution for murder has steadily diminished. Professor James Liebman's exhaustive studies of capital appeals reveal that about 67 percent of U.S. death sentences are thrown out on appeal. About 140 persons wrongly sentenced to death have also had their convictions thrown out because of post-verdict discoveries of innocence. More basically, at the inception of homicide charges, prosecutors seek the death penalty in only 1–2 percent of all murder cases, meaning that a death sentence is not "on the table" for more than 90 percent of all murder trials. These data suggest that the likelihood of a death sentence for a murder is very low.

As to severity, while an execution is severe, of course, the U.S. Supreme Court has repeatedly said that state governments cannot impose on the offender the degree of pain inflicted on the victim. Mirroring the circumstances of the original crime—raping the rapist, torturing the torturer—cannot be accomplished in our present legal system, in part because courts have said such behaviors reduce the government to the level of a criminal. So Beccaria's third requirement of pain is a near impossibility.

Beccaria's final requirement of public execution fares no better. While it is true that during the colonial and revolutionary periods executions usually occurred in town squares or similar public gathering places, today's executions via lethal injection occur in a specially equipped prison room before an audience usually numbering around 30 persons, none of whom is likely to be a potential murderer in the future. The relative privacy of today's executions means that Beccaria's final requirement has also been frustrated.

Instead of achieving Beccaria's four requirements for crime deterrence, today's executions display their opposites: they are not speedy, they are statistically infrequent, they cannot seek pain, and they do not broadly communicate a warning message to a large population. The conclusion from this fourfold analysis is that deterrence is a near impossibility under today's legal practices.

The foregoing analyses of kinds of deterrence research are neither exhaustive nor the last word. Because of its importance the deterrence hypothesis is likely to remain as a controversial topic in criminal justice theory and practice.

Rudolph J. Gerber is a retired judge who served on the Arizona Court of Appeals for more than 10 years before turning to private practice and teaching. He has taught courses on law and philosophy at the University of Notre Dame, Arizona State University, and the University of San Diego. He is the author of numerous works including The Top Ten Death Penalty Myths: The Politics of Crime Control *(2007),* Cruel and Unusual *(1999),* Lawyers, Courts, and Professionalism: The Agenda for Reform *(1989), and* Legalizing Marijuana: Drug Policy Reform and Prohibition Politics *(2004), as well as articles for the* Stanford Law Review, *the* American Journal of Jurisprudence, *and* Ethics and Public Policy. *He earned an LLM degree from the University of Virginia, a JD from the University of Notre Dame, and a PhD from the Université Catholique de Louvain. He is currently an adjunct faculty member at the Thomas Jefferson School of Law in San Diego, California.*

The Death Penalty Should Be Abolished— For Very Practical Reasons
Richard C. Dieter

From a practical perspective, it is becoming increasingly clear that the death penalty no longer serves the public interest. Given the enormous risks, costs, and divisiveness of this extreme punishment, there is no reasonable justification for retaining it.

Risks of Wrongful Executions

The primary reason why the death penalty is already on the decline in the United States is written across the faces of the 138 people who have been exonerated and freed from death row since death sentencing resumed in 1973. With so many documented mistakes, the idea that the death penalty threatens innocent lives is no longer a theoretical argument. Advances in science, coupled with the crucial time between sentencing and execution, have exposed a justice system that poses a high and unnecessary risk to innocent lives. For every nine executions that have been carried out in modern times, one inmate on death row has been found who was wrongly convicted and has now been cleared of all charges.

Unfortunately, these exonerations are not a sign that the system works. Anthony Porter was spared execution in Illinois because journalism students investigated his case as an academic exercise and wound up finding the true killer who confessed to the crime. Kirk Bloodsworth was freed in Maryland because the science of DNA testing had advanced to the point where it could exclude him from the crime for which he was sentenced to death. Eventually, the same science pointed to the real perpetrator. The justice system failed in these and many other cases because it is a fallible process. It is not necessary to abandon the whole justice system; but it is possible to make sure that none of its mistakes are irrevocable.

Cameron Willingham was executed in Texas in 2004, having been convicted of arson resulting in the death of his three children. Subsequent investigation by forensic fire experts has revealed that the evidence presented at Willingham's trial should not have led to a conclusion of arson. Current science pointed to a number of other causes for the fire. Some of these revelations came out before his execution, but went unheeded. Now the execution of an innocent person may be the ultimate condemnation of Texas's often criticized system of justice.

Eyewitnesses at the scene of the crime make errors; some people do not tell the truth; prosecutors occasionally withhold critical evidence; and defense lawyers do not always investigate all the facts. The consequences of these predictable failings are that innocent people will inevitably slip through the safety nets. Some risks are unavoidable, but with the sentence of life without parole, society can be kept safe and criminals severely punished without the danger of executing the innocent. For that reason alone, the death penalty can no longer be justified.

Costs of Capital Punishment

There is another practical reason for abolishing the death penalty that has grown in importance as states grapple with the difficult choices of cutting public services. The death penalty is exactly the kind of government program that is ripe for elimination: its costs have grown, but it is producing little or nothing in return.

As the exonerations from death row grew in the late 1990s, the justice system reacted in a number of ways. Death sentences dropped 60 percent in the past decade, and executions have declined by half as doubts about convictions permeated jury rooms and even state legislatures. Four states have abolished the death penalty in the past four years, after years of stalemate. The response of other states to the problem of innocence was to incorporate reforms. But while efforts have been made to lessen the mistakes of the death penalty system, it has become much more expensive and time consuming.

Courts, including the Supreme Court, have begun to expect more of lawyers and specialists to satisfy the demands of constitutional death penalty representation. Lawyers with capital case experience are now typically assigned in capital cases, and these lawyers will cost the state more than inexperienced public defenders. Preparation for trial means investigating the defendant's past and early childhood, and sometimes requires visits to other states or countries. Prosecutors and judges must be better prepared as well, as scientific evidence and questions of mental disabilities bring new challenges. Appeals, too, cannot be casually dismissed with the defendant's life on the line.

Although there are numerous restrictions on the time for filing appeals and the issues that can be raised, no one wants to face the prospect of executing an innocent person.

The cost of this system is breaking the back of county and state budgets. By the 1990s, Illinois had more exonerations than executions, and the governor finally declared a moratorium on carrying out the death penalty. The legislature made a few reforms, but the system remained broken by most accounts. Illinois spent more than $100 million over 7 years preparing death penalty cases. No one was executed and the state finally decided in 2011 to abolish the death penalty. New Jersey spent over $250 million for its years of capital punishment; again, no one was executed and the punishment was stricken from the books in 2007. New York spent over $170 million after it reinstated the death penalty in 1995. Not only was no one executed, but every death sentence was overturned on appeal. The practice has been abandoned and the state capital defender offices have been closed, immediately saving the state millions of dollars.

Even states that have carried out executions are doing so at enormous costs. A recent report by a senior federal judge and a law professor in California found that the state had spent $4 billion on the death penalty since its reinstatement in 1978, resulting in 13 executions. That translates to a cost of $308 million per execution. Such expenditures represent thousands of police officers not hired, libraries and schools closed, or even prisoners released early because of overcrowding. And there is no sign that the costs of the death penalty will be going down. The report stated that California would have to spend even more money in the future to fix this broken system. The state has over 700 people on an overcrowded death row and has not carried out an execution in over 5 years.

A study by the Urban Institute of Maryland's death penalty costs projected state expenditures of $187 million to produce 5 executions, or roughly $37 million per execution. That is less expensive than in California but still impossible to justify when so many worthwhile programs have to be cut back.

Why Is the Death Penalty So Expensive?

Preparing for a death penalty trial means that two defense lawyers and two prosecutors will be working on a single case for at least a year. Experts in mental health, forensics, and social-history investigation will be hired by both sides. Pretrial hearings will consume many hours of court time. Jury selection in a capital case can take weeks or even months because each potential juror has to be quizzed about his or her views on capital punishment. The guilt-innocence phase of the trial is followed by the sentencing phase that may take even longer.

All of this time and expense comes before a sentencing verdict is even rendered. Years of appeal and high-security detention on death row will follow. Death row inmates are kept in closely watched single cells, rarely work in the prison, and have their meals delivered. These costs are two to three times more expensive than ordinary incarceration. While both death- and life-sentenced inmates have appeals, those on death row will most likely have lawyers paid at public expense.

Typically, a capital case will be reversed and tried a second time if the death sentence is to be preserved. The whole process is far more expensive than trying and sentencing an individual to life without parole. The study by the Urban Institute in Maryland found that the total cost of a death sentence was $3 million, while the total cost of a life sentence was $1.1 million, with incarceration and appeals included in both instances.

Life sentences are rarely overturned, and the defendant usually slips into anonymity, instead of reopening the wounds of victims' families who have to return to court again and again for appeals and retrials. Many family members are now asking the prosecution not to seek the death penalty, and more prosecutors are willing to accept a plea bargain that essentially ends the case immediately and starts the punishment. In capital cases, the punishment is often delayed for 15 years or more, and may never be carried out.

The problem is not just that the death penalty is expensive; states are getting virtually nothing for all their expenditures.

While the death penalty appears to be on its way out, states are spending hundreds of millions of dollars just to maintain it, only occasionally carrying out an execution. In 2010, there were approximately 15,000 murders in the United States and the country executed 46 inmates, the majority in just two states (Texas and Ohio). Most states with the death penalty carry out less than one execution per year—a meaningless act toward the purported justifications of deterrence and retribution. Over 99 percent of murders will never result in an execution.

Even if viewed from the perspective of efficiency, the death penalty is a failed system. According to the Bureau of Justice Statistics' most recent data, the average time between sentencing and execution has lengthened to 14 years. Many death sentences are overturned on appeal because states failed to protect the constitutional rights of defendants facing execution. When these cases are retried or disposed of by plea bargains, about 80 percent receive a sentence of less than death. Thus, for most defendants in most states, the death penalty is simply a very expensive form of life without parole.

Political Influence

The death penalty is more a part of the political process than of the criminal justice system. Many elected officials continue to support this costly system out of fear of being called "soft on crime." Even elected judges campaign on their willingness to impose and uphold death sentences. The public, however, is more interested in being "smart on crime." While supporting the death penalty in theory, they are willing to replace it with a sentence that keeps society safe and is less expensive and risky than the death penalty. A 2010 survey by Lake Research Partners found that 61 percent of registered voters supported replacing the death penalty with alternative sentences. That explains why death sentences are declining so dramatically and why many states have either abolished or are considering ending the death penalty.

The same survey found that the public would rather see their taxes go to public services and creating jobs than for the death penalty. If they supported a candidate, most respondents said it would either make no difference if that candidate voted to end the death penalty, or that such a vote would even increase their support.

Arbitrariness

The death penalty does not follow the logic of the criminal justice system, where the goal is to match the crime with the punishment in a rational way. Instead, the death penalty picks out a few cases based on arbitrary factors—rather than the worst cases—for execution. Defendants with the shoddy lawyers, those who killed a white person rather than a black person, and those in certain counties in a handful of states are far more likely to be executed than those who committed the worst crimes.

Gary Ridgway in Washington received a life sentence even though he admitted to killing 48 women. Teresa Lewis, on the other hand, a woman with an IQ of 72, was executed in 2010 in Virginia for conspiracy to murder, while the actual killers, who probably led her along for insurance money, received life sentences. Terrorists, organized crime bosses, and other serial killers who were arguably among the worst offenders in recent history have received life sentences or less, but an incidental killing in a robbery gone wrong may result in an execution. That is the picture of the death penalty in America today.

Theodore Kaczynski (the Unabomber), Eric Rudolph (who killed people at the Atlanta Olympics and killed abortion providers), Zacarias Moussaoui (who pled guilty to the 9/11 conspiracy), Brian Nichols (who killed a judge in his courtroom and three others while escaping in Georgia), Terry Nichols (who was found guilty of conspiracy in the Oklahoma City bombing), Stephen "the Rifleman" Flemmi (an organized crime figure who killed 11 people), all received life sentences.

There may be good reasons why these and similar defendants did not receive the death penalty, but those same reasons apply to many others guilty of much less heinous offenses, who did receive a death sentence and were executed. This is not a fair system.

Only 15 percent of those who have been sentenced to death have been executed since the death penalty was reinstated in 1976. Over 80 percent of the executions have occurred in the South. Even within states, the death penalty tends to cluster in certain counties as prosecutors with more resources, or simply more inclination, seek the death penalty often, while others do not seek it at all. For many years, if you committed a murder in Houston or Philadelphia you were far more likely to get the death penalty than if you committed the same crime in Dallas or in Pittsburgh. Such distinctions make little sense. This kind of arbitrariness was part of the reason the death penalty was struck down in 1972. As Supreme Court Justice Potter Stewart wrote at the time, a sentence that is akin to being "struck by lightning" is a cruel and unusual punishment.

Race

Race plays a disturbing role in determining which cases are prosecuted as capital cases. A report by Professor David Baldus to the American Bar Association found statistical evidence of racial bias in over 20 states. The key finding in almost all of these studies was that those who murder a white victim are much more likely to be sentenced to death than those who killed a black person. Over 75 percent of the executions that have occurred since the death penalty was reinstated in 1976 involved a crime with a white victim, even though whites are victims of murder in less than 50 percent of the murders committed. This disparity is equivalent to putting a higher value on white lives than on black lives.

In many cases, a black defendant accused of killing a white victim faces an all-white system to determine his fate. The district attorney is white, the judge is white, even his defense attorney is white. Because potential jurors who express doubts about the death penalty can be struck from serving on death penalty juries (or because of racial bias by the prosecutor), a black defendant may have an all-white jury, as well. The death penalty remains one of the most divisive issues in our society.

Conclusion

For many people, the death penalty is a moral question. However, for an increasing number of Americans, the key question is not whether capital punishment can be supported in theory, but whether this clearly broken system is worth keeping. From a practical perspective, the death penalty unnecessarily risks innocent lives, is far more expensive than the alternative of life in prison with no parole, remains arbitrary and unfair in its application, and gives nothing to society in return. The rest of the world is moving away from the death penalty, and its practice in the United States is on the decline. As many states have already found, the death penalty will not be missed when it is gone.

Richard C. Dieter is the executive director of the Death Penalty Information Center in Washington, D.C.

Capital Punishment Should Not Be Abolished in the United States
Brett R. Meltzer

There are many arguments on why the federal and state governments should not abolish the death penalty. In this essay, I will focus on the three most persuasive ones. First, the United States Constitution authorizes the use of the death penalty so the federal government and the individual states should have the punishment available to use. Second, the death penalty serves as a proportional punishment for offenders in certain circumstances. Finally, the death penalty deters offenders from committing murders. At the conclusion of this essay, the reader should be persuaded that there exist enough procedural safeguards to ensure a fair and just application of the punishment, so the penalty's benefit to society far outweighs any costs.

The Death Penalty Is Constitutional

In 1791, Congress proposed and the state governments ratified the Fifth and Eighth Amendments to the United States Constitution. The Fifth Amendment of the U.S. Constitution, which applies to the federal government, clearly provides that "no person shall be . . . deprived of life, liberty, or property, without due process of law." As it plainly states, the use of death as a legal punishment was permitted as long as the federal government did not deprive a person of life without first providing the requisite due process of law (which is the opportunity to challenge the charge and sentence through a process that provides a fair and honest trial and appellate procedure). In 1868, Congress and the state governments reaffirmed the above principle by adopting the Fourteenth Amendment to the U.S. Constitution. The Fourteenth Amendment, which applies to the state governments, provides that "nor shall any State deprive a person of life, liberty, or property, without due process of law." Thus, it is clear from these two amendments that the text of the U.S. Constitution permits capital punishment. This would be consistent with the time periods, as hanging was the most chosen method of punishment for those found guilty for crimes such as treason, espionage, or murder.

The Eighth Amendment of the U.S. Constitution prohibits "cruel and unusual" punishment. Abolitionists, or people who oppose capital punishment and seek to have it abolished, argue that the manner in which the government administers the penalty is unconstitutional because it is "cruel and unusual" punishment. They have two main arguments. First, abolitionists argue that the methods used to execute a prisoner are unconstitutional because of their inhumanity. They attack as cruel the standard methods of hanging, electric chair, firing squad, or lethal injection. Although the courts have generally found that all these methods do not constitute "cruel and unusual" punishment, the federal government and all of the states that permit the death penalty primarily use lethal injection. The combination of drugs involved with lethal injection ensures that the prisoner experiences little or no pain at death, since the prisoner is first rendered unconscious by one drug before the other drugs kick in to collapse the lungs and stop the heart. Regardless of the method currently used, it is clear, though, that the drafters of the Eighth Amendment were concerned with preventing "tortures" and other "barbarous" methods of punishment like brutality that caused excessive pain, dismemberment, or lingering death.

As stated above, death by hanging was the most common mode of execution at the time of the enactment of the Eighth Amendment. Interestingly, the drafters considered hanging the most humane method at the time, since it led to a relatively quick and painless death. The drafters, instead, were concerned about cruel punishments like "burning at the stake" or "public dissection," which are extremely painful and destroy the body. The drafters wished to prevent punishments that intended to inflict serious pain and anguish. The drafters were not concerned with punishments that might cause some pain or death, as the Fifth Amendment was drafted and approved by the same people who wrote the Eighth Amendment. Logically, if the drafters believed the death penalty was a "cruel and unusual" punishment in violation of the Eighth Amendment, they would not have permitted death as a punishment through the Fifth Amendment.

If administered correctly, lethal injection is the most humane method to carry out the death penalty since the prisoner is placed unconscious at the beginning, ensuring little or no pain at death. Lethal injection involves a three-drug combination where the first drug renders the prisoner unconscious, the second drug paralyzes the lungs, and the third drug stops the heart. Abolitionists raise concerns that the prisoner could feel great pain if not given enough of the first drug. They fear the possibility that the prisoner would be conscious, thus feeling pain of asphyxiation as his lungs collapse or the pain of cardiac arrest as his heart stops. But, that possibility is remote or nonexistent as trained professionals administer the drugs. Plus, there are no proven cases where lethal injection was ever administered incorrectly. Any method of execution presents risks that the prisoner will experience some pain, but it is clear that lethal injection, properly administered, causes no pain. Thus the method of lethal injection is not cruel or inhumane, and this should not be argued as a reason to abolish the death penalty.

The abolitionists' other main argument that the death penalty is unconstitutional is that the sentences are imposed arbitrarily, excessively, and discriminatorily. Death penalty abolitionists also argue that the process is unfair as some who deserve to die are executed while others are saved. But, the process is the fairest devised. Currently, there exist enough procedural safeguards to ensure a fair and just application of the punishment. Faith in the judicial system, the cornerstone of our democracy, squarely places the offender's peers as the deciders of whether a life is worth saving. And there is no better group of people to make the decision on who deserves the death penalty than the jury who heard the evidence, determined guilt beyond a reasonable doubt, and considered the aggravating and mitigating circumstances of the crime and the person.

The United States Supreme Court has consistently found that as long as the punishment of death is not doled out unfairly or in a manner where it is as random as being struck by lightning, then it is not a "cruel and unusual" punishment. The Court found that by applying the death penalty to specific, carefully defined crimes, it prevented any arbitrary imposition of the death penalty. Furthermore, by requiring a jury in a capital case to carefully consider both the guilt of the offender and any aggravating or mitigating circumstances, the penalty is limited to the most brutal of crimes. Finally, by mandating appeals in such cases, the appellate courts safeguard against capricious and weak prosecutions, or egregiously erroneous jury determinations unsupported by the evidence. Thus, with these safeguards in place the offender is afforded due process.

Accordingly, since the United States Supreme Court has consistently ruled that the death penalty is constitutional, then it should be available to use. It is up to the will of the people and not the judges to decide otherwise. If the public at some point determines that the "evolving standards of decency" change, then the American people will seek amendment to the U.S. Constitution or pass legislation abolishing the punishment. But since the public believes that the penalty is just in certain circumstances (which also explains why the federal government and 31 out of the 50 states permit the sanction), then the American people should have the punishment available. If the people in some states want to keep the penalty while the people in others want to abolish it, then that is the beauty of our federalist governmental system. As United Supreme Court Justice Potter Stewart wrote:

> Following the laws that the people enact is an important purpose in promoting the stability of a society governed by law. When people begin to believe that organized society is unwilling or unable to impose upon criminal offenders the punishment they "deserve," then there are sown the seeds of anarchy—of self-help, vigilante justice, and lynch law.

Since capital punishment is constitutional, there is no legal reason to abolish it. It should be left to the democratically elected legislature to determine what punishments to use to control crime.

Some Offenders Deserve the Death Penalty

Another reason to not abolish the death penalty is that to remain a civilized society the people need to mete out punishments in proportion to the crime. The primary purpose in sentencing offenders is to punish. For certain offenders, the punishment of death seems the only reasonable outcome. The typical individual sentenced to the death penalty is a white male with an average age of 44 years old, a 12th grade education, with felony priors who has committed a clear act of premeditated murder, often involving aggravating factors like grave cruelty, multiple victims, or the killing of a law enforcement officer. But as the typical death penalty case involves shocking circumstances, the most extreme cases even more clearly justify the necessity of the death penalty.

Ted Bundy admitted to killing 30 people in several states in the 1970s. Danny Rolling terrorized a college town in Gainesville, Florida, in 1990 by murdering five college students in a burglary spree, and then decapitating and mutilating the bodies. Jeffrey Dahmer killed 17 men and boys between 1978 and 1991 and kept the human remains in his bedroom and refrigerator. Timothy McVeigh detonated a truck bomb in front of a federal building killing 168 people and injuring 800 more. All these offenders took pleasure in others' pain.

These are just some examples of heinous crimes committed across this country in recent years. Innately, it does not seem appropriate that these offenders receive the same punishment of life in prison as those who commit lesser crimes. In our system of justice, the more serious the crime you commit, the more serious your punishment. When the offender commits a DUI, then the sentence is proportional to that crime. The offender pays a fine, is placed on probation, and may be sentenced to jail. If the offender commits a burglary of a home, then he is usually sentenced to prison for no more than 15 years. If a drug dealer traffics in 30 kilograms of heroin, then he usually faces 30 years in prison. The idea is that the more serious the crime, the more time you spend in prison.

Other than death, the most serious punishment an offender faces is life in prison without the possibility of parole. Bernie Madoff, for example, was sentenced to 150 years in federal prison for embezzling more than $20 billion from investors.

His sentence is tantamount to a life sentence. Although he will spend the remainder of his life in prison, he recently stated in an interview with journalist Barbara Walters that he is happier in prison than on the outside. No matter the harshness of prison, inmates who are sentenced there still get to enjoy some of the benefits of life.

Since the punishment of death can never be undone, it should be used only in certain circumstances (like in cases of murder where the punishment fits the crime). If people are going to have any confidence in the judicial system that offenders are justly punished, then the death penalty needs to be available to punish the most serious violators of the law.

The death penalty is a proportionate penalty for those offenders who commit murder, since death for the murderer and the victim are both final. In sum, by executing those murderers who commit heinous crimes, justice so requires that they get their just deserts. Innately, there is a feeling that the prisoner deserves it. Without the death penalty, the likes of Ted Bundy, Danny Rolling, and Timothy McVeigh, all murderers, would be walking around in prisons the same as Bernie Madoff. They would all breathe the same air, enjoy the same food, and watch the same movies. In this example, the punishment of a life sentence for these violent murderers does not seem proportional or just to the punishment levied against a despicable thief. Thus, the penalty of death needs to be available to use for those offenders where life in prison is not a proportionate penalty for the crime they committed.

The Death Penalty Deters Crime

Another reason not to abolish the death penalty is that the empirical evidence shows that the penalty is a useful deterrent to murder. Since another purpose of sentencing is to deter people from committing crimes, this evidence is a very persuasive reason to keep the death penalty.

A series of academic studies over the past six years confirm that the death penalty acts as such a deterrent. One such study in 2003 by Naci Mocan, an economics professor at Louisiana State University, and a 2006 study that reexamined the data found that each execution results in five fewer homicides, and commuting a death sentence means five more homicides. Interestingly, Dr. Mocan is a proponent in abolishing the death penalty. But he admits that the data support the conclusion that the death penalty deters prospective murderers. He stated that, "Science does really draw a conclusion. It did. There is no question about it. The conclusion is that there is a deterrent effect."

Among the conclusions of the above and other studies:

- Between three and 18 lives would be saved by the execution of each convicted killer.
- Each execution deters an average of 18 murders, according to a 2003 nationwide study by professors at Emory University. (Other studies have estimated the deterred murders per execution at 3, 5, and 14.)
- The Illinois moratorium on executions in 2000 led to 150 *additional* homicides over the following four years, according to a 2006 study by professors at the University of Houston.
- Speeding up executions would increase the deterrent effect. For every 2.75 years cut from time spent on death row, one murder would be prevented, according to a 2004 study by an Emory University professor.

Intriguingly, this empirical evidence jibes with common sense. I bet that most people believe that the fear of death is greater than the fear of life imprisonment. Consequently, if one prospective murderer is deterred by the threat of death over that of life imprisonment, then the option of using the death penalty served its purpose by controlling crime. Sir James Fitzjames Stephen, an English judge, said it best:

> Some men, probably, abstain from murder because they fear that if they committed murder they would be hanged.

Hundreds of thousands abstain from it because they regard it with horror. One great reason why they regard it with horror is that murderers are hanged.

The threat of the death penalty has a powerful deterrent effect against future murderers. The people should have this penalty available so that it can protect itself.

Conclusion

The abolitionists' best argument is that since the death penalty is irrevocable there is a risk that an innocent person may die for a crime he never committed. But abolishing the death penalty creates a risk that an innocent victim dies by the hand of a murderer. Indeed, the risk of an innocent person dying by the death penalty is so small that it does not outweigh the cost of abolishing capital punishment. There are sufficient safeguards in place to prevent innocent people from being executed. As a former federal and state prosecutor, I have never seen or heard, during my years of practice, of an innocent person sentenced to death in the current American system. Neither can any of the United States Supreme Court justices. There has not been one proven example of an innocent person executed in our current legal system. Jurors do not impose the death penalty swiftly. Jurors want to see DNA evidence, corroborating witnesses, and confessions before they find guilt. They want to hear about the mitigating circumstances of the person's life to see whether it should be saved. The appellate process ensures that the offender was treated fairly.

While there is a very small risk that an innocent person may be executed, that is not a sufficient reason to abolish the penalty. Over the past few years, about 16,000 homicides a year occurred in the United States; each year around 115 convicted murderers were sentenced to death; and fewer than 50 a year are actually executed. The risk of an innocent person dying is so small, that it is worth the risk. Risks are inherent in any system, because we are human and vulnerable. But by abolishing the death penalty, we risk way more. We risk giving up our constitutional rights. We risk not punishing the offender proportionally to the crime they committed. We risk giving up a powerful tool in deterring future murderers. That risk is too high. I think for all the above reasons, capital punishment should not be abolished in the United States.

Brett R. Meltzer is an instructor of law with the Department of Legal Studies at the University of Central Florida.

Retaining the Death Penalty: Sociopolitical Support
Kim MacInnis

The battle between advocates and the opponents of the death penalty continues in the United States. The United States remains one of the few developed nations to still incorporate the death penalty as an important component of its criminal justice system, virtually always for the offense of first degree homicide after 1977. In 1977, in *Coker v. Georgia*, the United States Supreme Court held that the sentence of death for a rape of a female adult was excessive punishment and unconstitutional under the Eighth Amendment. Amplifying on this decision, in 2008, the Supreme Court held in *Kennedy v. Louisiana* that the imposition of a sentence of death was constitutionally impermissible even for the offense of raping a child, so long as the victim did not die as a result of the crime. Currently, there are 31 states with capital punishment statutes: Alabama, Arizona, Arkansas, California, Colorado, Florida, Georgia, Idaho, Indiana, Kansas, Kentucky, Louisiana, Mississippi, Missouri, Montana, Nebraska, Nevada, New Hampshire, North Carolina, Ohio, Oklahoma, Oregon, Pennsylvania, South Carolina, South Dakota, Tennessee, Texas, Utah, Virginia, Washington, and Wyoming, as well as the U.S. Government and U.S. Military. There are a variety of moral arguments for and against the death penalty, but the "sociopolitical environment" of the United States pertaining to the use of the death remains the most persuasive argument in support of a death penalty practice. This sociopolitical environment is characterized by a society that believes in harsh punishment and expects the state to accommodate its wishes. Given the public support of the death penalty, it must remain as the ultimate punishment for serious crimes.

Politically and socially, the United States has a long history of death penalty practices. The death penalty was a fact of life in colonial America; it was used as a means of maintaining order. Continuing into the late 19th century, there was little federal criminal law jurisprudence in the area of capital punishment. Nearly 900 people were legally executed in the 1880s and 1,215 people were legally executed in the 1890s, the highest proportionate execution rate in American history. There were also extra-judicial killings, illegal executions, and the use of lynching (particularly in southern states), reaching 1,540 in the 1890s.

According to Ronald J. Tabak, any public discussion about capital punishment in the United States since the 19th century has tended to be "incident-driven and incident-focused," not "issue-driven or issue-focused." Historically, a majority of Americans have agreed that some criminals should forfeit their lives as a just punishment for unacceptable societal behavior. This belief continues to be a persistent theme regarding the death penalty. This is evident in a 2010 Gallup poll concerning the death penalty—in which two-thirds of Americans were still in support of it. Sixty-nine percent of those polled supported the death penalty; 27 percent opposed it, and 4 percent had no opinion. The Harris, Rasmussen Telephone, and Pew Research polls reported similar numbers concerning the public's support for the death penalty. The majority of those polled believed in using the death penalty for purely punitive reasons. In fact, the circumstances of the crime will often dictate support for the propriety of capital punishment as a suitable societal remedy (to wit, the more heinous the circumstances of the crime, the more the support that exists for imposition of capital punishment). These sentiments are important components of political support for retaining the death penalty in the United States. Politicians want the support of their constituents and people want politicians who support their values.

Before examining the sociopolitical approach to the death penalty, it is important to present briefly the three most common theoretical perspectives supporting capital punishment: utilitarian, retributive, and egalitarian.

Utilitarian arguments focus mainly on deterrent effects of the death penalty. Dating back to original works of Jeremy Bentham and Cesare Beccaria, deterrence theory assumes that offenders exercise rational judgment and are reasonably aware of the potential costs and benefits associated with criminal acts. Utilitarianism is an ethical theory—stating that the moral worth of an action is solely determined by its contribution to overall utility. The emphasis is on consequences, not intentions. The classical utilitarianism theory of John Stuart Mill and Jeremy Bentham purported that actions are judged by the virtues of their consequences and also added that the pursuit and production of happiness should be taken into consideration. In short, according to utilitarianism, our duty is to do whatever will increase the amount of happiness in the world. Punishing someone by putting them to death via state execution would be of benefit to the rest of society. The remaining population would be protected from this criminal. In addition, capital punishment might force others to think twice before committing heinous crimes. This deterrent argument holds little weight since most murders are committed impulsively or as a crime of passion. Additionally, the highest rates of murders occur in states that implement the death penalty.

The remaining two theoretical perspectives used in support of the death penalty focus on punishment and fairness. Retributive arguments focus on sheer punishment with no regard for deterrence or rehabilitation. Retribution is one of the oldest theories of punishment, dating back to ancient societies and adherence to the *lex talionis*. It is the belief articulated in the

Old Testament of the Bible that "an eye for an eye, a tooth for a tooth" was a permissible societal response to criminal offenders. *Lex talionis*, or the Law of Retaliation, continues to be widely accepted and is the most cited argument for retaining the death penalty in the United States today. The idea is that if someone takes another's life, that someone deserves to die as well. The offender must experience what the victim experiences. Egalitarian arguments are also appeals to equity; people in the same position should be treated the same. There is some logic to thinking of egalitarian arguments as a subset of retributive arguments: people, of course, deserve to be treated fairly. But in the context of the death penalty, at least, egalitarian arguments are persuasive. If someone murders another person, they should be put to death as well. This seems fair. There is not necessarily a vengeful element in this argument.

The sentiment that the death penalty is an appropriate response to heinous crime remains strong in the United States. There were 1,233 executions in the United States from 1977 through 2010. There were fifty-two executions in 2009 and forty-six in 2010. American society is a punishing society. There does not necessarily have to be a logical, scientific reason for implementing harsh punishment. One of the founding fathers of sociology, Emile Durkheim, argued that the essence of punishment in society and the evolution of penal methods lie in the anger and passion triggered by crimes that violate people's most important values. There is no science involved. Durkheim believed that state officials react to punishment based on what the "onlookers" (public) demand. Thus, the United States must retain the death penalty mainly because of the popular retributive response to violent crime.

Why is the United States as a culture, so punitive? Tradition is one answer. Today, the main reason for being so punitive directly relates to political culture. The political elite, supported by the media, have bolstered an increasingly punitive crime-control approach to social problems. This is despite the fact that since 1994, violent crime rates (murder, rape and sexual assault, robbery, and assault) have declined, reaching the lowest level recorded in 2009. The barrage of "crime shows" and crime documentaries on television support the image of a violent society. The public accepts this image and, as a result, supports a punitive approach to violent crime. This relationship between the public and the state is an important reason to retain the death penalty, especially in terms of reelection. American politicians are reluctant to deviate drastically from public demands and abolishing the death penalty may be perceived as drastic and weak.

Although slightly dated, Patrick Fisher and Travis Pratt's explanation of political culture lends credence to the support of the death penalty. This culture is based on the utilitarian conception that politics should work like a marketplace. The government should handle functions demanded by the people. This is the essence of democracy. Good government is measured by the degree to which it supports the public good as well as how it controls the population. If two-thirds of the population support a utilitarian or retributive approach to the death penalty, then so be it. Sociopolitical values have more influence on public policy than scientific or moral arguments against the death penalty. According to this belief, if the majority of the people in the United States did not support the death penalty, it would be abolished. Other countries arguably would follow suit, to the extent their populations were opposed to the use of the death penalty. In most European countries, supporters of the death penalty form a minority. Indeed, this at least partially explains why the death penalty is now universally outlawed among all twenty seven nations of the European Union. The Charter of Fundamental Rights of the European Union (as well as the European Convention on Human Rights) expressly and flatly forbids states from employing capital punishment.

Related to political culture are constitutional arguments that do not necessarily support the death penalty but also do not discourage its usage. The Eighth Amendment to the U.S. Constitution prohibits the imposition of "cruel and unusual punishments." This has been construed collectively by the federal courts as meaning that the infliction of unnecessary pain in the administration of the death penalty would be a violation of the Eighth Amendment. This aspect of the Constitution would be the strongest argument against the death penalty. However, at least according to the United States Supreme Court, the Eighth Amendment does not guarantee a pain-free death. Punishment is by definition supposed to be somewhat painful, emotionally, physically, or both. Death in most cases involves some level of pain. The issue is whether the punishment is "cruel" or "unusual." Historically, being put to death meant being hanged, flogged, electrocuted, or shot—and, at that time, these methods were not held to be a violation of the Eighth Amendment. Today, these very same methods would be perceived as cruel or unusual by the courts. The Eighth Amendment is more clearly affected by societal change than any other amendment in the Constitution, because the very nature of the phrase "cruel and unusual" appeals to evolving societal standards. Chief Justice Earl Warren, writing for the 1958 Supreme Court case *Trop v. Dallas*, stated that the Eighth Amendment ". . . must draw its meaning from the evolving standards of decency that mark the progress of a maturing society."

Today, almost all of the states that employ or allow for the death penalty use the three-drug protocol. Lethal injections arose in reaction to the perceived brutality of electrocutions, as well as to the contention in *Gregg v. Georgia* (1976) that the death penalty is not, in itself, unconstitutional. Lethal injections appear to be a more humane way to execute someone. The assumption is that the capital felon simply goes to sleep, painlessly. This is now debatable. Critics argue that the drug process induces paralysis and suffocation, not unlike hanging, and thus is perceived as cruel. However, the death penalty is perceived as constitutionally acceptable because it cannot be scientifically proven that unnecessary pain is being inflicted and that the state is attempting to be "cruel"; rather, it is simply intending to be effective and to minimize the possibility of unnecessary pain (to the best extent possible). Thus, the question arises of "how can one implement constitutional boundaries of pain?" Additionally, capital punishment is not "unusual." It has been used as a form of punishment for hundreds of years and thus cannot be considered a sudden change in justice. As such, retaining the death penalty can be considered constitutional. Interestingly enough, the length of time prisoners spend in the condemned cell—or on death row in tiny cells in virtual solitary confinement prior to execution—and the uncertainty of eventual execution as various stays are granted and then overturned (particularly in the United States, where it is an average of over 12 years) has not been not considered cruel and unusual punishment by the federal courts. It is interesting to note that many international human rights activists and jurists have opined that America's "death row" holding areas do constitute a violation of human rights. Therefore, is confining one in a tiny cell for 23 out of 24 hours a day humane? This may be perceived as cruel and unusual to many—thus cruel and unusual remain relative.

Cost is another very consistent factor voiced in the arguments regarding the death penalty. Anti-capital-punishment campaigners in the United States cite the higher cost of executing someone compared to life in prison, but this, while true for the United States, has to do with the endless appeals and delays in carrying out death sentences that are allowed under the United States legal system (where, as just noted, the average time spent on death row is over 12 years). Jon Gould and Lisa Greenman found that "the median cost of a case in which the attorney general authorized seeking the death penalty was nearly eight times greater than the cost of a case that was eligible for capital prosecution but in which the death penalty was *not* authorized." The report found that the median cost for defense representation in a death case that went to trial was $465,602, including $101,592 for experts. If the authorized case was settled by a plea, the median cost was $200,933, still far greater than the median cost of a death-eligible case in which the death penalty was *not* sought—$44,809. In other words, it is the seeking of the death penalty that considerably raises the costs, even if the case results in a plea bargain and no trial, not the death penalty itself. These figures do not include prosecution and judicial costs.

Proponents of the death penalty argue that if the convicted felon was put to death in a timely fashion, costs would be drastically reduced. It certainly appears that the death penalty is extremely expensive and that taxpayers bear the brunt of the bill. However, states that implement capital punishment have the support of the people. Again, if we remain committed to a democratic argument supporting the death penalty while simultaneously living in a country devoted to punishment, costs experiences of confinement are irrelevant for the moment. According to the *New York Times*—as well as virtually every major media outlet in the United States—on May 2, 2011, when Osama Bin Laden was killed by American Navy Seals, Americans celebrated in every state and other parts of the world. Most families who lost loved ones to the 9/11 terrorist attack expressed the justice inherent in Bin Laden's death. There was a clear "eye for an eye" reaction to his death. For Americans who support the death penalty, vengeance is an important factor. This was never so apparent as with the death of Bin Laden. Capturing and jailing Bin Laden for life would have been perceived as a betrayal to the American people.

As long as the majority of Americans wish to retain the use of the death penalty for specific crimes, it will continue to be used. Cost and deterrence are irrelevant because retribution is paramount. A democracy is government by the people; *especially* rule of the majority. A democratic government is one in which the supreme power is vested in the people and exercised by them directly or indirectly through a system of representation. In sum, and in short, from a sociopolitical perspective, the United States must retain the use of the death penalty—or it would no longer be perceived as democratic.

Kim MacInnis is a professor of sociology at Bridgewater State University. She received her bachelor's degree in sociology/criminology from St. Francis Xavier University in Antigonish, Nova Scotia, Canada, and her master's degree in sociology/criminology from Dalhousie University in Halifax, Nova Scotia, Canada. She received her doctoral degree in sociology from Northeastern University in Boston, Massachusetts.

Gender and Capital Punishment
Elizabeth Rapaport

The question of whether the death penalty is applied in a discriminatory fashion has been fiercely contested since the first half of the 20th century. Critics of capital punishment argue that there are no rich men on death row and that racial minorities, especially African Americans, are over represented. Also contentious is the question of gender discrimination: Are women murderers spared the ultimate penalty while no more guilty or blameworthy men are executed? In 1976, the United States Supreme Court instituted a series of reforms aimed at purging the capital punishment system of bias. The Court held that henceforth capital punishment would be reserved for the worst of the worst murderers and subject to enhanced procedural safeguards intended to insure even-handed justice. These constitutional reforms have by no means satisfied critics. Among the enduring areas of contention is equality of treatment of men and women who kill. Since 1976, over 1,400 men but only 15 women have been executed. A small trickle of women have been executed, approximately one a year, since 2000. Does this stark numerical disparity prove that women are spared while men are exposed to the full rigors of capital justice?

Women comprise about 2 percent of death row, typically, in contemporary times. For some critics, the meaning of such statistics is manifest: Women commit one in eight homicides in the United States so one in eight death sentences should be meted out to women. Therefore death row statistics prove that women are protected by cultural or even more fundamental inhibitions from paying the ultimate price for taking life. For opponents of capital punishment gender bias is one more powerful reason for condemning capital punishment.

These statistics are misleading. Although women commit one in eight homicides, they commit a very small percentage of offenses that are eligible for capital punishment. Demonstrably, the single most important explanatory factor accounting for the sparse representation of women on death row is the low rate of commission of death-penalty echelon offenses by women. The death penalty is reserved for offenses and offenders our society regards as the most reprehensible. Two-thirds of women who kill, kill family members and lovers. Our law reflects the societal belief that these stereotypically hot-blooded or passionate crimes are less heinous than coldblooded killing. Homicides whose victims are family or other intimates seldom result in death sentences regardless of the sex of the killer. Homicide of intimates may result in a death sentence when the crime has a coldblooded motive, money not passion, or there are multiple victims or the crime is exceptionally brutal. More than 75 percent of those on death row killed in the course of committing a violent felony such as robbery or rape. These are the offenses that are most severely condemned by our society. Women's rate of participation in these offenses is very low. Women commit 4 percent or slightly less of killings of strangers, of robbery-murders and rape-murders. They commit 7 percent of killings with multiple victims.

Another important factor is the criminal history compiled prior to prosecution for murder. If the individual has previously been convicted of a violent felony, he or she is both eligible for prosecution for capital murder and more likely to be sentenced to death. Women killers are far less likely than men to have prior histories of violence.

The combination of reserving capital punishment for a small minority of homicides deemed the most reprehensible and the statistical profile of female killers results in very few women on death row. Women commit only one in eight homicides of any kind. The homicides they commit are rarely death penalty–eligible crimes. And rarely do they face homicide charges with a prior record of violent felonies. It is difficult if not impossible to disprove whether gender bias ever plays a role in the fate of persons convicted of murder. It is however demonstrable that the most powerful factors accounting for the gross statistical disparities are propensity to commit homicide, type of homicide committed, and criminal history.

The ultimate fate of men and women sentenced to die takes years and frequently decades to resolve. Modern death penalty law is complex, legal errors in these cases are rife, and there are multiple opportunities to appeal a conviction or sentence. Only 16 percent of persons sentenced to die had been executed by year's end 2012. The average time elapsed between condemnation and execution reached 12 and one-half years. A man or woman sentenced to die is far more likely to be living on death row or to have left death row due to a reduction in sentence, or more rarely an overturned conviction, than to suffer execution. Forty percent of persons sentenced to die have had their convictions or sentences overturned. Six percent have died on death row. Thirty-eight percent remain on death row. This flux makes it difficult to compare the relative success of men and women in avoiding execution after being placed under sentence of death.

To date, a smaller percentage of women under sentence of death have been executed (9% versus 16%). A slightly smaller percentage of women remain on death row (35% versus 38%) and a larger proportion of women have been resentenced to life, had their convictions lifted, received executive clemency, or died on death row (55% versus 40%). These comparisons must be treated with caution because the number of women is so small and the time horizon of death row incumbency is so long. Any explanation of the apparent success of women in avoiding execution must be tentative if not speculative. One explanation would be bias against executing women. Another is that because women on death row are so rare, their cases get greater scrutiny, and therefore greater likelihood of the discovery of legal error or the granting of executive clemency. Any hypothesis is vulnerable because a small change in the number of sentences or executions would produce a big swing in the statistical profile of women sentenced to die.

Elizabeth Rapaport is Hatch Professor of Law (emerita) at the University of New Mexico School of Law. She previously taught at a number of universities including Boston University and Duke University. She has also led the University of New Mexico School of Law Clemency Project.

Death Row Exonerations and Conviction Integrity
John Rago

Many years ago, I struggled with a legal issue. Help arrived from my dear friend and colleague, Professor Bob Taylor when he said to me ". . . do your best to work through it, but understand this, in the end, *all truth rebels against contradiction.*"

Many of us try to live our lives anchored in this absolute. Whether guided by philosophical, religious, scientific, or historical reasoning, we struggle with challenges reminded that truth requires us to recognize our errors, whenever we encounter them, and correct them as far as we can.

Undoubtedly, we make mistakes in our system of criminal justice. Three hundred and 44 post-conviction DNA exonerations—twenty from death row—provide incontrovertible certainty that factually innocent individuals have been sentenced to death. As the debate over the death penalty in a just society continues, my own pursuit of truth in this very narrow but highly consequential journey reminds me of Professor Taylor's instruction.

Society demands integrity from an imperfect criminal justice system, not inerrancy. We must always be prepared to recognize our errors and correct our mistakes, as fully as it lies within our means. Our nation's DNA exonerations provide a treasure trove of mistakes to examine. By extension, as deeply disquieting as these exonerations are, the consequences we face if we fail to correct our mistakes are even more disturbing. The stakes are high. Certainly, no American would countenance the risk of executing a factually innocent individual.

Since the 1988 cymbal-crash arrival of DNA in a criminal case, Lady Justice often has looked in the mirror and blanched. We now know with complete certainty that if we are to continue to use the death penalty, our system needs some careful and immediate attention. In particular, our reoccurring mistakes are manifest largely in the form of eyewitness misidentification, junk science, false confessions, government misconduct, incentivized witnesses, and bad lawyering. Consider one such case—the first DNA death row exoneration in 1993 from the State of Maryland involving Kirk Noble Bloodsworth.

On July 25, 1984, a horrific crime shocked the small, semi-rural community of Fontana Village located a few miles outside of Baltimore. Police found the body of nine-year-old Dawn Hamilton in a wooded area near a spot known as Becky's Pond. She had been brutally raped and murdered. Just a few miles away from where Dawn Hamilton's body lay, a 23-year-old honorably discharged Marine was struggling to make a life for himself while trying to mend a breaking marriage. That day, Bloodsworth's life began its fall into an unimaginable nightmare.

Two young boys were the last to see Dawn Hamilton alive. They were fishing when they saw her walk into the woods to look for her friends. She was followed by her assailant. The mothers of these two young eyewitnesses, aged 10 and 8, brought their sons to the police station to look at a photospread. Polaroids were shown to Chris and Jackie. Jackie could not identify anyone, and Chris thought that Bloodsworth looked like the man, but that his hair color was wrong—it was too red. The investigators felt that they had enough to secure a warrant for Bloodsworth's arrest. On August 9, Bloodsworth was arrested for the rape and murder of Dawn Hamilton. The evidence against him was largely based upon eyewitness identifications.

As he prepared to leave the police station for processing following his arrest and interrogation, Bloodsworth declined to shield his face from news cameras. This was a terrible decision. He walked defiantly through a gauntlet of news cameras and reporters, refusing to hide his face from anyone because he knew that he had done nothing wrong. Meanwhile, police informed several of their witnesses that an arrest had been made. The witnesses were told not to watch television because a line-up was imminent and it would be better if they did not see the accused until they were at the precinct station. The witnesses watched the news.

On August 13, Jackie and Chris were again brought to the police station by their mothers, this time to participate in a line-up identification. Both boys appeared to be extremely nervous. Six individuals were placed in the line-up. Bloodsworth was number six. Jackie identified number three, a police officer, as the perpetrator. Chris shook his head (indicating "no") when he was asked if he could identify anyone. Detective Capel testified at trial that, once outside of the line-up room, Chris regained his composure. "He said he knew all the time that it was Number 6, but he did not want the man to hear his voice because the man could tell it was him because it was a little kid's voice." Nearly four weeks later, Jackie returned to the station with his mother, who explained that her son was too afraid to name the real killer. She indicated that he said "Number 6" was the real killer. At trial, Jackie did not identify Bloodsworth as the man he saw on July 25. Chris made a positive, in-court identification, as did the woman who was the last to see Dawn and the man with curly blonde hair walking down the wooded path. In all, five eyewitnesses claimed to have seen Bloodsworth with the girl on July 25. One claimed to have seen Bloodsworth alone as early as 6:00 a.m.

With no physical evidence linking Bloodsworth to the crime, and despite ten alibi witnesses, the jury returned a verdict within two hours after beginning deliberations Bloodsworth was convicted on March 8, 1985, of sexual assault, rape, and first-degree premeditated murder. Baltimore County Judge J. William Hinkel sentenced Bloodsworth to death.

Nearly ten years following Bloodsworth's 1993 exoneration, DNA from Dawn Hamilton's panties was collected and uploaded into CODIS (Combined DNA Index). The test revealed Kimberly Shay Ruffner as the individual who raped and killed this nine-year-old girl. Ironically, Ruffner slept in the same cellblock as Bloodsworth in the Maryland penitentiary. At his sentencing for the Hamilton murder, Bloodsworth argued against the imposition of the death penalty.

While the debate for many over the death penalty will continue, my work with Bloodsworth and others who have been exonerated through DNA has moved me much closer to my own truth.

Society may not be prepared to abandon capital punishment, and remarkably, despite this accounting, I have my moments when I still can see its value. But the plight of my dear friend Kirk has delivered me to a new way of thinking. At a bare minimum, death penalty advocates must insist upon a hastened pace for responding to these errors with evidence-based practices for examining eyewitnesses, electronic recording of custodial interviews and interrogations, or any number of steps proven to be the best available means for sustaining conviction integrity.

I recognize that the law is slow to cut down errors as soon as they make their appearance. But on the question of capital punishment and factual innocence, we can no longer allow our errors to pile up. In these instances, our mistakes can be the forerunner and companion of truth, but only if we move on the lessons of these 344 DNA exonerations (and those yet to come). Only when truth is within our collective field of vision can our conversation about the death penalty move closer to its final angle of repose.

John Rago is an associate professor at Duquesne University School of Law. He chaired a 51-member statewide committee formed by the Pennsylvania State Senate to study wrongful convictions (2007–2011). He has served on the Innocence Project's Northeast Policy Board and the Governor's Advisory Board on Probation. He is frequently consulted on matters of conviction integrity and postconviction claims of actual innocence.

Capital Punishment and Public Confidence in the Criminal Justice System
Gov. Tom Corbett

Our nation has long engaged in a running argument over capital punishment. Politically, this issue has invigorated partisan views; however, this is not a clear-cut issue of Right versus Left.

The landmark 1972 case of *Furman v. Georgia* placed a *de facto* moratorium on the death penalty in America opening wide the door to intense and often passionate political conversation. By invitation of the Court, many states amended their laws to comply with the mandates of *Furman* while others took another direction. Today, the death penalty is followed in 31 states with 19 adopting the course of abolition.

Death penalty advocates and abolitionists argue with equal vigor that their views reflect the conscience of society. Ironically, both sides argue that justice can be elusive, biased, and imprecise. These conditions and the socioeconomic settings that drive them will not diminish any time soon. America's appetite for capital punishment appears to be slowly diminishing. Conservative writer George Will recently opined: ". . . without a definitive judicial ruling or other galvanizing event, a perennial American argument is ending. Capital punishment is withering away." Statistically speaking, he has a point; however, these statistics may overshadow a growing and deeply troubling condition that will affect all of us.

A recent Report by the Pew Foundation suggests the political divide between Republicans and Democrats on the death penalty has become more pronounced. In 1994, 85 percent of Republicans and 75 percent of Democrats supported the death penalty. Today, support for the death penalty has declined to 76 percent and 49 percent respectively among Republicans and Democrats. While two-thirds of Americans support the use of the death penalty, the downward trend in support for capital punishment offers some insight to questions that should have all of our attention.

We should ask ourselves, what lessons reside in these statistics?

Even though a clear majority of Americans continue to support the death penalty, public doubt over its ongoing efficacy is more than casual. For some, this is worrisome news. In my view, these statistics are a troubling harbinger for a different and perhaps a more elemental reason as they may reflect a lessening of public confidence in our criminal justice systems.

The single most critical imperative of any government is to secure through wise and appropriate laws a greater measure of public safety for all citizens. My adherence to this bedrock value was profoundly formed first as a prosecutor, and continuously shaped by my experiences as U.S. attorney, attorney general, and most recently, as governor of the Commonwealth of Pennsylvania. My experiences with the criminal justice system have taught me that freedom in society cannot long endure in the midst of disorder and that disorder will follow if we lose our faith in the Rule of Law. Herein lies my concern.

An ordered society is deeply rooted in our regard for the rule of law and in our faith in those institutions committed to seeing that the ends of rule of law are achieved. Cast aside the death penalty debate and consider how much of this statistical decline is the product of a diminishing faith in the rule of law or, more precisely, confidence in the institutions charged to carry out the rule. Trust in law enforcement, a properly functioning judicial system, and the Executive's faithful discharge of his or her constitutional and statutory duties are essential ingredients for sustaining public confidence in our criminal justice system. Absent these features, confidence in the rule of law may break down. Perhaps this is what lurks beneath the Pew Report's statistics.

Turning to the death penalty, as governor, I signed 48 death warrants. Following a thorough review of the record, I signed these warrants because it was my duty as stated in the Pennsylvania Supreme Court's Opinion in the case of *Morganelli v. Casey*, 646 A. 2d 744–1994 which preceded my tenure as governor. But to be clear, I also signed these warrants because of my respect for the law, my respect for the juries who painstakingly rendered their penalty phase verdict, my regard for the families of the victims of these evil acts, and my confidence in law enforcement. All sides of the death penalty issues ask, are we perfect? No, of course we are not perfect. For many, this admission is enough reason not to impose a sentence of death. But signing a death warrant is not the same as countenancing imperfection. A very careful review of these 48 cases left me no doubt of the defendant's factual guilt and eligibility for the penalty fixed by the jury.

I understand and can empathize with conventional arguments against the death penalty: racial bias, inadequate representation, economic conditions, and certainly, factual innocence.

But I cannot imagine any moral reasoning supporting the conclusion that an injustice will be done when the death penalty finally is administered to Richard Baumhammers who killed five people during a racially motivated shooting spree in Allegheny and Beaver Counties in April 2000, with a sixth victim who died of his wounds nearly seven years later.

Baumhammers killed Anita Gordon, 63, his Jewish next-door neighbor, and set fire to her house. He subsequently opened fire in a Scott Township grocery store, killing Anil Thukar, 31, and leaving Sandeep Patel paralyzed from the neck down. Patel later died from these wounds in 2007. Baumhammers's evil killing spree continued with the shooting deaths of Ji-Ye Sun, 34, and Thao Pham, 27, at the Ya Fei Chinese Cuisine Restaurant in Robinson Township. The carnage ended with the shooting death of Gary Lee, 22, a customer at C.S. Kim

Karate in Center, Beaver County. But for the heroic efforts of law enforcement on this day, the bloodshed and carnage could have continued.

Baumhammers was convicted and sentenced to death on September 6, 2001. As compelled by *Morganelli* and in fulfillment of my obligations under the laws of our Commonwealth, I signed Baumhammers' second death warrant on October 6, 2014 setting the date of his execution for December 4, 2014. The United States District Court for the Eastern District of Pennsylvania stayed his execution on October 30, 2014. His case is pending.

Abraham Lincoln believed in the rule of law, believing that the government was obligated to take actions based on established law rather than personal whim and desires. As governor, I was very much aware of the public stirrings against capital punishment. I was well informed on the arguments of abolitionists, wrongful-convictions advocates, faith-based groups, and others. But political dissonance is not relevant to the functions of the capital-qualified jury, the judicial reasoning that led to conviction and sentencing, or the governor's role in carrying out the sentence imposed.

Finally, while I continue to believe the death penalty supports the construct of a just society, the subject matter is deserving of serious political discussion.

My own sense springs from the transcendent message found in the Pew Report. Public confidence in the rule of law is contingent upon public confidence in our criminal justice institutions. Perhaps the Pew Report suggests some level of creeping compromise. A boundary crossed?

The Pew Report is an awakening. Depending upon our response, the new day can be met with peril or promise . . . or both.

Tom Corbett is a practicing attorney who served as governor of Pennsylvania from 2011 through 2015. He also served as U.S. attorney for the Western District of Pennsylvania (1989) and Pennsylvania attorney general (1995–1997 and 2004–2010). Previously, he was an assistant district attorney in Allegheny County, Pennsylvania.

Introduction

Capital punishment in the United States has had three distinct eras: the social, the legal, and the political. The death penalty was a social issue from the founding of the nation to *Furman v. Georgia* (1972), a relatively minor one within larger debates within America about crime and punishment and about racial justice. It was primarily a legal issue for almost three decades after *Gregg v. Georgia* (1976), as the Supreme Court set the limits on who could be executed and what procedures were required. In the last decade, legal development continues but is overshadowed by political trench warfare, as each execution, judicial appointment, and election revisit a now-familiar set of issues. This chapter is a guide to some of the people and organizations from each era.

American Bar Association

The American Bar Association (ABA) was founded in 1878 and has approximately 400,000 members, making it the world's largest association of legal professionals. In 1997, the ABA called for a moratorium on executions, claiming that there were serious flaws in five areas: the competence of counsel, the

---

Sister Helen Prejean, famous for the book *Dead Man Walking* about her work with death row inmates, speaks at Belmont University in Nashville, Tennessee, on September 23, 2015. (AP Photo/Mark Humphrey)

thoroughness of habeas corpus review, racial discrimination in the selection of capital cases, the imposition of the death penalty on the mentally retarded, and the imposition of the death penalty on those who committed murder before age 18. The last two concerns were made moot by *Atkins* and *Roper*, but the adequacy of counsel remains a concern. In 2001, with revisions in 2010, the ABA promulgated standards for adequate representation by counsel in capital cases that call for the following: there should be two lawyers at each stage of the proceeding, one particularly to concentrate on guilt phase, the other to focus on penalty; the budget for capital defense should allow the lawyers to retain experts appropriate to the case; and there should be automatic stays of execution during the appeals process. Additionally, the prosecution should be required to preserve all biological evidence indefinitely, and during post-conviction challenges and habeas corpus proceedings, the defendant should continue to be represented by counsel, and defense counsel should be allowed to conduct investigations and discovery using the prosecution's evidence.

Between 2006 and 2013, the ABA conducted studies of Alabama, Arizona, Florida, Georgia, Indiana, Kentucky, Missouri, Ohio, Pennsylvania, Tennessee, Texas, and Virginia, the 12 states that account for approximately two-thirds of executions since *Gregg*. The studies evaluated each state's performance in the pretrial process (law enforcement conduct of investigations and especially eyewitness identification) at trial (judicial independence and clarity of jury instructions, prosecutorial conduct, and competence of defense counsel) and in post-trial proceeding (court review of the death sentence, including review of challenges based on claims of mental retardation, mental illness, and racial discrimination, and executive branch procedures for clemency). Although the ABA did not give grades to the states evaluated, it called attention to some practices it considered outliers. Florida leads the nation in persons exonerated from death row (24), while in Kentucky, 52 of the first 78 death sentences were overturned on appeal or by gubernatorial clemency. In Alabama, where judges are elected and which allows judge overrides of jury recommendations, 90 percent of overrides are in the direction of imposing a death sentence. Pennsylvania is the only state in the country that funds its defender services at the county level, thus exposing capital defendants to widely varying levels of defense depending on the locality of the trial (ABA 2001).

The ABA's role as the largest and most prestigious association of lawyers means that it has an influential role in approving federal judges, particularly at the district court and Court of Appeals level, which are frequently the final forums for reviewing whether an execution will take place. Because the ABA has widely been regarded as taking a more liberal position on several issues including capital punishment, in 2001, President George W. Bush abandoned the practice of having the ABA evaluate candidates before nominations. President Obama returned to the use of ABA rankings in his judicial nominating decisions (Tobias 2010, 777).

American Law Institute

The American Law Institute (ALI) was founded in 1923 by a group of academics, lawyers, and judges including Chief Justice William Howard Taft, ABA president and future chief justice Charles Evans Hughes, and future justice Benjamin Cardozo. Between 1923 and 1944, the ALI developed a series of treatises known as the Restatements, analyzing and summarizing fields of civil law in the United States. The success of the project led to a second series in 1952, and a third series that began in 1987. The ALI's Restatements are the modern equivalents in their educational impact on American lawyers of Coke's *Institutes* and Blackstone's *Commentaries*. In 1962, the ALI officially adopted a Model Penal Code that officially took no position on capital punishment but in Section 210.6 recommended standards and procedures for jurisdictions that retained the death penalty. The code recommended that death be retained as a penalty only for murder, and only when there were defined aggravating circumstances that outweighed mitigating circumstances. Death was prohibited in cases of "residual doubt" where the jury found the murder proved beyond a reasonable doubt but not beyond "all doubt" about guilt. The code also exempted from execution persons under 18 at the time of the murder and persons whose physical or mental condition "calls for leniency." There were two sentencing options: a penalty phase before a jury, after which a judge could accept or override a jury's recommendation of death (but not life), or a penalty phase before a judge alone.

In 2009, the ALI voted to withdraw Section 210.6, thus officially endorsing the position that further legal study or attempt to reform the death penalty is futile (ALI 2009). The ALI report in support noted that capital punishment was a political and moral issue that presented several "intractable" legal problems: the conflict between the two goals mandated by the Supreme Court that the legislature clearly define in advance what aggravating factors made a subset of murders deserving of the death penalty and the requirement that in each case the jury make an individual determination of deservingness; the impossibility of addressing by legal rule the statistical disparity in the race of defendants executed; the cost of administering a system that still could not claim that defendants were receiving adequate representation; the likelihood that advances in DNA testing would conclusively show that some persons executed were in fact innocent; and the politicization of judicial elections caused by candidates' and incumbents' need to campaign on their personal views on the issue.

Antiterrorism and Effective Death Penalty Act of 1996

For hundreds of years, a writ of habeas corpus was a simple order for a warden to bring a prisoner to court. As we noted in Chapter 1, by the founding of this country, the writ had come to be seen as a fundamental protection against detention without trial. After the Civil War, Congress gave federal courts the power to issue writs of habeas corpus to state courts, and lawyers with no other argument began to claim that proceedings in court had been so lacking in due process that their clients were in effect being detained without a "real" trial. At first this did not succeed. In *Frank v. Mangum* (1915), the Supreme Court denied a writ to Leo Frank, attempting to overturn his capital murder conviction in Georgia for strangling Mary Phagan, a teenage girl employed in Frank's factory. Frank's attorneys argued that the threat of mob violence dominated the trial and deprived him of due process. The Supreme Court stated the orthodox doctrine: errors of law committed by a criminal court were to be reviewed on appeal, not in habeas corpus. After the governor of Georgia commuted Frank's sentence to life imprisonment, an organized group of vigilantes kidnapped Frank from prison and hanged him.

The Court reconsidered in *Moore v. Dempsey* (1923). The petitioners were five black men condemned to death for the murder of a white man during a riot in Arkansas that had resulted in the deaths of several hundred people. The petitioners alleged that a white mob was on its way to lynch them and stopped only when promised by the prosecution that if the mob would just wait, the defendants would get a fair trial and *then* be hanged. The outcome of the 45-minute trial was never in doubt: the defendants were represented in a joint trial by one attorney who called no witnesses and who did not challenge the exclusion of black jurors or the use of whippings and other coercion to obtain testimony for the prosecution. The jury deliberated for five minutes.

Beginning a tradition of special scrutiny to criminal prosecutions in the South, the Court sent the petition to the federal district court for a hearing, over a dissent that complained that this would "prevent prompt punishment." The delay allowed the public excitement over the riot to die down, and eventually negotiations led to the governor commuting the sentences and later releasing the petitioners.

By the 1940s, the Supreme Court suggested that it would examine not just the atmosphere surrounding trial but the evidence presented too and, by the 1960s, held in *Townsend v. Sain* (1963) that federal judges must hold evidentiary hearings even if the state courts had resolved the merits of a petitioner's claim, as long as the petitioner had not received a "full and fair" hearing.

As for defendants who had not attempted to bring their claims in state court at all, *Fay v. Noia* (1963) held that as long as a petitioner had not *deliberately* bypassed an issue in state court he could raise that issue in a federal habeas corpus petition. Since the Supreme Court was in case after case expanding the Fourth Amendment protections against searches, the Fifth Amendment protections against self-incrimination, and the Sixth Amendment guarantee of the right to counsel, there were new claims every year for defendants to raise in federal court.

Since habeas corpus had never been designed as a post-trial remedy, there was no limit on how many petitions an inmate could file and no limit on how long after conviction they could be filed, as long as some federal judge would hear them. This practically ended the death penalty long before *Furman v. Georgia* (1972).

After *Gregg v. Georgia* (1976), the late 1970s and 1980s saw the Court under Chief Justice Burger and Chief Justice Rehnquist limit or overrule many of the expansive habeas corpus decision of the Warren Court including *Fay v. Noia* and *Townsend v. Sain*, but death penalty decisions continued to spark petitions as death row inmates sought to apply new rulings to increasingly old convictions. By 1988, the average time from capital crime to execution had grown to eight years and the delay caused by repetitive petitions had drawn enough complaints that Chief Justice William Rehnquist appointed retired justice Lewis Powell to study reform of the process (Powell 1989). In 1989, the Powell Committee reported three major problems: repetitiveness, the lack of any counsel or good counsel for poor defendants once their direct appeals ended, and the strain of litigating with executions imminent. That same year, the Rehnquist Court decided *Teague v. Lane* (1989), holding that courts could no longer retroactively apply new decisions by the Supreme Court in habeas corpus matters unless the decision was one that abolished the power of the state to impose a penalty (like the juvenile death penalty in *Roper v. Simmons*) or announced a "fundamental" procedural rule like the right to counsel. The Court has not declared any procedural rule to be that fundamental since *Teague v. Lane*. As a result, by the 1990s, many defendants whose appeals had ended could now be executed even if they were convicted under statutes held unconstitutional during their stay on death row.

Congress addressed many of the problems studied by the Powell Committee in the Antiterrorism and Effective Death Penalty Act of 1996, generally known as AEDPA. Congress reformed habeas corpus law for all crimes by requiring petitions to be filed within a year after a conviction became final, by limiting petitioners to one petition, and by requiring federal courts to defer to state court legal rulings unless they were not only wrong but unreasonably wrong interpretations of Supreme Court cases.

Congress added a new chapter to the statute specifically to address the delay in capital punishment cases caused by federal judges ordering a stay of execution and then putting the petition on the back burner to prevent a sentence from ever being carried out. AEDPA's Section 2266 now imposes a 450-day limit from the filing of the application for a writ by a capital defendant to the district court's decision, with a single 30-day extension; the Court of Appeals must enforce those time limits, and must decide the appeal of the decision within 120 days after the last brief is filed.

To ensure that the new limits on federal court delay would not rush courts into considering poorly presented issues or incomplete records, Congress specified that the time limits would apply only to cases arising in states certified to have established adequate assistance of counsel for defendants by providing funding for the appointment and compensation of competent counsel and for the payment of reasonable expenses in litigating death penalty cases.

The problem with this orderly statutory procedure is that from 1996 to 2006 when the certification decision was in the hands of the courts, no court ever certified a state to have adequate procedures for death penalty counsel, and California, Pennsylvania, Ohio, and Virginia were specifically found to be inadequate. After 2006, Congress moved the certification decision to the attorney general, and no attorney general has ever certified any state to be in compliance. Regulations to implement the statute were issued by the George W. Bush administration in 2008, withdrawn by the Obama administration in 2010, and not finally promulgated until 2013, 17 years after AEDPA. The regulations define *competent counsel* as one admitted to the bar for at least five years with at least three years of experience in state court collateral procedures or habeas corpus. More significantly, to be presumed competent, counsel must be compensated at approximately at the same level as the prosecutor and have access to reasonable funding for investigators, mitigation specialists, mental health experts, forensic scientists, and clerical support. The regulations were immediately challenged by California death row inmates, but the Court of Appeals for the Ninth Circuit dismissed the litigation in March 2016 because the attorney general has still not made any certification decisions.

Most states retaining the death penalty have moved to upgrade their standards for appointment and funding of counsel but few now see any prospect of trimming the time spent in federal habeas corpus proceedings.

Bedau, Hugo Adam (1926–2012)

A philosophy professor at Tufts until his death in 2012 (In Memoriam: Hugo A. Bedau 2016), Hugo Bedau was the most prominent academic opponent of the modern death penalty. Together with Michael Radelet and Constance Putnam, Bedau authored *In Spite of Innocence* (1992), a collection of case histories of wrongful convictions in capital prosecutions. Written for a popular audience, the book helped to draw public attention to exoneration projects that began in the early 1990s. Beginning in 1973, Bedau also wrote successive generations of the pamphlet "The Case against the Death Penalty" for the American Civil Liberties Union's Capital Punishment Project (Bedau 2012), summarizing arguments Bedau made in books and scholarly articles. Bedau's arguments against the death penalty after *Gregg* were, first, that capital punishment was a relic of the early days of penology like slavery, branding, and other outmoded forms of corporal punishment. Second, although murderers demonstrate disrespect for human life, a society should not deliberately kill human beings to show that killing is wrong. Third, the capital punishment system violates due process by being irrevocable and thereby depriving defendants of any opportunity to benefit from new evidence that could result in the setting aside of a death sentence. Fourth, the death penalty violates the Equal Protection Clause because it is imposed most frequently upon those whose victims are white, on minority defendants, and on the poor and uneducated. Fifth, changes since *Furman v. Georgia* have not eliminated the defects identified by the Supreme Court. Sixth, the death penalty fails as a deterrent, ranked even by police chiefs as the least effective crime control measure, behind curbing drug use, additional police officers, longer sentences, and gun control. Seventh, capital punishment is expensive and time-consuming for judges, prosecutors, defense counsel, and corrections personnel. Finally, every nation in Western Europe has abolished the death penalty, and the UN General Assembly has urged countries to abolish it. It is now inappropriate in civilized society.

Blackmun, Justice Harry A. (1908–1999)

Harry Blackmun, who served on the Supreme Court from 1970 to 1994, became one of the most controversial justices for his authorship of *Roe v. Wade* (1973), but almost as controversial was the transformation of his views on the death penalty. Justice Blackmun was bracketed by other justices from an early age, attending school in St. Paul Minnesota with Warren Burger. After earning a degree in mathematics from Harvard, Blackmun graduated from Harvard Law School in 1932, one year behind William Brennan. Justice Blackmun began his career as a law clerk to Judge Sanborn of the Court of Appeals for the Eighth Circuit and then practiced law, most prominently as counsel for the Mayo Clinic. Appointed to the Eighth Circuit by President Eisenhower in 1959, in his decade on the Court of Appeals Blackmun dealt with only a handful of capital punishment cases, most notably *Maxwell v. Bishop*, and became known as a conservative. In 1970, he was confirmed for the Supreme Court, 94–0, as a noncontroversial choice after two earlier nominees of President Nixon had been rejected by the Senate. At the time, he and Chief Justice Warren Burger, confirmed a year earlier, were referred to by some lawyers as the "Minnesota Twins" for what many believed would be Blackmun's similarity to Burger's conservatism.

Justice Blackmun's death penalty jurisprudence illustrates several modern themes. One is the influence of law clerks, who have been employed at the Court since the late 19th century. Justice Blackmun succeeded the Court of Appeals judge he clerked for, and Supreme Court Justice Byron White clerked for Chief Justice Fred Vinson, Chief Justice William Rehnquist clerked for Justice Robert Jackson, Justice John Paul Stevens clerked for Justice Wiley Rutledge, Justice Stephen Breyer clerked for Justice Art Goldberg, Chief Justice John Roberts clerked for Justice Rehnquist, and Justice Elena Kagan clerked for Justice Thurgood Marshall (Frequently Asked Questions 2016). Hundreds of lower court judges began their careers as law clerks, and service as a law clerk is a near universal credential of law professors.

There have been frequent complaints for decades that law clerks exert too much influence on judges. One notable example is Justice Blackmun's impassioned dissent in *Callins v.*

Collins (1994), which was a lightly edited draft prepared by his law clerks for use in a generic death penalty case (Greenhouse 2005, 177–178).

A related theme is the perceived tendency of justices to move in a more liberal direction once confirmed to the Supreme Court. At his confirmation hearing, Blackmun had replied to a senator's question about capital punishment with the statement that, although he personally was not convinced that capital punishment was a deterrent to crime, with the exception of absurd situations like imposing the death penalty on a pedestrian for crossing against a red light, it was a matter for legislative discretion (Stephenson 1994, 279–280).

Blackmun's early capital punishment decisions on the Court were consistent with this philosophy, although, even in dissent in *Furman v. Georgia*, Blackmun expressed his personal opinion that if he were a legislator he would vote against the death penalty. As procedural issues began to come to the Court after *Gregg v. Georgia*, Blackmun's votes on the Court began to reflect a distinction between cases involving procedural safeguards, where Blackmun usually voted to reverse a capital punishment decision, and the Eighth Amendment itself, which Blackmun did not believe prohibited death as a sentence for murder. In 1984, Blackmun wrote the majority opinion in *Spaziano v. Florida* and in 1985 the majority opinion in *Baldwin v. Alabama*, permitting death sentences to be imposed by a judge despite a contrary recommendation by a jury, but by the latter half of the 1980s had become a reliable vote for the defendant facing capital punishment. Most notably, in 1987, Blackmun dissented in *McCleskey v. Kemp*, adopting the position that he appeared to reject in *Maxwell v. Bishop* that statistics could show that the death penalty was being applied in a racially discriminatory fashion. That same year, he reversed his earlier support for mandatory sentences, writing the majority opinion in *Sumner v. Shuman* that rejected Nevada's mandatory death sentence for murder by a prisoner serving a life without parole. In 1988, Blackmun wrote *Mills v. Maryland* for the Court, holding that it was unconstitutional to require jurors to find mitigating factors by a unanimous vote.

By the 1990s, after Justice Brennan retired in 1990 and Justice Marshall retired in 1991, Justice Blackmun became the justice voting most often against imposition of the death penalty. In the related area of habeas corpus review, Justice Blackmun, often in the minority as the Court grew more conservative, increasingly protested what he saw as the Court's abdication of its duty to ensure that federal courts provide thorough review of claims of error in capital cases. What Justice Blackmun described in one 1992 case as an "ever-growing skepticism" that the death penalty could be imposed fairly in light of what he called a "skewed value system" that was more concerned with efficiency than human life ripened in 1994 into his outright rejection of the death penalty in *Callins v. Collins*.

Justice Blackmun retired in 1994 and passed away five years later. He was succeeded by Justice Stephen Breyer.

Brennan, Justice William J. (1906–1997)

Justice William J. Brennan Jr. served on the Supreme Court from 1956 to 1990, was its dominating intellectual force for 30 years, and wrote pivotal opinions on voting rights, free speech, and due process. Even when he was not in the majority, Justice Brennan's energy and ability to achieve consensus influenced the Court's method of analyzing legal issues. Brennan grew up in an Irish Catholic family in Newark, New Jersey, and attended the University of Pennsylvania and then Harvard Law School, graduating in 1931. Justice Brennan was taught by professors who believed in an evolutionary interpretation of the Constitution, and on the Court, he became an ardent proponent of interpreting the Eighth Amendment by reference to evolving standards of decency. After practicing labor law in Newark and service in the army during World War II, Brennan was in 1949 appointed to successively higher New Jersey courts, eventually becoming a justice of the New Jersey

Supreme Court in 1952. In 1956, Brennan came to the attention of Herbert Brownell, President Eisenhower's attorney general, as Justice Sherman Minton was retiring and as Eisenhower was campaigning for reelection. The political advantages of appointing a Catholic Democrat from New Jersey led Eisenhower to put Brennan on the Court in a recess appointment before the election; Brennan appeared briefly before the Senate Judiciary Committee the following February and was confirmed without objection in March 1957 (Bigel 1994, 16–18).

Justice Brennan was widely regarded as the architect of the Warren Court's "due process revolution," which imposed the criminal law provisions of the Bill of Rights on state criminal procedures. The Warren Court never directly addressed capital punishment, although Justice Brennan joined Justice Goldberg's call in 1963 for the Court to strike down the death penalty. As noted in earlier chapters, the death penalty was practically ended by Justice Brennan's opinion in *Fay v. Noia* (1963), expanding the scope of habeas corpus, and by other opinions altering standards for admissibility of confessions, the suppression of evidence, and the right to counsel.

Justice William Brennan recognized that President Nixon's appointment of four justices would move the Supreme Court away from the expansive federal review of constitutional claims that he had championed in the 1950s and 1960s. He also recognized that he and Justice Marshall were the only two votes on the Court for the proposition that the death penalty was always and in every circumstance unconstitutional. As a result, Brennan wrote many dissents and few opinions for the Court on capital punishment. His influence was nonetheless great due to the views he expressed in speeches and influential articles (Brennan 1964, 1977), stressing that in a federal system the Constitution was a floor and not a ceiling and urging state judges to interpret their own constitutions to provide more liberal protections to criminal defendants.

Many state courts have accepted Brennan's invitation. Even before *Furman*, the California Supreme Court decided *People v.*

Anderson (1972), holding California's death penalty unconstitutional under the *state* constitution. In 2004, New York's highest court declared the state's 1995 death penalty law invalid in *People v. LaValle* (2004). In 2016, Delaware's Supreme Court decided *Rauf v. State* (2016), holding that the state constitution prohibited Delaware's sentencing system in which a jury recommended a penalty but the final decision was made by a judge; later in 2016, Florida's Supreme Court held that Florida's revised death penalty statute, passed after *Hurst v. Florida* (2016), was still in violation of Florida's constitution.

Justice Brennan saw many of his due process opinions restricted during the 1980s but continued to insist, as he did in a 1986 lecture at Harvard Law School, that "a majority of the Supreme Court will one day accept that when the state punishes with death, it denies the humanity and dignity of the victim and transgresses the prohibition against cruel and unusual punishment" (Brennan 1986, 331). Justice Brennan resigned from the Court in 1990 after suffering a stroke, and passed away in 1997.

Breyer, Justice Stephen (1938–)

Stephen Breyer began his legal career after earning degrees from Stanford University, Oxford University, and Harvard Law School, with a 1964 clerkship for Justice Arthur Goldberg. Returning to Boston, Breyer taught at Harvard Law School and in the 1970s worked as counsel to the Senate Judiciary Committee during the periods of Democratic control of the Senate, and he was chief counsel in 1979–1980 during Senator Edward Kennedy's chairmanship of the committee. President Carter appointed Breyer to the Court of Appeals for the First Circuit in 1980. Breyer served on the First Circuit until 1994, when President Clinton made him his second appointment to the Supreme Court. Because there was not another new appointment on the Court for 11 years, until 2005 Justice Breyer was the junior justice on the Court for 11 years.

As such, he has not authored many death penalty decisions, but Justice Breyer is important for his part in the debate within the Supreme Court over the extent to which foreign countries' laws, particularly their abolition of the death penalty, should similarly be considered. Together with Justice Kennedy, Justice Breyer has consistently suggested that considering evolving standards of decency requires considering international law.

International law is already part of U.S. law, including human rights treaties, to which the United States is a party, that restrict or prohibit the death penalty. For instance, the International Covenant on Civil and Political Rights bans capital punishment for pregnant women and persons below 18 years of age. The United States ratified this treaty in 1992 with the express reservation that the death penalty would continue to be governed by American constitutional law, which at the time permitted the execution of 16-year-olds. This was overturned in *Roper v. Simmons* (2005), a decision that Justice Breyer joined.

Dissenting in *Glossip v. Gross* (2015), Justice Breyer revived the request made in 1963 by Justice Goldberg, asking the Court to call for briefing on the basic question whether all death penalty laws violate the Eighth Amendment. Quoting the statements of previous justices, Justice Breyer also stated that despite the constitutional principle that most important decisions be made by legislatures, legal challenges to the death penalty are "quintessentially judicial matters" and in deciding those matters "the Constitution contemplates that in the end our own judgment will be brought to bear on the question of the acceptability of the death penalty." In making that judgment, Justice Breyer stated that "primarily" U.S. federal and state practice should be relied on, but noted that 95 members of the United Nations have formally ended capital punishment and another 42 have abolished it in practice, that in 2013 only 22 countries carried out executions at all, and that the United States was one of only 8 countries to execute more than 10 individuals.

In an interview at Harvard Law School on January 25, 2016, Justice Breyer seemed to discard his statement that domestic law should be primarily relied on:

The Founders don't say what the words "cruel and unusual" mean. Does the word "unusual" mean "unusual" in the United States, or does it mean "unusual" in the world? They don't say. Some people think yes. Some people think no. I wrote about the death penalty with respect to the world. (Severson 2016, 260)

Justice Breyer has also succeeded Justice Stevens in urging capital sentences to be overturned due to what are called *Lackey* claims, after Clarence Lackey, eventually executed in 1997 for a 1977 murder. In *Lackey v. Texas* (1995), the Court denied review to the novel claim that because his lengthy stay on death row violated the Eighth Amendment, Lackey could not be executed. Justice Stevens wrote that extensive delays diminished any retributive benefit or deterrent effect society might receive from an execution, and he invited state and lower federal courts to study the issue. Four years later, in *Knight v. Florida* (1999), Justice Breyer dissented from the Court's refusal to hear the same claim by Thomas Knight, who was on death row for stabbing a prison guard to death in 1980 while already on death row for a double murder in 1974. Justice Breyer noted that more than a third of Florida's death row inmates attempted suicide and remarked that as a constitutional issue any retributive or deterrent effect that justified the death penalty was weakened by lengthy delays. Justice Breyer urged the full Court to consider the claim because at that time approximately 125 inmates had been on death row for more than 20 years. Justice Thomas replied that no court since *Lackey* had accepted the claim that executions could be challenged on the grounds of delay, and suggested that "the Court should consider the experiment concluded."

A decade later, the Court denied certiorari in *Thompson v. McNeil* (2009), after William Lee Thompson claimed that despite conviction for kidnapping, torture, and murder in 1976, his 32 years on death row should prevent his execution. Justices Stevens and Breyer dissented, observing that the average delay in executions had by this time grown to 13 years, and that since there had been more than 100 exonerations from death sentences, which had on average taken about a decade to achieve, the solution was not to speed up the process but to recognize that the inescapable delay was "unacceptably cruel." Justice Thomas again answered them, this time recounting the facts of the crime and asserting that it is the crime and not the punishment or the delay that was unacceptably cruel.

In the next term of Court, Justice Breyer resumed the debate in *Johnson v. Bredesen* (2009). This time the Court denied a last minute stay of execution and refused to address the technical question about how many times and by what means Cecil Johnson could claim that his 29 years on Tennessee's death row for three murders committed in a 1980 robbery were enough to prevent his execution. Johnson was executed in December 2009, within hours of the Supreme Court's ruling. Knight was eventually executed in January 2014 after further legal challenges, four decades after his first murders. Thompson remains on death row in 2017, awaiting word whether the Court's decision in *Florida v. Hurst* (2016) will apply retroactively and require a new sentencing hearing.

Given his judicial and public comments, it seems likely that Justice Breyer will soon become the first completely abolitionist justice since Justice Blackmun's retirement.

Federal Death Penalty Act (1994)

Because the United States is more diverse than any single state, it is not surprising that federal legislation is slower to respond to social trends than is state legislation. Although the Congress acted relatively quickly in passing a federal kidnapping act in 1932 shortly after the Lindbergh baby kidnapping and in passing anti-hijacking legislation in 1958 after the first wave of air piracy in the 1950s, compared to the swift response of death penalty states to *Furman v. Georgia* (1972), it took the federal government almost 20 years to reenact a comprehensive death penalty statute.

In 1988, the Anti-Drug Abuse Act had made it a capital offense to commit homicide in the course of operating a continuing enterprise that has five or more persons engaged in criminal activities: the act became more simply known as the Drug Kingpin Act. In 1994, in an attempt to repel Republican attacks that the Democratic Party was soft on crime, Senator Joseph Biden introduced sweeping criminal legislation ("the Biden Bill"), a portion of which was enacted as the Federal Death Penalty Act (FDPA; Tirschwell and Hertzberg 2009, 76–77). It was signed into law by President Clinton in September 1994 at the height of public support for the death penalty. The FDPA, driven by concern about violent crime that had grown dramatically in the 1970s and 1980s but which was already dropping through the 1990s, prescribes the death penalty for approximately 60 crimes.

Why so many capital offenses, given the Supreme Court cases that limit the death penalty to murder? As is sometimes overlooked, the Constitution only permits federal criminal enforcement in matters relating to powers given to the national government. Simple murder, for example, is not a federal crime, but assassination of a federal official or committing a murder in a federal park or government building is. The FDPA attempts to remain within constitutional boundaries by making it a capital crime "when death results" in the course of committing a crime already within federal jurisdiction. For instance, the Constitution commits foreign relations to the national government, and so the FDPA punishes murder of a foreign official or murder related to the smuggling of aliens. Federal law can also punish crimes that have some effect on interstate commerce or which uses some instrumentality of interstate commerce, like death resulting from hijacking an aircraft or carjacking. Finally, Congress has the power to pass legislation in support of the Fourteenth Amendment's guarantee of equal protection; that is the basis for hate crimes laws. Federal district judges have struck down the FDPA several times, but each time the Courts of Appeals have reversed them; the Supreme Court has never ruled on the law's constitutionality.

There are three capital crimes that do not require proof that death resulted: espionage; treason; and trafficking in drugs that results in more than $20 million per year or more than 60 kilograms of heroin, 300 kilograms of cocaine, or similar amounts of other drugs. The constitutionality of these last provisions has not been tested.

Federal criminal prosecutions are ordinarily approved and supervised by the 94 U.S. Attorneys that the president appoints as the chief federal law enforcement officers within each federal district. Beginning with Janet Reno in the Clinton administration, since the FDPA was enacted the Attorney General has centralized the decision whether to seek the death penalty in the Department of Justice in Washington, D.C. There is an obvious political reason for this: the fallout from the decision to charge or not to charge Oklahoma City bomber Timothy McVeigh, 9/11 conspirator Zacarias Moussaoui, Boston Marathon bomber Dzhokar Tsarnaev, or church gunman Dylann Roof would be national in scope, and an attorney general is generally unwilling to delegate that decision. Different administrations follow different policies. A sampling of the prosecutions for the 76 persons condemned under federal law since 1988 illustrates this: there are inmates on the federal death row at the federal corrections institution in Terra Haute, Indiana for murders of witnesses in federal cases and murders of police officers during drug crime, for murders by inmates of fellow inmates and prison guards, and for murders by escaped inmates. There are also persons prosecuted under the FDPA in states that do not have the death penalty because the Attorney

General believes that the crime was so horrific that the invest-
ment of federal resources to seek a harsher punishment than life
imprisonment was appropriate. Sometimes this is controversial
and sometimes it even backfires: in one well-known case, a jury
in Puerto Rico acquitted defendants in what effectively was
a political protest against the federal government seeking the
death penalty over the objections of local officials that the laws
of Puerto Rico do not permit the death penalty.

The other reason for centralizing the process is to ensure
uniform enforcement of federal law. The process for seeking
the death penalty is set forth in the *United States Attorneys'
Manual*. The first step is for the U.S. Attorney to submit the
case to the Capital Case Section, a committee in the Department of Justice that advises the attorney general. The confi-
dential application must be submitted before the indictment,
and must contain the local prosecutor's summary of the facts
of the case, the defendant's criminal history, what federal
interest is served by the prosecution, and what aggravating
and mitigating factors appear to exist. A victim impact statement, if one can be obtained, is required, but to the extent
possible the application must avoid disclosing the race of the
defendant or victims. Defense counsel has the opportunity to
argue against the death penalty even before the defendant is
charged, including by arguing that there is some geographic or
racial bias in the decision to seek the death penalty. An effective defense presentation, which can last from 45 to 90 minutes, can literally be a life saver (Little 1999, 425). The Capital
Review Committee makes a nonbinding recommendation,
and the U.S. Attorney's support or opposition for the death
penalty is given weight, but the final decision is the Attorney
General's alone.

Innocence Protection Act (2004)

On October 30, 2004, President George W. Bush signed into
law the Innocence Protection Act of 2004. Although the impe-
tus for the law was the many exonerations of death row inmates

that began with the exoneration of Kirk Bloodsworth in 1993, the Innocence Protection Act permits any defendant convicted of a federal crime to challenge his conviction, despite the running of any statute of limitations that may otherwise apply, if he can set forth a plausible claim that he is actually innocent. The defendant must have maintained his innocence: the act does not allow a defendant to invoke this law if he has pleaded guilty and waived his right to DNA testing. The claim of innocence cannot be inconsistent with the defense previously raised: that is, a defendant cannot claim to have killed in self-defense and then seek DNA testing to prove that someone else did the killing. A plausible theory of innocence does not allow the defendant to reopen the case to look for new evidence, but does give rise to a right to have evidence in the possession of the government tested by up-to-date scientific methods. If the evidence was previously subject to DNA testing, the act does not require retesting unless there has been some technological advance that makes a new method substantially more probative. If the results of testing are exculpatory, the defendant can move for retrial or resentencing.

The Innocence Protection Act affects state capital punishment cases as well, authorizing grants to states to defray the cost of DNA testing under state laws, and grants to improve the quality of both defense representation and prosecution in death penalty cases tried in state courts. The law also established the Kirk Bloodsworth Post-Conviction DNA Testing Grant Program, authorizing grants to help states pay for postconviction DNA testing for claims of actual innocence by defendants convicted in state courts. The law also updated a federal law that provided compensation to defendants exonerated of federal crimes: a person erroneously sentenced to death in federal court can now receive up to $100,000.

Kasi, Mir Aimal (1964–2002)

In other entries, we discuss the diplomatic complications in extradition of a fugitive wanted for murder in the United States from a country critical of capital punishment. Sometimes law enforcement officers simply bypass the extradition process.

Consider the case of Mir Aimal Kasi, a national of Pakistan living in Reston, Virginia, near the Langley, Virginia, headquarters of the CIA. Kasi worked as a driver for a local courier service and, on January 25, 1993, pulled in behind the line of cars waiting to drive onto CIA property. Kasi moved among the stopped automobiles firing an AK-47 on, killing two CIA employees and wounding three. Kasi fled the next day to Pakistan, and two days later was reported by his roommate as a missing person. Virginia indicted Kasi for capital murder. For the next four and a half years, FBI and CIA agents searched for Kasi in Pakistan and Afghanistan, locating him in Pakistan in June 1997. An FBI agent abducted Kasi from his hotel room and took him to a prison not operated by Pakistan, and then flew him by military aircraft to Virginia. After 15 pretrial hearings and a 10-day jury trial in November 1997, Kasi was convicted. He was sentenced to death in February 1998. After Virginia's highest court affirmed his sentence Kasi sought habeas corpus relief in federal court. The Court of Appeals for the Fourth Circuit ruled in August 2002 that it was a well-settled principle of United States law that a criminal, even if abducted in violation of an extradition treaty, does not thereby acquire a defense to the power of a court to try and sentence him. The Supreme Court denied Kasi's petition for a writ of certiorari and his motion for a stay of his execution on November 14, 2002, and Virginia executed him that same day (Nath 2003, 212).

Other judicial decisions have similarly rejected challenges from criminal defendants abducted from other countries, and in *United States v. Alvarez-Machain* (1992), the Supreme Court held that a Mexican abducted from Mexico City to stand trial in federal court for murder of a DEA agent could not use the violation of the United States–Mexico extradition treaty as a defense; the Supreme Court later held that the kidnapped defendant could not sue his abductors after his acquittal either.

Because Mexico's extradition treaty provides that Mexico, unlike Canada, will not extradite in a capital case without a guarantee that the death penalty will not be sought, it appears that, unless an American prosecutor is willing to violate international law and risk being prosecuted for kidnapping in Mexico, reaching Mexico will insulate a defendant from a death sentence. Mexico has become well-known as a destination for fugitives seeking to avoid the risk of capital punishment.

Kennedy, Justice Anthony (1936–)

The nation's death penalty jurisprudence is made by justices *not* selected for their stance on capital punishment, because, when they were nominated, issues such as desegregation, abortion, and more recently LGBTQ rights were more prominent. Beginning with Justice O'Connor, confirmation hearings had been televised, and both publicity and partisanship became permanent features of Senate scrutiny of nominees. In 1988, Justice Kennedy was President Ronald Reagan's third nominee to succeed Justice Powell after the Senate rejected Judge Robert Bork over Bork's opposition to abortion and after the forced withdrawal of the nomination of Judge Douglas Ginsburg. Justice Kennedy, who had authored more than 400 opinions in 13 years as a well-regarded conservative judge on the increasingly liberal Court of Appeals for the Ninth Circuit, was confirmed 97–0 after relatively mild questioning. Shortly afterward, one commentator described him as an "unknown, stealth appointee" and wrote "Justice Kennedy is a competent jurist and *may* become a leader on the Court" (Silverstein 1994, 164, 122–123). Three decades later, Justice Kennedy has been the most influential justice of both the Rehnquist Court and the Roberts Court.

As the shift from *McGautha* to *Furman* shows, new justices can produce abrupt changes in the Court's jurisprudence, so presidents now choose justices with an eye for ideology and for longevity: of the justices appointed since *Furman*, only Justice

Souter stepped down before serving two decades on the Court. Justice Kennedy is the longest serving justice on the current Court and since the retirement of Justice O'Connor, Justice Kennedy has been the fifth vote in more 5–4 decisions than any other justice. Either because the chief justice needs to secure his vote or because he is the senior associate justice and can control opinion assignments himself, Justice Kennedy is likely to write important death penalty decisions for years to come.

Justice Kennedy has tended to vote with the conservative wing of the Court on criminal cases, but is widely regarded as a liberal for his high-profile opinions in the juvenile life sentence cases and in the death penalty cases *Hall v. Florida* (2014), *Kennedy v. Louisiana* (2008), *Panetti v. Quarterman* (2007), and *Roper v. Simmons* (2005). All four limit the power of states to impose the death penalty on categories of defendants (mentally retarded, rapists who do not kill, incompetents, and juveniles) and do so in large part on the basis of Justice Kennedy's belief that the justices should consider "our own judgment" rather than exclusively examine what states are doing to see if there is a national consensus.

Justice Kennedy has taken a conservative approach in non–death penalty cases, concurring in *Harmelin v. Michigan* (1991) that the Eighth Amendment forbids only extreme sentences that are grossly disproportionate to the crime. In *Harrington v. Richter* (2011), Kennedy's opinion for the Court held that federal courts can overturn state court convictions only when an error is so clear that "no fair-minded jurist" could ignore it. Though not headline material, Kennedy's impact here is substantial: in the 60 most recent cases where Courts of Appeals overturned state court rulings, the Supreme Court has reversed the defendants' victory more than three-fourths of the time.

Justice Kennedy, born in 1936, was raised in Sacramento, California, where his father was a lawyer associated with Republican Party politics. Kennedy obtained an undergraduate degree from Stanford University in 1958, and spent his senior year at the London School of Economics. After obtaining his law degree from Harvard Law School in 1961, Kennedy returned to California and practiced law in San Francisco. He also enlisted in the California Army National Guard and became a private, first class. In 1963, Kennedy's father died and Kennedy took over his father's law practice in Sacramento. Familiar with many politicians in the state capital including future attorney general Ed Meese, in 1973, Kennedy helped then governor Ronald Reagan draft a proposed tax-cut amendment. On Reagan's recommendation, in 1975, President Ford appointed Kennedy to the Court of Appeals for the Ninth Circuit, and at the time he was the youngest Court of Appeals judge in the country (Jelliff 2012, 337–338). Kennedy has been on the faculty of the McGeorge School of Law since 1965, and as a Supreme Court justice has during the Court's summer recess regularly taught a summer session in Salzburg, Austria, where the focus is on international law (McGeorge School of Law, 2012).

NAACP Legal Defense and Educational Fund, Inc.

In 1998, Amherst College political scientist Austin Sarat estimated that there was a community of about 200 lawyers who constitute the death penalty bar in the United States (Sarat 1998, n.55). Many of them have been litigating death penalty cases for decades. One of the earliest organized efforts was the NAACP Legal Defense and Educational Fund, Inc. (LDF), originally founded in 1939 as an offshoot of the NAACP primarily to allow Thurgood Marshall to litigate the school desegregation cases culminating in *Brown v. Board of Education* (1954). By 1961, Marshall had become a judge of the Court of Appeals for the Second Circuit, and leadership of the expanded LDF passed to Jack Greenberg, who in addition to the desegregation cases had for a decade been handling appeals of black men sentenced to death. Under Greenberg, the LDF initially focused on challenges based on the racial disparity of death sentences imposed, especially for rape, and then expanded to an attack on the death penalty generally. Attorneys for the LDF began distributing "Last Aid Kits" containing federal habeas corpus petitions and motions for stay of execution (Labi 2007, 12) and filing class action suits raising the entire range of constitutional arguments against each execution (Muller 1985, 170). As a practical matter, this halted use of the death penalty in most states by 1967. The legal battle continued in states without stays: in 1967, Anthony Amsterdam, a former law clerk for Justice Frankfurter, then a young professor at the University of Pennsylvania Law School and LDF attorney, argued before the Eighth Circuit that an Arkansas warrant for the execution of William Maxwell for rape was unconstitutional. Then Court of Appeals judge Harry Blackmun wrote the opinion denying relief, rejecting a claim that the statistical imbalance of black men sentenced to death for rape of white women was so extreme as to make the death sentence a denial of equal protection of law. In 1970, however, Amsterdam, Greenberg, and Michael Meltsner persuaded the Supreme Court in *Maxwell v. Bishop* (1970) to overturn the sentence on the less controversial grounds that opponents of the death penalty had been unconstitutionally excluded from the jury. Before *Furman v. Georgia*, the LDF also appeared as amicus curiae in *Boykin v. Alabama* (1969), a capital case in which Edward Boykin, a young black man, had been sentenced to death by a jury after his guilty plea to five armed robberies. The LDF advanced an unsuccessful attack on the death penalty itself as well as the narrow ground that the Court relied on to overturn the death penalty, that there was no indication that Boykin knew of the consequences of his guilty plea. Over the next three decades, the LDF would appear before the Court to advance the claim invited by Justice Goldberg and accepted by Justices Brennan, Marshall, and eventually Blackmun that the death penalty inherently violated the Eighth Amendment. Amsterdam argued many of the cases discussed in this book, including *McGautha v. California* (1971), *Furman v. Georgia* (1972), *Woodson v. North Carolina* (1976), *Roberts v. Louisiana* (1976), *Lockett v. Ohio* (1978), *Enmund v. Florida* (1982),

Zant v. Stephens (1983), *Barefoot v. Estelle* (1983), *Lockhart v. McCree* (1986), *McCleskey v. Kemp* (1987), and *Mills v. Maryland* (1988). Amsterdam is a professor at New York University Law School. Greenberg, who passed away in October 2016, later served as a dean of Columbia University Law School. Meltsner, the author of *Cruel and Unusual: The Supreme Court and Capital Punishment* (1973), is a professor at Northeastern University Law School. The LDF's impact extends into the next generation: the standard work on federal habeas corpus and some of the most widely cited studies of errors in the death penalty process are by Columbia Law School professor James Liebman, who was junior counsel to Greenberg, Amsterdam, and Meltsner at the LDF (Gelman 2004, 210, 216).

O'Connor, Justice Sandra Day (1930–)

Sandra Day O'Connor would be of historic importance if her only claim was to be the first woman to serve as a Supreme Court justice, but her impact on the Court's jurisprudence has been far more profound than that. As one commentator expressed it, the "dominant mode of jurisprudence" is Justice O'Connor's jurisprudence (Sullivan 2006, 1252).

Sandra Day was born in Texas in 1930 and grew up on her parents' 155,000-acre ranch in Southeastern Arizona near the New Mexico border. She entered Stanford University at age 16 and entered Stanford Law School after her junior year. She was graduated with classmate and future colleague William Rehnquist and with John O'Connor, a fellow editor of the law review, whom she married in 1952. As is legendary in the legal community, despite being graduated third in her class, O'Connor was only offered employment as a legal secretary. She worked for free in the San Mateo County Attorney's Office until she was offered a paid position, and then from 1954 to 1957 worked for the U.S. Army in Frankfurt, Germany, while her husband was serving there in the army's Judge Advocate General Corps (Bales 2006, 1705–1707).

Returning to the United States, the O'Connor family settled in Phoenix, Arizona. O'Connor practiced law, raised three children, and worked in Republican political campaigns. She worked in the Arizona Attorney General Office from 1965 to 1969, when she was appointed to fill an unexpired term in the Arizona Senate. She campaigned for election in her own right and was reelected in 1970 and 1972, becoming in 1972 the Senate majority leader. In 1974, O'Connor was elected to the Maricopa County Superior Court. Arizona filled its appellate courts by gubernatorial appointment, and in 1979, Governor Bruce Babbitt appointed her to the Arizona Court of Appeal, in part because Babbitt, a Democrat, wanted to avoid having her run against him for governor (Hoffer et al. 2016, 403).

Fellow westerner Ronald Reagan was elected in 1980 after campaigning on the general Republican theme of appointing conservative judges and on the specific promise to appoint a woman to the Supreme Court if a vacancy arose. When Justice Potter Stewart retired in 1981, O'Connor was recommended by Senator Goldwater and Justice Rehnquist. President Reagan enthusiastically nominated her in July 1981 and she was confirmed 99–0 in time for the October 1981 term.

Justice O'Connor was and has been the only justice in the last half century who has won electoral office, and is one of the few with experience in state government. Having served in all three branches of Arizona government, she brought unique practical experience in how the electoral process works, how legislation is passed, and how state courts decide cases. Initially she was more conservative than the justice she replaced and most of the more senior justices on the Burger Court, but the Court shifted around O'Connor after successive conservative appointments by President Reagan. By the end of Reagan's term of office and with the retirement of Justice Powell and early conservatism of Justice Kennedy, Justice O'Connor had become the decisive vote in most of the Rehnquist Court's 5–4 decisions as the Court continued to define the limits of capital punishment and to limit or overturn more liberal procedural rulings of the Warren and Burger Courts.

As an example of this trend, early in her tenure, Justice O'Connor wrote a dissent in *Enmund v. Florida* (1982), which barred executions of defendants convicted of murder in the course of a felony but who did not kill or intend to kill. Five years later, she limited this in *Tison v. Arizona* (1987), approving capital punishment for those who do not kill but who are major participants in felony murder. Her characteristic approach was to examine state legislation to determine whether there was a national consensus as to a practice. Justice O'Connor followed this method in her concurrence in *Thompson v. Oklahoma* (1988) and in her opinion for the Court in *Penry v. Lynaugh* (1989). Many of her opinions, like *Wiggins v. Smith* (2003), addressed a key concern of Justice O'Connor that she expressed in many speeches and articles: how competent does defense counsel have to be to ensure a fair trial (Ashley 2002, 407–408). Others, such as *Teague v. Lane* (1989) and *Coleman v. Thompson* (1991), addressed how constitutional claims could be pursued in habeas corpus proceedings, and typically tended toward less federal oversight of state court decisions.

Justice O'Connor submitted her resignation in July 2005 to be effective upon the qualification of her successor, and retired in January 2006. In 2009, Justice O'Connor founded iCivics to promote civic education. Its website is https://quest.icivics.org.

Powell, Justice Lewis F. (1907–1998)

Justice Lewis F. Powell served on the Supreme Court during the years of its most fertile development of Eighth Amendment law, from 1972 to 1987, and was, in the 66 capital punishment opinions during his tenure on the Court, the justice most likely to provide the fifth vote in a 5–4 decision. Justice Powell was appointed to the Court by President Nixon after the retirement of Justice Hugo Black. President Nixon had campaigned on a slogan of appointing "strict constructionists" to the Court, in other words judges opposed to further expansion of the criminal procedure rulings of the Warren Court. Powell, known as a moderate to conservative corporate lawyer, was believed to fit this criterion. He was also a southerner, like Justice Black, and a Democrat, allowing Nixon to demonstrate bipartisanship to a Senate controlled by Democratic senators. Powell's confirmation hearings in 1971 were, as Scalia's would be in 1986, relatively smooth because of the more contentious confirmation processes for William Rehnquist at the same time. Powell disclaimed any overall judicial philosophy but stated six points he thought should guide the Court: respect by the Court for the other branches of the federal government, respect for states in a federal system, judicial restraint, respect for precedent, deciding on the particular facts of a case, and determination to uphold the Bill of Rights (Howard 1972, 450–451). Powell was asked only one question about capital punishment, and stated that he had not taken a position on the subject (Jeffries 1999, 598). He was confirmed with only one negative vote, and took his seat on the Court in time for *Furman v. Georgia* (1972).

Justice Powell grew up in Richmond, Virginia, and graduated from Washington and Lee College in 1929 and Washington and Lee Law School in 1931, and then obtained a master's degree in law from Harvard Law School. Returning to Richmond in 1932, he practiced law before the outbreak of World War II, becoming partner at a prestigious law firm where he would stay until 1971. After Pearl Harbor, the 34-year-old Powell volunteered for service and spent four years in the Army Air Corps, working for the intelligence service in North Africa and England on code-breaking. Powell achieved the rank of colonel and earned the Legion of Merit and a Bronze Star (Rehnquist 1999, 590). Turning down an offer to head the Securities Exchange Commission, Powell returned to his law practice in Richmond, participating in Democratic Party politics, serving as the chair of the Richmond School Board from 1952 to 1961 and, over opposition, insisting on beginning the desegregation of Richmond schools after *Brown v. Board of Education* (Kuhn and Butler 1991, 421–425).

Powell served in 1969 on the commission to adopt a new constitution for Virginia. From 1964 to 1965, Powell was the president of the ABA, and worked with Senator Birch Bayh on the ratification of the Twenty-Fifth Amendment; in 1966, he served as a member of President Johnson's Crime Commission; from 1969 to 1970, he was president of the American College of Trial Lawyers; and from 1969 to 1971, he was also president of the American Bar Foundation (Kuhn and Butler 1991, 413, 427).

Taking his seat on the Court at the age of 64, Powell was described as the consummate southern gentleman and a buffer between the conservative and liberal wings of the Court (Galloway 1988, 379–380). Justice Powell dissented from *Furman v. Georgia* (1972), as did all four Nixon appointees, and in 1976, he was a joint author of the plurality opinion in *Gregg v. Georgia* that became the framework for subsequent analysis of capital punishment. Other notable death penalty opinions by Powell include *Eddings v. Oklahoma* (1982), establishing the necessity of permitting mitigation evidence, and *McCleskey v. Kemp* (1987), rejecting the claim that statistics proved racial discrimination in particular capital punishment cases.

As a result of health problems, Justice Powell retired from the Court in 1987. He continued to serve on the Court of Appeals for the Fourth Circuit, and in 1988, Chief Justice Rehnquist appointed him to study the most difficult legal issue in capital punishment jurisprudence, the role of federal habeas corpus. The Powell Committee's analysis of the issues was substantially adopted in the enactment in 1996 of the Anti-terrorism and Effective Death Penalty Act.

Justice Powell passed away in 1998.

Prejean, Sister Helen (1939–)

In the 14th century, a religious order was formed in the Catholic Church to care for the spiritual needs of those to be executed. Brothers of the order accompanied the condemned to the block carrying a *tavoletta*, a religious painting of the crucifixion of Jesus, for the person to concentrate on before his beheading. This not only obscured the approaching executioner, but also affirmed the continuing humanity of the condemned and emphasized the hope from repentance (Johnson 1990, 165–166). In the modern era, that work is done by death row chaplains and spiritual counselors, among the most famous of whom is Helen Prejean, a Catholic Sister of the Congregation of St. Joseph. Sister Prejean is the author of *Dead Man Walking: An Eyewitness Account of the Death Penalty in the United States* (1993), a book about her work with death row inmates at Louisiana's Angola State Prison. It was made into a movie in 1995 that won a Best Actress Academy Award for Susan Sarandon, who portrayed Prejean. Sean Penn portrayed Matthew Poncelet, a role based on Elmo Patrick Sonnier, who was electrocuted at Angola in 1984 for the abduction and murder of two teenagers. Prejean is also the author of *The Death of Innocents: An Eyewitness Account of Wrongful Executions* (2005), recounting her involvement in attempting to halt Virginia's 1997 execution of Joseph O'Dell and Louisiana's 1999 execution of Dobie Gillis Williams (Prejean 2016).

Sister Prejean was born in Louisiana in 1939, graduated from St. Mary's Dominican College in New Orleans in 1962, and received a master's degree from St Paul's University in Ottowa in 1973. She began working in prison ministry in New Orleans in 1981. From 1985 to 1995, she was on the board of the National Coalition to Abolish the Death Penalty.

It is possible that Sister Prejean has indirectly changed the death penalty in the United States. The Catholic Church has traditionally taught that in cases of extreme gravity, public authorities had the "right and the duty" to punish malefactors with appropriate penalties, including even the death penalty. Sister Prejean recounts that in 1997 she sent an impassioned letter to Pope John Paul II calling for him to reject the death penalty, a topic the Pope had spoken and written about, most notably in a 1995 encyclical, *Evangelium Vitae* (Abercrombie 2005). The Church's catechism was revised in 1997 to restrict the permissibility of the death penalty to cases when it is the "only practicable way" to defend human life, and to add, in Section 2267, the Pope's words from *Evangelium Vitae* that such cases are "very rare if not practically non-existent" (Flannery 2007, 411). Although the attention American Catholics pay to papal pronouncements varies, it is worth noting that the states that have abandoned capital punishment by legislative action—New Jersey (2007), New Mexico (2009), Illinois (2011), Connecticut (2012), and Maryland (2013)—all have significant Catholic populations.

Meanwhile, Sister Prejean and Susan Sarandon are currently campaigning together for a halt to the execution of Richard Glossip, the petitioner in *Glossip v. Gross* (2015), on the grounds that he is innocent. As of 2017, Glossip's execution has been stayed.

Rehnquist, Chief Justice William H. (1924–2005)

William Hubbs Rehnquist presided over the Supreme Court as chief justice for 19 years from 1986 to 2005, longer than anyone since the 19th century, and he served as an associate justice for 14 years before that. As an associate justice and as chief justice during the Court's most turbulent period, Rehnquist attempted to reduce the intervention of federal courts in state court judicial decisions, particularly in capital punishment cases, and strove to curb the Warren Court's tendency to seek out controversial issues. In many respects, the death penalty jurisprudence of the Court after *Furman v. Georgia* can be viewed as a struggle between Justice Brennan and Chief Justice Rehnquist over the interpretation of the Constitution and the role of the Court.

Rehnquist was born in 1924 and grew up in Milwaukee, Wisconsin. He dropped out of college and enlisted in the Army Air Corp during World War II, serving as a weather observer in

North Africa. Discharged as a sergeant, Rehnquist attended Stanford on the G.I. Bill and worked as a busboy. Obtaining a bachelor's and master's from Stanford, and then another master's from Harvard, Rehnquist attended Stanford Law School, graduating first in the class of 1952. He clerked for Justice Robert Jackson, and then practiced law in Phoenix, Arizona, and became active in Republican politics (O'Connor 2005, 3–4). He served as an assistant attorney general in President Nixon's first term, in the Office of Legal Counsel, the section of the Department of Justice that evaluates potential judges, and was nominated by President Nixon to fill Justice Harlan's seat in 1971. He and Justice Powell joined the Court in January 1972 (Hoffer et al. 2016, 398).

When Chief Justice Warren Burger retired in 1986, President Reagan nominated him to become chief justice. Rehnquist's two confirmation hearings illustrate how the selection of justices has become increasingly partisan. Although the Senate, with a Democratic majority from 1955 to 1981, passed a resolution in 1960 calling for the end of recess appointments, as late as the end of the Eisenhower administration, Chief Justice Warren and Justices Brennan and Stewart were appointed to the Court before any Senate hearings, and justices were often confirmed by voice vote without extensive hearings. In 1968, President Nixon began the Republican tradition of campaigning against the Supreme Court's liberal decisions exemplified by Earl Warren. The Democratic majority in the Senate scrutinized President Nixon's picks relatively carefully, but despite controversy over conservative memos and public statements, including one in which Rehnquist had decried the influence of liberal law clerks on their justices, he was still confirmed by a 68–26 vote. He was known as the Lone Ranger for his frequent conservative dissents until the Court's personnel changed with succeeding Republican appointments. Nominated for the center seat during the end of Republican control of the Senate, after 14 years on the Court, Rehnquist was confirmed by a weaker 65–33 vote, with almost every Democratic senator outside the South in opposition (O'Brien 2005, 72–73).

Like William Brennan, William Rehnquist was well liked even by ideological opponents and was highly respected for his efficient management of the Supreme Court and his fair assignment of opinion writing (Ginsburg 2005, 6). As chief justice, Rehnquist presided over the impeachment trial of President Clinton, wrote the plurality opinion in the *Bush v. Gore* (2000) decision ending the election dispute of 2000, and was responsible for appointing Justice Breyer to head a committee to study judicial misconduct and retired Justice Powell to head a committee to study habeas corpus reform. Although petitions for certiorari almost doubled from the beginning to the end of his tenure as chief justice, the Court granted review in far fewer cases and issued fewer opinions per term than had the Warren Court or the Burger Court.

Because the Rehnquist Court's personnel did not change between 1994 and 2005, its voting patterns were usually predictable, with a conservative bloc of the Chief Justice and Justices Scalia and Thomas, a center bloc of Justices O'Connor and Kennedy who more often than not joined the conservatives in 5–4 cases, and a liberal bloc of four justices: Stevens, Souter, Ginsburg, and Breyer (Rosen 2005). This meant that the Chief Justice, rather than attempt to write the Court's opinion, could better use his opinion assignment power to secure the center votes, and although his tenure was notable for reversing most of the precedents allowing expansive federal review of state convictions, he authored few key capital punishment decisions. One exception is *Herrera v. Collins* (1993). Leonel Herrera had been convicted of murdering two police officers in 1981 and received the death sentence for one. Several years after his appeals ended and his execution was scheduled, Herrera filed a petition for a writ of habeas corpus, claiming that he had uncovered new evidence that he was innocent because his brother who died in 1984 had actually committed the murders. In 1992, Justices Blackmun, Stevens, O'Connor, and Souter voted to have the Court consider whether innocence unaccompanied by a claim that some constitutional error affected the trial was a basis for relief. But the four could not persuade a fifth justice to grant a stay. The Texas Court of Criminal Appeals granted Herrera a stay because *it* felt that it would be improper to have Herrera executed while his case was under certiorari review by the U.S. Supreme Court. One year later, the chief justice wrote in *Herrera v. Collins* that claims of actual innocence based on newly discovered evidence were not a basis for habeas corpus relief. The Court noted that Herrera's evidence was of doubtful quality but stressed that safeguards against legal error and not claims of innocence were the purpose of a writ of habeas corpus. Four months later, after a flurry of last minute appeals and requests for clemency, Herrera was executed. Some of the issues about when a claim of actual innocence can or should be heard were resolved by the Innocence Protection Act and similar state laws, but the controversy about the role of habeas corpus in hearing claims of innocence remains a real issue for the Roberts Court.

Chief Justice Rehnquist died in office in 2005, the first justice to die in office since his former employer, Justice Jackson, in 1954.

Roberts, Chief Justice John (1955–)

Chief Justice Roberts was appointed by President George W. Bush in 2005 to be the 17th chief justice, two years after President Bush appointed him to the Court of Appeals for the District of Columbia, often considered as the "farm team" for the Supreme Court. After graduating from Harvard University in 1976 and Harvard Law School in 1979, Roberts followed a traditional path to the Supreme Court by clerking for Chief Justice Rehnquist, then working in the Reagan and George H. W. Bush administrations before joining a Washington, D.C., law firm and representing clients in matters before the Supreme Court. Originally projected to replace Justice O'Connor, Roberts was renominated to be chief justice after Rehnquist's death.

Chief Justice Roberts illustrates several modern trends in selecting members of the Supreme Court: Presidents of both parties prepare dossiers on potential nominees well in advance of any vacancy, prefer judicial experience as a Court of Appeals judge, and seek nominees who will maintain a philosophy consistent with the president's but who do not have a lengthy paper trail that might lead to controversy during the confirmation process (Gonzales 2014, 652–654).

In his first decade on the Court, Roberts has been seen as continuing his predecessor's conservative stance not only in deciding cases but also in management style, and has appeared to attempt to reduce the splintering of Supreme Court opinions by deciding cases on narrow grounds, and by using his power as chief justice to assign opinions to justices who cast the deciding vote in close cases. Chief Justice Roberts has written little in death penalty cases, with the important exceptions of *Baze v. Rees* (2008), discussed in Chapter 2, and *Medellin v. Texas* (2008).

Jose Ernesto Medellin was a Mexican citizen living since childhood in Houston, Texas. In 1993, Medellin and members of his gang first raped and then murdered two teenaged girls. Medellin was arrested, tried, convicted, and sentenced to death. The United States is a party to the Vienna Convention on Consular Relations, which requires notice to foreign citizens that they have the right to contact their nation's consul for assistance if arrested. In several cases, the International Court of Justice (ICJ) has held that foreign nationals from Paraguay, Germany, and Mexico on death row in Virginia, Arizona, and Texas were not given the required notice by the United States, and in 2004, the ICJ decided in *Mexico v. United States (Avena)* that states must remedy this even when defendants had not raised the claim at trial or on appeal.

President George W. Bush issued a memorandum declaring that states must give effect to the *Avena* decision. Oklahoma agreed, but Texas would not. In *Medellin v. Texas* (2008), Chief Justice Roberts held that Texas was right: the decisions of the

ICJ were enforceable in the United States only when Congress provides that they are, and presidents do not have the power to override the decisions of state courts. On August 5, 2008, the Court denied a stay of Medellin's execution sought on the chance that Congress might implement the *Avena* decision; Medellin was executed the same day.

An example of Chief Justice Roberts's behind-the-scenes influence came in November 2016, when he voted to stay Alabama's execution of Tommy Arthur. Arthur alleged that in light of *Hurst v. Florida*, Alabama's similar capital sentencing procedure should be struck down.

Under Supreme Court rules it requires four justices to vote to grant a petition, but *five* votes to grant a stay of execution. Since *Barefoot v. Estelle* (1983), stays are virtually automatic while the lower courts considered an appeal, but once the matter is before the Supreme Court, a stay requires a significant possibility of reversal of the lower court's adverse decision. Without the chief justice's vote, Arthur might have been executed while waiting for a decision. That has happened before. Justice Powell consistently provided a courtesy fifth vote for a stay when four members of the Court wished to grant review to a claim. After Justice Powell's retirement in 1987, when four members of the Supreme Court voted to hear a petition by Alexzene Hamilton claiming that her son, James Edward Smith, was incompetent to waive his appeals, they could not secure a fifth vote. The Court's denial of a stay in *Hamilton v. Texas* (1990) was issued on June 26, 1990, and Smith was executed that day. Chief Justice Roberts has acted to prevent a repeat of that scenario, writing that he was voting to stay the execution because four justices wanted additional time to review Arthur's petition for certiorari. Chief Justice Roberts's action might signal a new approach to the death penalty on the Court, or perhaps a step toward greater civility between the justices regardless of how the Court might rule on the merits of a claim.

Scalia, Justice Antonin (1936–2016)

Almost exactly 30 years behind Brennan, Antonin Scalia was graduated from Harvard Law School in 1960, and although his often harsh criticisms of opinions that he disagreed with reduced his ability to build a coalition for his views, he succeeded Brennan as the dominating intellectual force on the Supreme Court for the 30 years from his appointment in 1986 until his death in 2016. Perhaps influenced by his father, a professor of languages, Justice Scalia was an opponent of the "evolving Constitution" and became the most prominent exponent of the "original meaning" school of constitutional interpretation. Like Justice Brennan, Justice Scalia's ideas influenced the Court even when the majority of the justices opposed the result they led to.

Scalia studied at Georgetown University and the University of Fribourg before attending law school, and after graduating practiced law in Cleveland for six years before becoming a professor at the University of Virginia Law School, leaving to work in the Nixon administration, including as head of the Office of Legal Counsel. Having returned to teaching at the University of Chicago Law School, Scalia was nominated to the Court of Appeals for the District of Columbia Circuit in 1982, and when in 1986 Justice Rehnquist was nominated to be chief justice, President Reagan nominated Scalia to fill his seat. Following the storm over Rehnquist's appointment, Justice Scalia's confirmation hearings produced a 76-word report, five minutes of debate, and a vote of 98–0 to confirm (O'Brien 2005, 73). He took office in September 1986, just before the beginning of the term.

In 2012, Justice Scalia summed up his belief about the original meaning of the Eighth Amendment:

> A Cruel and Unusual Punishments Clause ensuring merely that future generations do nothing *they* consider cruel—a clause that means, in effect, "to thine own self be true"—is of little use."

> . . .

So the Eighth Amendment's prohibition of cruel and unusual punishments prohibits neither the death penalty nor any manner of imposing that penalty that is less cruel than hanging, which was an accepted manner in 1791. It is not left to future judges to determine in the abstract, with no governing standards, whether electrocution or lethal injection is "cruel." Otherwise they might be equally free to find that burning at the stake is not cruel. (Scalia and Garner 2012, 407)

But even Justice Scalia's views evolved. Shortly after joining the Court, Justice Scalia wrote that he had lost any enthusiasm for the classic narrow case-by-case development of law and had come to embrace the position that it was more important for the Supreme Court, given the tiny proportion of cases it could review, to announce clear rules for the guidance of lower courts (Scalia 1989, 1177–1178).

Justice Scalia's rejection of ambiguous rules moved him to repeatedly criticize the contradiction between the goal stressed in *Furman* and *Godfrey* that eligibility for death be restricted in advance to the worst of offenders and jury discretion be channeled to produce consistency, and the goal announced in *Lockett* and *Eddings* of removing restrictions on mitigation evidence to produce individualized sentencing. In *Walton v. Arizona* (1990), Scalia wrote that the two doctrines were flatly irreconcilable and that since he could find no support in history for the claim that the Eighth Amendment required juries to engage in individualized sentencing he would never support such a claim.

Twelve years later, Justice Scalia concurred in *Ring v. Arizona* (2002), overturning *Walton* and abolishing capital sentencing by judges with the explanation that although the Eighth Amendment related only to the extent of the punishment, the Sixth Amendment was vital to the process by which it was imposed. He wrote:

[M]y observing over the past 12 years the accelerating propensity of both state and federal legislatures to adopt "sentencing factors" determined by judges that increase punishment beyond what is authorized by the jury's verdict . . . cause[s] me to believe that our people's traditional belief in the right of trial by jury is in perilous decline. That decline is bound to be confirmed, and indeed accelerated, by the repeated spectacle of a man's going to his death because *a judge* found that an aggravating factor existed. We cannot preserve our veneration for the protection of the jury in criminal cases if we render ourselves callous to the need for that protection by regularly imposing the death penalty without it.

In *Hurst v. Florida* (2016), one of his last cases, Justice Scalia joined the majority, holding Florida's capital sentencing by judges to be invalid.

Justice Scalia, though a conservative who loudly decried the policy choices in issues like abortion and gay marriage that he felt were no business of the judicial branch, never doubted that it was the Supreme Court's role to expound on what the Constitution meant. In *Kansas v. Carr* (2016), one of Scalia's last opinions, the Court reversed by an 8–1 vote the Kansas Supreme Court's interpretation of federal law. Reginald and Jonathan Carr were sentenced to death after a joint sentencing proceeding for their roles in a December 2000 crime spree that involved robbery, kidnapping, and rape, and ended in the torture and murder of four out of five victims. The fifth victim survived the gunshot wound to her head and testified at trial. The Supreme Court has held that sentencing requires individual consideration by a jury of each defendant's deservingness of the death penalty. The Kansas Supreme Court vacated the sentences, holding that "individualized" meant separate hearings, because each defendant's presentation of mitigating evidence about himself "put a thumb on death's scale" for the other brother. Justice Scalia wrote that the Eighth Amendment did not mean that the jury cannot consider the death penalty for two or more defendants at the same time. Justice Scalia went on to add that a joint sentencing for multiple defendants might even be preferable because having the same jury consider the defendants would at least promote consistency.

Replying to the lone dissent by Justice Sotomayor suggesting that the Court should not have taken the case, Justice Scalia admitted that it "generally would have been none of our business" if the Kansas Supreme Court had relied on the Kansas constitution, but "what a state court cannot do is experiment with our Federal Constitution and expect to elude this Court's review so long as victory goes to the criminal defendant."

Sellin, Thorsten (1896–1994)

Since Beccaria's time, it has been a perennial question whether the death penalty or life imprisonment is more effective in deterring crime. Although crime statistics remain fuzzy to this day because different states collect data more or less efficiently, define crimes differently, and impose different punishments for them, since about the 1930s academics have had data on the question whether the death penalty deters crime. A driving force behind the collection of reliable crime statistics and one of the most influential authorities on that data was Professor Thorsten Sellin, a founder of the modern discipline of criminology in the United States.

Johan Thorsten Sellin was born in Sweden in 1896, emigrated to Canada with his family, and attended Augustana College in Illinois, earning his bachelor's degree in 1915 at age 18. He earned his master's degree from the University of Pennsylvania in 1916, and after teaching in Minneapolis returned to Philadelphia and received a Ph.D. in sociology in 1922. Sellin was a professor at Penn from 1921 until taking emeritus status in 1967, serving as chair of the Sociology Department from 1945 to 1959, and as editor of the *Annals of the American Academy of Political and Social Sciences* from 1929 to 1968. In the 1930s, Sellin was a consultant to the Census Bureau in developing its database of crime statistics. In the 1940s, Sellin was invited to draft the Uniform Criminal Statistics Act and in

1950 became secretary general of the International Penal and Penitentiary Commission (Lejins 1987, 975–986). His major works include *Culture Conflict and Crime* (1938), a seminal work in the study of crime, *The Death Penalty* (1959), *Capital Punishment* (1967, ed.), and *The Penalty of Death* (1980). Before his death in 1994, Sellin was honored by governments and universities throughout the world.

In numerous books, articles, and studies, including work as a consultant to the Swedish Penal Code Commission and for the United Kingdom's Royal Commission on Capital Punishment when the United Kingdom was debating the end of the death penalty, Professor Sellin concluded that the death penalty was not a deterrent compared to life imprisonment. His methodology was relatively simple, comparing homicide rates in states with the death penalty (whether they in fact carried out the death penalty during the period studied) to those in neighboring states without the death penalty. He observed that there were no significant differences. He also examined the effectiveness of the death penalty by comparing homicides in Philadelphia before five executions between 1927 and 1932, and noted that the homicide rate was slightly higher after execution (Bailey 1974, 417). From this and similar studies, Sellin and other opponents of capital punishment drew the conclusion in the 1950s and 1960s that deterrence was a failed theory of punishment.

In 1975, Isaac Ehrlich, now an economics professor at the University of Buffalo, published one of the first prominent pro–death penalty articles based on deterrence. As a member of the law and economics movement begun at the University of Chicago Law School, Ehrlich analyzed the death penalty as a cost of crime, asking whether raising the price of crime would reduce its frequency. Ehrlich reported that each execution might deter as many as eight homicides, a statistic cited by Solicitor General Robert Bork in support for the validity of the death penalty in 1976, and a statistic mentioned by the Supreme Court in *Gregg* itself (Fagan 2006, 255–256).

In the last 40 years, academic study of deterrence has in essence divided behind Sellin or Ehrlich. Depending on the data set chosen and method of analysis, some academic studies claim that each execution deterred even more murders than Ehrlich suggested, especially if the execution was publicized or carried out by electrocution, while many more found no deterrent effect or found that the data were simply inconclusive (Donohue and Wolfers 2005, 841).

Those who base their support for or opposition to capital punishment on retribution would not change their minds even if there were a conclusive answer on its deterrent effect. And recently some research suggests that deterrence does not matter as much as either Sellin or Ehrlich thought (Tyler 2006, 269). Most people would not commit a crime, and certainly would not murder, whether the penalty is harsh or light. To a non-criminal, deterrence is irrelevant.

Of the small subset of the population that commits crimes, some no doubt look at crime the way economic models suggest, to decide whether it is profitable for them. In a rough way, they estimate the likelihood of getting caught and the severity of the punishment they would receive and decide what to do in a rational manner. *Some* criminals no doubt think like this. The death penalty is a deterrent for them, but so are other factors. The drastic drop in crime through the 1990s may have been caused in part by some criminals concluding that the death penalty raised the stakes, but it is likely that the drop was also helped by the higher probability of being caught as a result of DNA testing, larger police forces, and almost universal surveillance of public places. Police in major cities like New York City, Chicago, and Washington, D.C., now deploy several thousand cameras, and since a significant percentage of capital murders are committed during robberies, the criminal who is deterred by thinking about the risk of getting caught for robbery may never become a murderer, without ever thinking about the death penalty.

But another subset of criminals is not deterred because they do not think like economists. Consider the motivations of a young drug dealer who kills a rival for turf or a gang member who kills for status. They act quite differently from the rational burglar or bank robber who decides not to take a weapon to avoid the risk of a more serious penalty if caught. Still other criminals are simply irrational, and can neither realistically estimate their likelihood of getting caught nor fathom the nuances in their jurisdiction's sentencing statutes. The Supreme Court has focused on the fraction of murderers with low IQs but others commit murder under the influence of drugs, alcohol, or blinding rage. These criminals have a sense of right and wrong, but it does not work very well as a restraining influence. Finally, a very small sliver of criminals, of which terrorists are the most prominent example, are not deterred and may be attracted by the finality of the death penalty and even by its celebrity status.

Soering, Jens (1966–)

Protocol 6 to the European Convention on Human Rights, ratified by 46 European states, prohibits the death penalty entirely. The European Union's abolition of the death penalty within its member nations leads to diplomatic complications when a fugitive wanted for murder in the United States is captured abroad.

In 1985, Jens Soering was an 18-year-old German citizen studying at the University of Virginia. Angry at the opposition by the parents of his American girlfriend to their relationship, Soering stabbed the parents to death in April 1985. Suspicion initially focused on the daughter, Elizabeth Haysom, but when police sought Soering for questioning, Soering fled to the United Kingdom, followed by Elizabeth. They were arrested there on unrelated fraud charges. Virginia sought Soering's extradition but would not give the United Kingdom, which had abolished capital punishment in 1956, an assurance that it would not seek to carry out the death penalty. When the United Kingdom indicated that it would extradite Soering, Soering sued in the European Court of Human Rights (ECHR). In *Soering v. United Kingdom* (1989), the ECHR held that Soering's extradition would violate the treaty's ban on torture and inhuman treatment. The court held that although capital punishment did not itself violate international law, the prolonged stay in the harsh conditions of death row caused a phenomenon it described as "death row syndrome" that would inflict cruel and unusual punishment. To secure extradition, Virginia agreed to drop the capital charge. Soering was convicted in 1990 and sentenced to two terms of life imprisonment. Elizabeth Haysom pleaded guilty and received a sentence of 90 years imprisonment (*Soering v. Deeds* 1998).

Soering's was not the last extradition affected by the European disfavor of the death penalty, nor was the death penalty the last point of disagreement over extradition. In 2014, the ECHR concluded that Belgium had violated the rights of Nizar Trabelsi by extraditing him to the United States to stand trial on terrorism charges without a guarantee that he would not be subject to a sentence of life without parole (*Trabelsi v. Belgium* 2014). As of 2017, Trabelsi's motion to dismiss his federal indictment remains pending.

Stevens, Justice John Paul (1920–)

The Supreme Court, originally six justices, has had nine justices since shortly after the Civil War. That makes the middle justices the key in controversial 5–4 decisions. With the increased polarization of political parties, that moderate middle of justices has shrunk from Justices Stewart, Powell, and Stevens in the 1970s to Justice Kennedy today.

That is in part because the justices, appointed by the president and subject to confirmation by a majority of the Senate, are often picked for their position on past controversial issues without consideration of likely future issues. Justice Stevens, who served on the Court from his appointment by President Ford in 1975 until his retirement in 2010, is an example of how the nation's death penalty jurisprudence was created and is shaped by justices *not* selected for their stance on capital punishment.

John Paul Stevens, born in 1920, witnessed his father, a Chicago businessman, prosecuted in the wake of a Depression-era business failure and then cleared as innocent by the Illinois Supreme Court. After service as an intelligence officer in the navy during World War II, Stevens graduated from Northwestern University Law School in 1947 and clerked for Justice Wiley Rutledge. Opening his own firm in 1952, he became known as an antitrust lawyer who also did volunteer criminal defense work, and in 1969 was appointed to a commission investigating allegations of impropriety by justices of the Illinois Supreme Court. The following year President Nixon appointed Stevens to the Court of Appeals for the Seventh Circuit, where Stevens served for five years without confronting a death penalty case (Smith 2010, 209–210). The Senate confirmed Stevens, 98–0, in December 1975.

In Stevens's first full year on the Court (1976), he joined Justices Stewart and Powell to form a three-justice plurality, approving the constitutionality of the death penalty in *Gregg v. Georgia*, *Proffitt v. Florida*, and *Jurek v. Texas*. Given an assured two votes by Justices Brennan and Marshall against any death penalty, the same plurality was responsible for striking down mandatory death penalties in *Woodson v. North Carolina* and *Roberts v. Louisiana*, and was a consistent vote during the late 1970s and early 1980s to narrow the crimes eligible for the death penalty (*Coker v. Georgia* 1977) to ensure that mitigating evidence could be considered (*Lockett v. Ohio* 1978) and that the jury was clearly instructed on what properly constituted aggravating factors justifying capital punishment (*Godfrey v. Georgia* 1980).

After Justice Stewart retired and was replaced by the more conservative Justice O'Connor, Stevens increasingly authored dissents in cases upholding the death penalty, although he did write for the plurality in *Thompson v. Oklahoma* (1988), striking down capital punishment for 15-year-olds. His major contribution to the current state of the law came in *Apprendi v. New Jersey* (2000) a non–death penalty case that led to the abolition of judge-based sentencing in capital cases in *Ring v. Arizona* (2002) and *Hurst v. Florida* (2016). Stevens also wrote the majority opinion in *Atkins v. Virginia* (2002), banning the execution of mentally retarded defendants.

The chief justice assigns opinions, but only if he is in the majority; otherwise it is the next senior member of the Court. As the senior associate, Justice Stevens was perceived as using the assignment power to cobble together a majority in *Roper v. Simmons* (2005) and *Kennedy v. Louisiana* (2008) by assigning the opinions to Justice Kennedy (Smith 2010, 243–244).

Justice Stevens's most famous death penalty opinion will be his concurrence in *Baze v. Rees* (2008), agreeing with the majority that Kentucky's lethal injection protocol does not violate the Eighth Amendment but expressing his *personal* opposition to the death penalty. Stevens wrote that current decisions to retain the death penalty were "the product of habit and inattention rather than an acceptable deliberative process that weighs the costs and risks of administering that penalty against its identifiable benefits," and concluded that the death penalty represents "the pointless and needless extinction of life with only marginal contributions to any discernible social or public purpose." Nevertheless, Stevens acknowledged that the Court's precedents upheld the constitutionality of the death penalty and established the framework for evaluating methods of execution. As a judge reviewing these standards, he found Kentucky's procedures constitutionally acceptable (Melusky 2016). Stevens also joined the other eight members of the Court in upholding the Ohio death sentence of Frank Spisak in *Smith v. Spisak* (2010). Responding to Spisak's claim that his attorney was wrong to argue to the jury that Spisak was "twisted" and "never going to be any different," Stevens agreed that this was wrong but wrote that not even Clarence Darrow could have prevented the jury from imposing the death penalty.

After retiring in 2010, Justice Stevens has given many interviews and delivered many speeches reiterating his personal opinion about the death penalty and his concern that the current jurisprudence of the Court fails to safeguard defendants (Stevens 2011). In a lecture on January 20, 2015, at the University of Florida Law School, Stevens said:

> Within the last year, Jim Liebman, who's a professor at the Columbia Law School and was a former law clerk of mine, has written a book . . . called *The Wrong Carlos*. . . . He has demonstrated, I think, beyond a shadow of a doubt that there is a Texas case in which they executed the wrong defendant, and that the person they executed did not in fact commit the crime for which he was punished. And I think it's a sufficient argument against the death penalty . . . that society should not take the risk that that might happen again, because it's intolerable to think that our government, for really not very powerful reasons, runs the risk of executing innocent people. (Nashrulla 2015)

Tucker, Karla Faye (1959–1998)

The English essayist Samuel Johnson once quipped that nothing so concentrates a man's thoughts as the knowledge he is to be hanged in a fortnight. One of the medieval justifications for the death penalty was that this maxim was true of the soul as well: a just penalty willingly accepted had the value of expiating the offense and redeeming the offender. Although public executions later became unruly spectacles, as late in history as colonial America it was traditional for ministers to deliver sermons to the crowds gathered at execution where they could hear the condemned's last contrite words. Sometimes the public could even purchase a printed copy at the gallows. Persons sometimes do reform on death row, and their cases present some of the deepest quandaries about capital punishment. To abolitionists, every sincere conversion is another piece of evidence that the death penalty turns its back on rehabilitation, while to retentionists giving a second chance to the inmate who is on death row for ending a life that will never be recovered is doubly unjust. After all, the victim was not given a second chance to live.

Consider the case of Karla Faye Tucker. While high on heroin she murdered two people with a pickaxe during a burglary in 1983. Tucker admitted her guilt and testified at her trial in 1984 that being pickaxed herself would not atone for her crime. A Texas jury sentenced her to death. She became a born-again Christian while on death row. In light of her gender and conversion, there were calls to commute her sentence to life imprisonment. On January 22, 1998, less than two weeks before her scheduled execution, the now-married Karla Faye Tucker Brown wrote to Governor George W. Bush requesting a stay of execution.

In her letter, she said that she previously tried to blame her mother, drugs, society, and everybody but herself for her actions but now that "God reigns in [her] heart" she "take[s] responsibility for [her] own actions." After giving her "heart to Jesus," she continued, she found the serenity and patience to cope with the "pressure cooker" that was life in prison. She had not succumbed to anger and violence during her 14 years in prison, proof, she said, would "never . . . act out in violence again" and that she was "no longer a threat to our society." Instead, she said that she had become a "positive contributor," helping others" and reaching them instead of hurting them:

> If my execution is the only thing . . . that can fulfill the demand for restitution and justice then I accept that. . . . Fourteen 1/2 years ago I was part of the problem. Now I am part of the solution. I come to you . . . asking you to please consider allowing me to continue on and reach out and help others keep from doing what I did. I am helping

save lives now instead of taking lives and hurting others. (Tucker 1998)

Governor Bush denied her request. On February 3, 1998, Karla Faye Tucker was executed.

Van Den Haag, Ernest (1914–2002)

By far, the weight of academic opinion is against continued use of the death penalty. One of the few prominent academic voices for capital punishment, Professor van den Haag was a psychoanalyst, a distinguished scholar at the Heritage Foundation, a fellow of the American Sociological Association and of the National Endowment for the Humanities, and, until his death in 2002, a professor of jurisprudence at Fordham University. In addition to scholarly articles, van den Haag was the author of *Punishing Criminals: Concerning a Very Old and Painful Question* (1975) and (with John Conrad) *The Death Penalty: A Debate* (1983). In a 1986 article published in the *Harvard Law Review*, van den Haag summarized his reasons for supporting capital punishment (van den Haag 1986).

Responding to the argument that capital punishment is immoral because it is applied in a discriminatory fashion, van den Haag asserted that how punishment is distributed has no effect on its morality. Although more equal distribution would be more equal, it would not be more just because punishment is not imposed on races, sexes, or ethnic groups: it is imposed on individuals. If a person who deserves to be executed escapes the punishment, the guilt of the individual who is executed is in no way diminished. Van den Haag conceded that maldistribution offends our sense of equality, but asserted that equality is a different interest than justice. Individuals are punished, not races or economic classes.

As for individual punishment, van den Haag conceded that capital punishment risked the execution of innocent persons, but noted that nearly all human activities—he cited trucking and construction as examples—cost innocent lives. He argued that a minimal number of such miscarriages of justice are offset by the social benefits of capital punishment. He also noted that opponents of the death penalty would oppose it even if it were error free.

As for deterrence, van den Haag stressed that the death penalty was justified *as retribution* even if it were shown that it failed to deter. While abolition would be required if the death penalty increased the murder rate, van den Haag felt no serious evidence supported any such claim, and in the absence of a definitive answer to the question whether capital punishment was a more effective deterrent than imprisonment, he suggested that it was reasonable to believe the death penalty had some deterrent effect because it is more feared than imprisonment. He concluded that even if executions did not deter all murderers, they had the net effect of saving the lives of some potential victims.

The argument that legal executions endorse or legitimize killing rested on a false analogy, according to van den Haag: imprisonment did not legitimize kidnapping, and fines did not legitimize robbery. The difference between crime and punishment is that the first is unlawful and undeserved and the second is a deserved punishment for an unlawful act.

Finally, citing the philosopher Immanuel Kant, van den Haag claimed that rather than degrading human dignity, the death penalty actually *affirms* the criminal's humanity by recognizing that he is fully responsible for his actions.

Vickers, Robert Wayne ("Bonzai Bob") (1958–1999)

Some inmates, like Karla Faye Tucker whose case is described elsewhere, find redemption while in prison. Tony Amadeo is another who found repentance. Condemned to death at 18 for a murder in Georgia, Amadeo's sentence was unanimously overturned by the Supreme Court in 1988. Convicted but given a life sentence at his retrial, Amadeo took college courses, graduating summa cum laude from Mercer University in 1995 (Bright 1996, 186).

But not all inmates mend their ways and turn their lives around. Many inmates do not even slow down, much less repent in prison. According to the Bureau of Justice Statistics, during the years 1985 to 1997, when there were 400 executions, there were 980 murders committed by inmates in prison. A member of this long list of inmates who do not repent is Robert Wayne Vickers, known as Bonzai Bob for carving a misspelled "banzai" into the body of his cellmate after Vickers strangled him for failing to wake Vickers for lunch. Once on death row, Vickers killed yet another inmate with a home-made incendiary device made of hair tonic and toilet paper. Arizona executed Vickers on May 5, 1999 (Allen and Shavell 2005, 630).

References

ABA Protocols on the Administration of Capital Punishment. 2001. *Death without Justice: A Guide for Examining the Administration of the Death Penalty in the United States* (revised 2010). http://www.americanbar.org/content/dam /aba/migrated/2011_build/death_penalty_moratorium /protocols2001.authcheckdam.pdf.

Abercrombie, Sharon. 2005. "Sister Helen Prejean Continues Campaign to End Death Penalty." *The Catholic Voice* 43 (14). Online edition at http://www.catholicvoiceoakland .org/2005/05-08-08/inthisissue9.htm.

ALI, Report of the Council to the Membership of the American Law Institute on the Matter of the Death Penalty (April 15, 2009). https://www.ali.org/media/filer_public/3f /ae/3fae71f1–0b2b-4591-ae5c-5870ce5975c6/capital_ punishment_web.pdf.

Allen, Ronald J. and Amy Shavell. 2005. "Further Reflections on the Guillotine." *Journal of Criminal Law & Criminology* 95: 625–636.

Apprendi v. New Jersey, 530 U.S. 466 (2000).

Ashley, Victoria 2002. "Death Penalty Redux: Justice Sandra Day O'Connor's Role on the Rehnquist Court and the Future of the Death Penalty in America." *Baylor Law Review* 54: 407–425.

Atkins v. Virginia, 536 U.S. 304 (2002).

Bailey, William C. 1974. "Murder and the Death Penalty." *Journal of Criminal Law and Criminology* 65: 416–423.

Bales, Scott. 2006. "Justice Sandra Day O'Connor: No Insurmountable Hurdles." *Stanford Law Review* 58: 1705–1712.

Barefoot v. Estelle, 463 U.S. 880, 895 (1983).

Baze v. Rees, 553 U.S. 35 (2008).

Bedau, Hugo A., et al. 2012. "The Case against the Death Penalty." American Civil Liberties Union. //www.aclu.org/other/case-against-death-penalty.

Bigel, Alan I. 1994. "Justices William J. Brennan, Jr. and Thurgood Marshall on Capital Punishment: Its Constitutionality, Morality, Deterrent Effect, and Interpretation by the Court." *Notre Dame Journal of Legal Ethics & Public Policy* 8: 11–163.

Boykin v. Alabama, 395 U.S. 238 (1969).

Brennan, William J., Jr. 1964. "Some Aspects of Federalism." *New York University Law Review* 39: 945–961.

Brennan, William J., Jr. 1977. "State Constitutions and the Protection of Individual Rights." *Harvard Law Review* 90: 489–504.

Brennan, William J., Jr. 1986. "Constitutional Adjudication and the Death Penalty: A View from the Court." *Harvard Law Review* 100: 313–331.

Bright, Stephen. 1996. "The American Bar Association's Recognition of the Sacrifice of Fairness for Results: Will We Pay the Price for Justice?" *Georgetown Journal on Fighting Poverty* IV: 183–188.

Brown v. Board of Education, 347 U.S. 483 (1954).

Bush v. Gore, 531 U.S. 98 (2000).

Callins v. Collins, 510 U.S. 1141 (1994).

Coker v. Georgia, 433 U.S. 584 (1977).

Coleman v. Thompson, 501 U.S. 722 (1991).

Donohue, John J., and Justin Wolfers. 2005. "Uses and Abuses of Empirical Evidence in the Death Penalty Debate." *Stanford Law Review* 58: 791–845.

Eddings v. Oklahoma, 455 U.S. 104 (1982).

Enmund v. Florida, 458 U.S. 782 (1982).

Fagan, Jeffrey. 2006. "Death and Deterrence Redux: Science, Law and Causal Reasoning on Capital Punishment." *Ohio State Journal of Criminal Law* 4: 255–320.

Fay v. Noia, 372 U.S. 391 (1963).

Flannery, Kevin, S. J. 2007. "Capital Punishment and the Law." *Ave Maria Law Review* 5: 399–427.

Frank v. Mangum, 237 U.S. 309 (1915).

"Frequently Asked Questions." 2016. www.supremecourt .gov/faq_justices.aspx.

Furman v. Georgia, 408 U.S. 238 (1972).

Galloway, Russell W., Jr. 1988. "Justice Lewis F. Powell, Jr." *Santa Clara Law Review* 28: 379–387.

Gelman, Andrew, James Liebman, Valerie West, and Alexander Kist. 2004. "A Broken System: The Persistent Pattern of Reversals of Death Sentences in the United States." *Journal of Empirical Legal Studies* 1: 209–261.

Ginsburg, Ruth B. 2005. "William H. Rehnquist: In Memoriam." *Harvard Law Review* 119: 6–10.

Glossip v. Gross, 135 S.Ct. 27126 (2015).

Gonzales, Alberto R. 2014. "In Search of Justice: An Examination of the Appointments of John G. Roberts and Samuel A. Alito to the U.S. Supreme Court and Their

Impact on American Jurisprudence." *William & Mary Bill of Rights Journal* 22: 647–712.

Greenhouse, Linda. 2005. *Becoming Justice Blackmun*. New York: Henry Holt and Company.

Gregg v. Georgia, 428 U.S. 153 (1976).

Hall v. Florida, 134 S.Ct.1986 (2014).

Hamilton v. Texas, 497 U.S. 1016 (1990).

Harmelin v. Michigan, 501 U.S. 957 (1991).

Harrington v. Richter, 562 U.S. 86 (2011).

Herrera v. Collins, 506 U.S. 390 (1993).

Hoffer, Peter C., Williamjames H. Hoffer, and N. E. H. Hull. 2016. *The Federal Courts: An Essential History*. New York: Oxford University Press.

Howard, A. E. Dick. 1972. "Mr. Justice Powell and the Emerging Nixon Majority." *Michigan Law Review* 70: 445–468.

Hurst v. Florida, 136 S.Ct. 616 (2016).

In Memoriam: Hugo A. Bedau. 2016 http://as.tufts.edu /philosophy/newsevents/faculty/bedauMemoriam.

Innocence Protection Act, codified in part at 18 U.S.C. § 3600, Title IV of the Justice for All Act of 2004, PL 108-405, October 30, 2004, 118 Stat 2260.

Jeffries, John C., Jr. 1999. "In Memoriam: Lewis F. Powell, Jr." *Harvard Law Review* 112: 597–602.

Jelliff, Anne. 2012. "Catholic Values, Human Dignity, and the Moral Law in the United States Supreme Court: Justice Anthony Kennedy's Approach to the Constitution." *Albany Law Review* 76: 335–365.

Johnson v. Bredesen, 558 U.S. 1067 (2009).

Johnson, Robert. 1990. *Death Work: A Study of the Modern Execution Process*. Pacific Grove, CA: Brooks/Cole Publishing Co.

Kansas v. Carr, 136 S.Ct. 633 (2016).

Kennedy v. Louisiana, 554 U.S. 407 (2008).

Knight v. Florida, 528 U.S. 990 (1999).

Kuhn, Clifford M., and George E. Butler. 1991. "'An Opportunity to Be Heard': An Oral Interview with Lewis F. Powell, Jr." *Georgia Journal of Southern Legal History* 1: 413–443.

Labi, Nadya. 2007. "A Man against the Machine." *The Magazine of the New York University School of Law* XVII: 10.

Lackey v. Texas, 514 U.S. 1045 (1995).

Lejins, Peter P. 1987 "Thorsten Sellin: A Life Dedicated to Criminology." *Criminology* 25: 975–988.

Little, Rory K. 1999. "The Federal Death Penalty: History and Some Thoughts about the Department of Justice's Role." *Fordham Urban Law Journal* 26: 347–508.

Lockhart v. McCree, 476 U.S. 162 (1986).

Lockhart v. Ohio, 438 U.S. 586 (1978).

Maxwell v. Bishop, 398 U.S. 262 (1970).

McCleskey v. Kemp, 481 U.S. 279 (1987).

McGautha v. California, 402 U.S. 183 (1971).

McGeorge School of Law. December 13, 2012. "Justices Kagan and Kennedy to Teach in Salzburg Summer Program." http://www.mcgeorge.edu/News/Justices_Kagan_and_Kennedy_to_Teach_in_Salzburg_Summer_Program.htm.

Medellin v. Texas, 552 U.S. 491 (2008).

Meltsner, Michael. 1973 "Litigating against the Death Penalty: The Strategy behind Furman." *Yale Law Journal* 82: 1111–1139.

Melusky, Joseph A. 2016. "The Executioner's Needle: The Supreme Court Revisits Lethal Injections." Paper presented at the National Technology and Social Science Conference, Las Vegas, NV, March 20–22, 2016.

Mexico v. United States (Case Concerning Avena and Other Mexican Nationals), 2004 I.C.J. 12 (Judgment of March 31, 2004).

Mills v. Maryland, 486 U.S. 367 (1988).

Moore v. Dempsey, 261 U.S. 86 (1923).

Muller, Eric. 1985. "The Legal Defense Fund's Capital Punishment Campaign: The Distorting Influence of Death." *Yale Law & Policy Review* 4: 158–187.

Nashrulla, Tasneem. 2015. "Former Supreme Court Justice Confirms Texas Once Executed an Innocent Man." *Buzzfeed News,* January 26, 2015; video of John Paul Stevens's discussion, quote begins at 57:00). https://www.buzzfeed.com/tasneemnashrulla/former-suprem e-court-justice-confirms-texas-once-executed-an?utm_term=.ck3w8MY67D#.cdXMeJA1yj (January 1, 2017).

Nath, Priya. 2003. "*Kasi v Angelone,* 300 F.3d 487 (4th Cir. 2002)." *Capital Defense Journal* 15: 203–212.

O'Brien, David M. 2005. *Storm Center: The Supreme Court in American Politics.* New York: W.W. Norton.

O'Connor, Sandra D. 2005. "William H. Rehnquist: In Memoriam." *Harvard Law Review* 119: 3–6.

O'Connor, Sandra D. and H. Alan Day. 2002 *Lazy B: Growing Up on a Cattle Ranch in the American Southwest.* New York: Random House.

Panetti v. Quarterman, 551 U.S. 930 (2007).

Penry v. Lynaugh, 492 U.S. 302 (1989).

People v. Anderson, 6 Cal.3d 628, 493 P.2d 880 (1972).

People v. LaValle, 3 N.Y.3d 88, 817 N.E.2d 341 (2004).

Powell, Lewis. 1989. "Ad Hoc Committee on Federal *Habeas Corpus* in Capital Cases, Judicial Conference of the United States, Committee Report. Reprinted in *Criminal Law Reporter* 45: 3239.

Prejean, Helen. 2005. *The Death of Innocents: An Eyewitness Account of Wrongful Executions.* New York: Random House.

Prejean, Sister Helen. 1993. *Dead Man Walking: An Eyewitness Account of the Death Penalty in the United States.* New York: Vintage Books/Random House.

Prejean, Sister Helen. 2016. http://www.sisterhelen.org /biography/.

Radelet, Michael L., Constance E. Putnam, and Hugo A. Bedau. 1992. *In Spite of Innocence: Erroneous Convictions in Capital Cases.* Lebanon, N.H.: Northeastern University Press.

Rauf v. State, 145 A.3d 430 (Delaware 2016).

Rehnquist, William H. 1999. "In Memoriam: Lewis F. Powell, Jr." *Harvard Law Review* 112: 589–590.

Ring v. Arizona, 536 U.S. 584, 611–12 (2002).

Roberts v. Louisiana, 428 U.S. 725 (1976).

Roe v. Wade, 410 U.S. 113 (1973).

Roper v. Simmons, 543 U.S. 551 (2005).

Rosen, Jeffrey. 2005. "Rehnquist the Great?" *The Atlantic* (April).

Sarat, Austin. 1998. "Recapturing the Spirit of *Furman*: The American Bar Association and the New Abolitionist Politics." *Law and Contemporary Problems* 61: 5.

Scalia, Antonin. 1989. "The Rule of Law as a Law of Rules." *University of Chicago Law Review* 56 (4) (Fall): 1175–1188.

Scalia, Antonin and Bryan Garner. 2012. *Reading Law: The Interpretation of Legal Texts.* St. Paul: Thomson/West.

Sellin, Thorsten. 1938. *Culture Conflict and Crime.* New York: Social Science Research Council.

Sellin, Thorsten. 1959. *The Death Penalty: A Report for the Model Penal Code Project of the American Law Institute.* Philadelphia: ALI.

Sellin, Thorsten. 1967. *Capital Punishment.* New York: Harper & Row.

Sellin, Thorsten, 1980. *The Penalty of Death*. Thousand Oaks, CA: Sage Publications.

Severson, Daniel S. 2016. "The Court and the World: An Interview with Associate Justice Stephen G. Breyer." *Harvard Journal of International Law* 57: 253–260.

Silverstein, Mark. 1994. *Judicious Choices: The New Politics of Supreme Court Confirmations*. New York: W.W. Norton & Co.

Smith, Christopher E. 2010. "Justice John Paul Stevens and Capital Punishment." *Berkeley Journal of Criminal Law* 15: 205–260.

Smith v. Spisak, 558 U.S. 139 (2010).

Soering v. Deeds, 255 Va. 457 (1998).

Soering v. United Kingdom, 11 ECHR 439 (1989).

Stephenson, D. Grier. 1994. "Justice Blackmun's Eighth Amendment Pilgrimage." *Brigham Young University Journal of Public Law* 8: 271–320.

Stevens, John Paul. 2011. *Five Chiefs: A Supreme Court Memoir*. New York: Little, Brown, and Co.

Sullivan, Kathleen M. 2006. "A Tribute to Justice Sandra Day O'Connor." *Harvard Law Review* 119: 1251–1256.

Teague v. Lane, 489 U.S. 288 (1989).

Thompson v. McNeil, 556 U.S. 1114 (2009).

Thompson v. Oklahoma, 487 U.S. 815 (1988).

Tirschwell, Eric A. and Theodore Hertzberg. 2009. "Politics and Prosecutions: A Historical Perspective on Shifting Federal Standards for Pursuing the Death Penalty in Non-Death Penalty States." *University of Pennsylvania Journal of Constitutional Law* 12: 57–98.

Tison v. Arizona, 481 U.S. 137 (1987).

Tobias, Carl W. 2010. "Postpartisan Judicial Selection." *Boston College Law Review* 51: 769–795.

Townsend v. Sain, 372 U.S. 293 (1963).

Trabelsi v. Belgium, ECHR No. 140/10, September 4, 2014, at http://hudoc.echr.coe.int/eng?i=001-146372.

Tucker, Karla Faye. 1998. "A Letter Written to Gov. George Bush, Ms. Tucker Asking for a 30-Day Stay of Execution." http://web.archive.org/web/20050406114222/http:/www .geocities.com/RainForest/Canopy/2525/karla2bush.html (July 11, 2016).

Tyler, Tom R. 2006. *Why People Obey the Law*. Princeton: Princeton University Press.

United States v. Alvarez-Machain, 504 U.S. 655 (1992).

van den Haag, Ernest. 1975. *Punishing Criminals: Concerning a Very Old and Painful Question*. New York: Basic Books.

van den Haag, Ernest. 1986. "The Ultimate Punishment: A Defense." *Harvard Law Review* 99: 1662–1669.

van den Haag, Ernest and John Conrad. 1983. *The Death Penalty: A Debate*. New York: Plenum Press.

Walton v. Arizona, 497 U.S. 639 (1990).

Wiggins v. Smith, 539 U.S. 510 (2003).

Woodson v. North Carolina, 428 U.S. 280 (1976).

Zant v. Stephens, 462 U.S. 862 (1983).

Introduction

This chapter presents tables displaying relevant data about the death penalty. It also includes excerpts from some pertinent documents, statements, and cases dealing with capital punishment. We encourage you to read unedited opinions and documents that are available in print and online.

Data

Sources of statistical information include the Bureau of Justice Statistics (http://www.bjs.gov/index.cfm?ty=tp&tid=18) and Amnesty International, "US Death Penalty Facts" (http://www.amnestyusa.org/our-work/issues/death-penalty/us-death-penalty-facts?gclid=COCM__vA_80CFY1bhgodBMwHJQ). Data are collected on yearly sentences and executions; trends; and offenders' sex, race, education, marital status, age, and more.

From 1976 through October 19, 2016, 1,438 executions were performed in the United States. Table 5.1 displays the number performed each year. Executions have dropped since they peaked in 1998. The number of death sentences has also dropped from 295 in 1998 to 49 in 2015.

A condemned inmate is led out of his east block cell on death row at San Quentin State Prison in San Quentin, California, on August 16, 2016. (AP Photo/Eric Risberg)

Table 5.1 Number of U.S. Executions since *Gregg v. Georgia* (1976)

Year	Number	Year	Number
1976	0	1997	74
1977	1	1998	68
1978	0	1999	98
1979	2	2000	85
1980	0	2001	66
1981	1	2002	71
1982	2	2003	65
1983	5	2004	59
1984	21	2005	60
1985	18	2006	53
1986	18	2007	42
1987	25	2008	37
1988	11	2009	52
1989	16	2010	46
1990	23	2011	43
1991	14	2012	43
1992	31	2013	39
1993	38	2014	35
1994	31	2015	28
1995	56	2016	20
1996	45	2017	10

Source: "Facts about the Death Penalty." DPIC. Updated April 28, 2017. http://www.deathpenaltyinfo.org/documents/FactSheet.pdf (accessed May 6, 2017).

Race and the Death Penalty

The Baldus Study that was discussed in *McCleskey v. Kemp* (1987) addressed the impact of race on capital punishment. Tables 5.2, 5.3, 5.4, and 5.5 provide statistics concerning the race and the death penalty. More than 75 percent of victims in cases that resulted in execution were white. Nationwide, however, "only" 50 percent of all murder victims are white. When a white person is murdered, chances for an execution increase.

Table 5.2   Race of Executed Defendants

Race	Percentage	Raw Number
White	55.7	808
Black	34.4	501
Hispanic	8.3	120
Other	1.6	23
Total	100.0	1,452

Source: "Facts about the Death Penalty." DPIC. Updated April 27, 2017. http://www.deathpenaltyinfo.org/documents/FactSheet.pdf (accessed May 6, 2017).

Table 5.3   Race of Victims in Cases Resulting in Execution

Race	Percentage
White	76
Black	15
Hispanic	7
Other	2

Source: "Facts about the Death Penalty." DPIC. Updated April 28, 2017. http://www.deathpenaltyinfo.org/documents/FactSheet.pdf (accessed May 6, 2017).

Table 5.4   Race of Death Row Inmates

Race	Percentage
White	42
Black	42
Hispanic	13
Other	3

Source: "Facts about the Death Penalty." DPIC. Updated April 28, 2017. http://www.deathpenaltyinfo.org/documents/FactSheet.pdf (accessed May 6, 2017). See also NAACP Legal Defense Fund, "Death Row USA" (October 1, 2016), for information about the number of death row inmates in each state. California has the nation's largest death row with 745 inmates.

Table 5.5   Interracial Murders and Execution Rates

White defendant and black victim	20
Black defendant and white victim	287

Source: "Facts about the Death Penalty." DPIC. April 28, 2017. http://www.deathpenaltyinfo.org/documents/FactSheet.pdf (accessed May 6, 2017).

Executions by State and Region

Where are executions performed? Tables 5.6 and 5.7 present data on state and regional execution rates. Note that 761 out of 1,438 executions—more than half—were performed in three states: Texas (the national leader by far), Oklahoma, and Virginia.

Table 5.6   Number of Executions in States since 1976

State	Number of Executions
TX	542
OK & VA	112 each
FL	92
MO	88
GA	69
AL	58
OH	53
NC & SC	43 each
AZ	37
AR	31
LA	28
MS	21
IN	20
DE	16
CA	13
IL & NV	12 each
UT	7
TN	6
MD & WA	5 each
ID, KY, MT, NE, PA, SD, & US GOVT	3 each
OR	2
CO, CT, NM, & WY	1 each
Total	1,452

Source: "Facts about the Death Penalty." DPIC. Updated April 28, 2017. http://www.deathpenaltyinfo.org/documents/FactSheet.pdf (accessed May 6, 2018).

Table 5.7   Executions by Region since 1976

Region	Number of Executions
South	1,184
Midwest	179
West	85
Northeast	4
TX, OK, & VA	766

Source: "Facts about the Death Penalty." DPIC. Updated April 28, 2017. http://www.deathpenaltyinfo.org/documents/FactSheet.pdf (accessed May 6, 2017).

Table 5.8   Murder Rates per 100,000

Region	Murder Rate (2014, per 100,000)
South	6.7
Midwest	5.3
West	5.5
Northeast	4.2

Source: "Facts about the Death Penalty." DPIC. Updated April 28, 2017. http://www.deathpenaltyinfo.org/documents/FactSheet.pdf (accessed May 6, 2017).

Table 5.9   Methods Used for Executions since 1976

Method	Number of Executions
Lethal injection	1,277
Electrocution	158
Gas chamber	11
Hanging	3
Firing squad	3

Source: "Facts about the Death Penalty." DPIC. Updated April 28, 2017. http://www.deathpenaltyinfo.org/documents/FactSheet.pdf (accessed May 6, 2017).

When regional execution rates are compared to regional murder rates (see Table 5.8), the deterrent effects of capital punishment are called into question. The South, with the highest execution rate, has the highest murder rate. Conversely, the Northeast has the lowest execution and murder rates.

Table 5.10   Opinions on the Death Penalty

Are You in Favor of the Death Penalty for a Person Convicted of Murder?

	Favor (%)	Not in Favor (%)	No Opinion (%)
October 7–11, 2015	61	37	2
October 12–15, 2014	63	33	4
October 3–6, 2013	60	35	5
December 19–22, 2012	63	32	6
October 6–9, 2011	61	35	4
October 7–10, 2010	64	29	6
October 1–4, 2009	65	31	5
October 3–5, 2008	64	30	5
October 4–7, 2007	69	27	4
October 9–12, 2006	67	28	5
May 5–7, 2006	65	28	7
October 13–16, 2005	64	30	6
October 11–14, 2004	64	31	5
October 6–8, 2003	64	32	4
May 19–21, 2003	70	28	2
October 14–17, 2002	70	25	5
October 11–14, 2001	68	26	6
February 19–21, 2001	67	25	8
August 29-September 5, 2000	67	28	5
June 23–25, 2000	66	26	8
February 14–15, 2000	66	28	6
February 8–9, 1999	71	22	7
May 11–14, 1995	77	13	10
September 6–7, 1994	80	16	4
June 13–16, 1991	76	18	6
September 25-October 1, 1988	79	16	5
September 9–11, 1988	79	16	5
January 10–13, 1986	70	22	8
November 11–18, 1985	75	17	8
January 11–14, 1985	72	20	8

(continued)

Table 5.10 *(continued)*

Are You in Favor of the Death Penalty for a Person Convicted of Murder?

	Favor (%)	Not in Favor (%)	No Opinion (%)
January 30-February 2, 1981	66	25	9
March 3–6, 1978	62	27	11
April 9–12, 1976	66	26	8
November 10–11, 1972	57	32	11
March 3–5, 1972	50	41	9
October 29-November 2, 1971	49	40	11
January 23–28, 1969	51	40	9
June 2–7, 1967	54	38	8
May 19–24, 1966	42	47	11
January 7–12, 1965	45	43	12
March 2–7, 1960	53	36	11
August 29-September 4, 1957	47	34	18
March 29-April 3, 1956	53	34	13
November 1–5, 1953	68	25	7
December 1–6, 1937	60	33	7
December 2–7, 1936	59	38	3

Source: Gallup Poll. http://www.gallup.com/poll/1606/death-penalty.aspx (accessed October 28, 2016).

How are executions performed in capital-punishment states? Methods of execution were described at length in another chapter. Table 5.9 summarizes the number of post-1976 executions that have been performed using different methods.

How does the general public feel about capital punishment? Table 5.10 summarizes results from Gallup polls from 1936 through 2015.

Documents

Code of Hammurabi (ca. 1780 BCE)

Hammurabi served as Babylonia's king from 1792 through 1750 BCE. His "Code of Laws" was written on a seven-foot stone slab that was discovered in 1901. The slab is preserved in the Louvre Museum in Paris.

1. If any one ensnare another, putting a ban upon him, but he can not prove it, then he that ensnared him shall be put to death.

2. If any one bring an accusation against a man, and the accused go to the river and leap into the river, if he sink in the river his accuser shall take possession of his house. But if the river prove that the accused is not guilty, and he escape unhurt, then he who had brought the accusation shall be put to death, while he who leaped into the river shall take possession of the house that had belonged to his accuser.

3. If any one bring an accusation of any crime before the elders, and does not prove what he has charged, he shall, if it be a capital offense charged, be put to death. . . .

6. If any one steal the property of a temple or of the court, he shall be put to death, and also the one who receives the stolen thing from him shall be put to death.

7. If any one buy from the son or the slave of another man, without witnesses or a contract, silver or gold, a male or female slave, an ox or a sheep, an ass or anything, or if he take it in charge, he is considered a thief and shall be put to death.

8. If any one steal cattle or sheep, or an ass, or a pig or a goat, if it belong to a god or to the court, the thief shall pay thirtyfold therefor; if they belonged to a freed man of the king he shall pay tenfold; if the thief has nothing with which to pay he shall be put to death.

9. If any one lose an article, and find it in the possession of another: if the person in whose possession the thing is found say "A merchant sold it to me, I paid for it before witnesses," and if the owner of the thing say, "I will bring witnesses who know my property," then shall the purchaser bring the merchant who sold it to him, and the witnesses before whom he bought it, and the owner shall

bring witnesses who can identify his property. The judge shall examine their testimony—both of the witnesses before whom the price was paid, and of the witnesses who identify the lost article on oath. The merchant is then proved to be a thief and shall be put to death. The owner of the lost article receives his property, and he who bought it receives the money he paid from the estate of the merchant.

10. If the purchaser does not bring the merchant and the witnesses before whom he bought the article, but its owner bring witnesses who identify it, then the buyer is the thief and shall be put to death, and the owner receives the lost article.

11. If the owner do not bring witnesses to identify the lost article, he is an evil-doer, he has traduced, and shall be put to death. . . .

14. If any one steal the minor son of another, he shall be put to death.

15. If any one take a male or female slave of the court, or a male or female slave of a freed man, outside the city gates, he shall be put to death.

16. If any one receive into his house a runaway male or female slave of the court, or of a freedman, and does not bring it out at the public proclamation of the major domus, the master of the house shall be put to death. . . .

19. If he hold the slaves in his house, and they are caught there, he shall be put to death. . . .

21. If any one break a hole into a house (break in to steal), he shall be put to death before that hole and be buried.

22. If any one is committing a robbery and is caught, then he shall be put to death. . . .

25. If fire break out in a house, and some one who comes to put it out cast his eye upon the property of the owner

of the house, and take the property of the master of the house, he shall be thrown into that self-same fire.

26. If a chieftain or a man (common soldier), who has been ordered to go upon the king's highway for war does not go, but hires a mercenary, if he withholds the compensation, then shall this officer or man be put to death, and he who represented him shall take possession of his house. . . .

109. If conspirators meet in the house of a tavern-keeper, and these conspirators are not captured and delivered to the court, the tavern-keeper shall be put to death.

110. If a "sister of a god" open a tavern, or enter a tavern to drink, then shall this woman be burned to death. . . .

116. If the prisoner die in prison from blows or maltreatment, the master of the prisoner shall convict the merchant before the judge. If he was a free-born man, the son of the merchant shall be put to death; if it was a slave, he shall pay one-third of a mina of gold, and all that the master of the prisoner gave he shall forfeit. . . .

129. If a man's wife be surprised (in flagrante delicto) with another man, both shall be tied and thrown into the water, but the husband may pardon his wife and the king his slaves.

130. If a man violate the wife (betrothed or child-wife) of another man, who has never known a man, and still lives in her father's house, and sleep with her and be surprised, this man shall be put to death, but the wife is blameless. . . .

153. If the wife of one man on account of another man has their mates (her husband and the other man's wife) murdered, both of them shall be impaled.

154. If a man be guilty of incest with his daughter, he shall be driven from the place (exiled).

155. If a man betroth a girl to his son, and his son have intercourse with her, but he (the father) afterward defile her, and be surprised, then he shall be bound and cast into the water (drowned). . . .

157. If any one be guilty of incest with his mother after his father, both shall be burned. . . .

229. If a builder build a house for some one, and does not construct it properly, and the house which he built fall in and kill its owner, then that builder shall be put to death.

230. If it kill the son of the owner the son of that builder shall be put to death. . . .

282. If a slave say to his master: "You are not my master," if they convict him his master shall cut off his ear.

Source: L. W. King, translator, *The Code of Hammurabi* (1915). Available online at http://avalon.law.yale.edu/subject_menus/ hammenu.asp.

The Bible, Book of Exodus (ca. 1300 BCE)

As recorded in the Book of Exodus, Moses received this list of laws, known as the Ten Commandments. The Book of Exodus then follows the Ten Commandments with a set of specific legal rules. The rules are stern, with many resembling the "eye for an eye" legal philosophy of Hammurabi's Code.

Exodus 20

1. I am the Lord your God, who brought you out of Egypt, out of the land of slavery. You shall have no other gods before me.

2. You shall not make for yourself an image in the form of anything in heaven above or on the earth beneath or in the waters below. You shall not bow down to them or worship them.

3. You shall not misuse the name of the Lord your God.

4. Remember the Sabbath day by keeping it holy.

5. Honor your father and your mother, so that you may live long in the land the Lord your God is giving you.

6. You shall not murder.

7. You shall not commit adultery.

8. You shall not steal.

9. You shall not give false testimony against your neighbor.

10. You shall not covet your neighbor's house. You shall not covet your neighbor's wife, or his male or female servant, his ox or donkey, or anything that belongs to your neighbor.

Exodus 21

Anyone who strikes a person with a fatal blow is to be put to death. However, if it is not done intentionally, but God lets it happen, they are to flee to a place I will designate. But if anyone schemes and kills someone deliberately, that person is to be taken from my altar and put to death.

Anyone who attacks their father or mother is to be put to death.

Anyone who kidnaps someone is to be put to death, whether the victim has been sold or is still in the kidnapper's possession.

Anyone who curses their father or mother is to be put to death.

If people quarrel and one person hits another with a stone or with their fist and the victim does not die but is confined to bed, the one who struck the blow will not be held liable if the other can get up and walk around outside with a staff; however, the guilty party must pay the injured person for any loss of time and see that the victim is completely healed.

If people are fighting and hit a pregnant woman and she gives birth prematurely but there is no serious injury, the offender must be fined whatever the woman's husband demands and the court allows. But if there is serious injury, you are to take life for life, eye for eye, tooth for tooth, hand for hand, foot for foot, burn for burn, wound for wound, bruise for bruise.

Exodus 22

If a thief is caught breaking in at night and is struck a fatal blow, the defender is not guilty of bloodshed; but if it happens after sunrise, the defender is guilty of bloodshed.

Anyone who steals must certainly make restitution, but if they have nothing, they must be sold to pay for their theft.

Source: THE HOLY BIBLE, NEW INTERNATIONAL VERSION®, NIV® Copyright © 1973, 1978, 1984, 2011 by Biblica, Inc.® Used by permission. All rights reserved worldwide.

The Twelve Tables (ca. 450 BCE)

The Twelve Tables of the Roman Republic consolidated Roman legal traditions and practices into a codified set of laws that lasted as long as the Empire itself. Only excerpts remain today. They were destroyed when the Gauls occupied Rome in 390 BCE.

Table I

1. If anyone summons a man before the magistrate, he must go. If the man summoned does not go, let the one summoning him call the bystanders to witness and then take him by force. . . .

Table II

. . . .

2. He whose witness has failed to appear may summon him by loud calls before his house every third day.

Table III

1. One who has confessed a debt, or against whom judgment has been pronounced, shall have thirty days to pay it in. After that forcible seizure of his person is allowed. The creditor shall bring him before the magistrate. Unless he pays the amount of the judgment . . . the creditor so shall take him home and fasten him in stocks or fetters. . . .

Table IV

1. A dreadfully deformed child shall be quickly killed.
2. If a father sell his son three times, the son shall be free from his father.
3. As a man has provided in his will in regard to his money and the care of his property, so let it be binding. If he has no heir and dies intestate, let the nearest agnate have the inheritance. If there is no agnate, let the members of his gens have the inheritance.
4. If one is mad but has no guardian, the power over him and his money shall belong to his agnates and the members of his gens.
5. A child born after ten months since the father's death will not be admitted into a legal inheritance.

Table V

1. Females should remain in guardianship even when they have attained their majority.

Table VI

1. When one makes a bond and a conveyance of property, as he has made formal declaration so let it be binding. . . .

Table VII

1. Let them keep the road in order. If they have not paved it, a man may drive his team where he likes. . . .

9. Should a tree on a neighbor's farm be bend crooked by the wind and lean over your farm, you may take legal action for removal of that tree.

10. A man might gather up fruit that was falling down onto another man's farm.

Table VIII

. . . .

2. If one has maimed a limb and does not compromise with the injured person, let there be retaliation. If one has broken a bone of a freeman with his hand or with a cudgel, let him pay a penalty of three hundred coins. If he has broken the bone of a slave, let him have one hundred and fifty coins. If one is guilty of insult, the penalty shall be twenty-five coins. . . .

3. If one is slain while committing theft by night, he is rightly slain. . . .

10. Any person who destroys by burning any building or heap of corn deposited alongside a house shall be bound, scourged, and put to death by burning at the stake provided that he has committed the said misdeed with malice aforethought; but if he shall have committed it by accident, that is, by negligence, it is ordained that he repair the damage or, if he be too poor to be competent for such punishment, he shall receive a lighter punishment.

12. If the theft has been done by night, if the owner kills the thief, the thief shall be held to be lawfully killed.

13. It is unlawful for a thief to be killed by day . . . unless he defends himself with a weapon; even though he has come

with a weapon, unless he shall use the weapon and fight back, you shall not kill him. . . .

23. A person who had been found guilty of giving false witness shall be hurled down from the Tarpeian Rock. . . .

26. No person shall hold meetings by night in the city.

Table IX

. . . .

4. The penalty shall be capital for a judge or arbiter legally appointed who has been found guilty of receiving a bribe for giving a decision.

5. Treason: he who shall have roused up a public enemy or handed over a citizen to a public enemy must suffer capital punishment.

6. Putting to death of any man, whosoever he might be unconvicted is forbidden.

Table X

1. None is to bury or burn a corpse in the city. . . .

3. The women shall not tear their faces nor wail on account of the funeral. . . .

Table XI

1. Marriages should not take place between plebeians and patricians.

Table XII

. . . .

5. Whatever the people had last ordained should be held as binding by law.

Source: Oliver J. Thatcher, ed., *The Library of Original Sources* (Milwaukee: University Research Extension Co., 1901), Vol. III: *The Roman World*, pp. 9–11.

The Magna Carta (June 15, 1215)

On June 15, 1215, at Runnymede, England, King John of England signed a charter of liberties known as the Magna Carta.

TO ALL FREE MEN OF OUR KINGDOM we have also granted, for us and our heirs for ever, all the liberties written out below, to have and to keep for them and their heirs, of us and our heirs:

. . . . Ordinary lawsuits shall not follow the royal court around, but shall be held in a fixed place.

. . . . For a trivial offence, a free man shall be fined only in proportion to the degree of his offence, and for a serious offence correspondingly, but not so heavily as to deprive him of his livelihood. In the same way, a merchant shall be spared his merchandise, and a husbandman the implements of his husbandry, if they fall upon the mercy of a royal court. None of these fines shall be imposed except by the assessment on oath of reputable men of the neighbourhood.

Earls and barons shall be fined only by their equals, and in proportion to the gravity of their offence.

. . . . In future no official shall place a man on trial upon his own unsupported statement, without producing credible witnesses to the truth of it.

No free man shall be seized or imprisoned, or stripped of his rights or possessions, or outlawed or exiled, or deprived of his standing in any way, nor will we proceed with force against him, or send others to do so, except by the lawful judgment of his equals or by the law of the land.

To no one will we sell, to no one deny or delay right or justice. . . .

All fines that have been given to us unjustly and against the law of the land, and all fines that we have exacted unjustly, shall be entirely remitted or the matter decided by a majority judgment of the twenty-five barons referred to below in the clause for securing the peace together with Stephen, archbishop of Canterbury, if he can be present, and such others as he wishes to bring with him.

. . . . Given by our hand in the meadow that is called Runnymede, between Windsor and Staines, on the fifteenth day of June in the seventeenth year of our reign (i.e. 1215: the new regnal year began on 28 May).

Source: British Library, "English Translation of the Magna Carta," http://www.bl.uk/magna-carta/articles/magna-carta-english-translation (accessed July 11, 2016).

The English Bill of Rights (1689)

This document limited the king's power. It is a precursor to the American Bill of Rights. Capping the "Glorious Revolution," it provided protections against excessive bails and fines and cruel and unusual punishments.

An Act Declaring the Rights and Liberties of the Subject and Settling the Succession of the Crown. . . .

Whereas the late King James the Second. . . did endeavour to subvert and extirpate the Protestant religion and the laws and liberties of this kingdom; [b]y assuming and exercising a power of dispensing with and suspending of laws and the execution of laws without consent of Parliament; . . . [a]nd excessive bail hath been required of persons committed in criminal cases to elude the benefit of the laws made for the liberty of the subjects;

And excessive fines have been imposed; [a]nd illegal and cruel punishments inflicted; . . .

All which are utterly and directly contrary to the known laws and statutes and freedom of this realm;

. . . . [T]he . . . Lords Spiritual and Temporal and Commons. . . for the vindicating and asserting their ancient rights and liberties declare:

. . . . That it is the right of the subjects to petition the king, and all commitments and prosecutions for such petitioning are illegal;

That the raising or keeping a standing army within the kingdom in time of peace, unless it be with consent of Parliament, is against law;

That the subjects which are Protestants may have arms for their defence suitable to their conditions and as allowed by law;

That election of members of Parliament ought to be free;

That the freedom of speech and debates or proceedings in Parliament ought not to be impeached or questioned in any court or place out of Parliament;

That excessive bail ought not to be required, nor excessive fines imposed, nor cruel and unusual punishments inflicted.

Source: United Kingdom. Parliament. *An Act Declaring the Rights and Liberties of the Subject and Settling the Succession of the Crown.* 1 William & Mary, Session 2, cap. 2, 1689.

The American Declaration of Independence (1776)

The Continental Congress approved a Resolution of Independence on July 2, 1776. Thomas Jefferson was charged with drafting a formal Declaration of Independence justifying the American Revolution in the eyes of the world. The final draft was approved on July 4, 1776.

The unanimous Declaration of the thirteen United States of America, When in the course of human events, it becomes necessary for one people to dissolve the political bands which have connected them with another, and to assume among the powers of the earth, the separate and equal station to which the Laws of Nature and of Nature's God entitle them, a decent respect to the opinions of mankind requires that they should declare the causes which impel them to the separation.

We hold these truths to be self-evident, that all men are created equal, that they are endowed by their Creator with certain unalienable rights, that among these are life, liberty and the pursuit of happiness.

That to secure these rights, governments are instituted among men, deriving their just powers from the consent of the governed. That whenever any Form of Government becomes destructive of these ends, it is the right of the people to alter or to abolish it, and to institute new government, laying its foundation on such principles and organizing its powers in such form, as to them shall seem most likely to effect their safety and happiness.

Prudence, indeed, will dictate that Governments long established should not be changed for light and transient causes; and accordingly all experience hath shewn, that mankind are more disposed to suffer, while evils are sufferable, than to right themselves by abolishing the forms to which they are accustomed.

But when a long train of abuses and usurpations, pursuing invariably the same Object evinces a design to reduce them under absolute despotism, it is their right, it is their duty, to throw off such government, and to provide new guards for their future security.

Such has been the patient sufferance of these colonies; and such is now the necessity which constrains them to alter their former systems of government. The history of the present King of Great Britain [George III] is a history of repeated injuries and usurpations, all having in direct object the establishment of an absolute tyranny over these states. To prove this, let facts be submitted to a candid world.

He has refused his assent to Laws, the most wholesome and necessary for the public good.

He has forbidden his Governors to pass Laws of immediate and pressing importance, unless suspended in their operation till his assent should be obtained; and when so suspended, he has utterly neglected to attend to them.

He has refused to pass other Laws for the accommodation of large districts of people, unless those people would relinquish the right of representation in the legislature, a right inestimable to them and formidable to tyrants only.

He has called together legislative bodies at places unusual, uncomfortable, and distant from the depository of their Public Records, for the sole purpose of fatiguing them into compliance with his measures.

He has dissolved representative houses repeatedly, for opposing with manly firmness his invasions on the rights of the people.

He has refused for a long time, after such dissolutions, to cause others to be elected; whereby the legislative powers, incapable of annihilation, have returned to the people at large for their exercise; the state remaining in the mean time exposed to all the dangers of invasion from without, and convulsions within.

He has endeavoured to prevent the population of these states; for that purpose obstructing the laws for naturalization of foreigners; refusing to pass others to encourage their migrations hither, and raising the conditions of new appropriations of lands.

He has obstructed the administration of justice, by refusing his assent to laws for establishing judiciary powers.

He has made judges dependent on his will alone, for the tenure of their offices, and the amount and payment of their salaries.

He has erected a multitude of new offices, and sent hither swarms of officers to harass our people, and eat out their substance.

He has kept among us, in times of peace, standing armies without the consent of our legislatures.

He has affected to render the military independent of and superior to the civil power.

He has combined with others to subject us to a jurisdiction foreign to our constitution, and unacknowledged by our laws; giving his assent to their acts of pretended legislation:

For quartering large bodies of armed troops among us:

For protecting them, by a mock trial, from punishment for any murders which they should commit on the inhabitants of these states:

For cutting off our trade with all parts of the world:

For imposing taxes on us without our consent:

For depriving us in many cases, of the benefits of trial by jury:

For transporting us beyond seas to be tried for pretended offences:

For abolishing the free system of English laws in a neighbouring province, establishing therein an arbitrary government, and enlarging its boundaries so as to render it at once an example and fit instrument for introducing the same absolute rule into these colonies:

For taking away our charters, abolishing our most valuable laws, and altering fundamentally the forms of our governments:

For suspending our own legislatures, and declaring themselves invested with power to legislate for us in all cases whatsoever.

He has abdicated government here, by declaring us out of his protection and waging war against us.

He has plundered our seas, ravaged our coasts, burnt our towns, and destroyed the lives of our people.

He is at this time transporting large armies of foreign mercenaries to complete the works of death, desolation and tyranny, already begun with circumstances of cruelty & perfidy scarcely paralleled in the most barbarous ages, and totally unworthy the head of a civilized nation.

He has constrained our fellow citizens taken captive on the high seas to bear arms against their country, to become the executioners of their friends and brethren, or to fall themselves by their hands.

He has excited domestic insurrections amongst us, and has endeavoured to bring on the inhabitants of our frontiers, the merciless Indian savages, whose known rule of warfare, is an undistinguished destruction of all ages, sexes and conditions.

In every stage of these oppressions We have petitioned for redress in the most humble terms: Our repeated petitions have been answered only by repeated injury. A prince whose character is thus marked by every act which may define a tyrant, is unfit to be the ruler of a free people. . . .

We, therefore, the Representatives of the United States of America, in General Congress, assembled, appealing to the Supreme Judge of the world for the rectitude of our intentions, do, in the name, and by authority of the good people of these colonies, solemnly publish and declare, that these United Colonies are, and of right ought to be free and independent states; that they are absolved from all allegiance to the British Crown, and that all political connection between them and the State of Great Britain, is and ought to be totally dissolved; and that as free and independent States, they have full power to levy war, conclude peace, contract alliances, establish commerce, and to do all other acts and things which independent states may of right do. And for the support of this Declaration, with a firm reliance on the protection of Divine Providence, we mutually pledge to each other our lives, our fortunes and our sacred honor.

[Signed by 56 representatives of New Hampshire, Massachusetts, Rhode Island, Connecticut, New York, New Jersey, Pennsylvania, Delaware, Maryland, Virginia, North Carolina, South Carolina, and Georgia.]

Source: U.S. National Archives & Records Administration, http://www.archives.gov/exhibits/charters/declaration_tran script.html (accessed July 11, 2016).

Ordinance of the Northwest Territory (1787)

The Articles of Confederation Congress passed this ordinance to provide for the political organization of the Northwest territories. The act described the basic rights and liberties of settlers. Article II described the rights of persons accused of crimes. The act provided that states carved out of this region would be admitted to the Union on an equal footing with the original states.

An Ordinance for the government of the Territory of the United States northwest of the River Ohio. . . .

Section 8. For the prevention of crimes and injuries, the laws to be adopted or made shall have force in all parts of the district. . . .

Section 14. It is hereby ordained and declared by the authority aforesaid, That the following articles shall be considered as articles of compact between the original States and the people and States in the said territory and forever remain unalterable, unless by common consent, to wit:

Article 1. No person, demeaning himself in a peaceable and orderly manner, shall ever be molested on account of his mode of worship or religious sentiments, in the said territory.

Article 2. The inhabitants of the said territory shall always be entitled to the benefits of the writ of *habeas corpus*, and of the trial by jury; of a proportionate representation of the people in the legislature; and of judicial proceedings according to the course of the common law. All persons shall be bailable, unless for capital offenses, where the proof shall be evident or the presumption great. All fines shall be moderate; and no cruel or unusual punishments shall be inflicted. No man shall be deprived of his liberty or property, but by the judgment of his peers or the law of the land; and, should the public exigencies make it necessary, for the common preservation, to take any person's property, or to demand his particular services, full compensation shall be made for the same. And, in the just preservation of rights and property, it is understood and declared, that no law ought ever to be made, or have force in the said territory, that shall, in any manner whatever, interfere with or affect private contracts or engagements, *bona fide*, and without fraud, previously formed.

Article 3. Religion, morality, and knowledge, being necessary to good government and the happiness of mankind, schools and the means of education shall forever be encouraged. The utmost good faith shall always be observed towards the Indians; their lands and property shall never be taken from them without their consent; and, in their property, rights, and liberty, they shall never be invaded or disturbed, unless in just and lawful wars authorized by Congress; but laws founded in justice and humanity, shall from time to time be made for preventing wrongs being done to them, and for preserving peace and friendship with them.

Sources: Northwest Ordinance, July 13, 1787 (National Archives Microfilm Publication M332, roll 9); Miscellaneous Papers of the Continental Congress, 1774–1789; Records of the Continental and Confederation Congresses and the Constitutional Convention, 1774–1789, Record Group 360; National Archives.

Amendments to the U.S. Constitution

The Fifth, Eighth, and Fourteenth Amendments relate to crime and punishment at the federal and state levels.

Amendment V (1791). No person shall be held to answer for a capital or otherwise infamous crime, unless on a presentment or indictment of a grand jury, except in cases arising in the land or naval forces, or in the militia, when in actual service in time of war or public danger; nor shall any person be subject for the same offense to be twice put in jeopardy of life or limb; nor shall be compelled in any criminal case to be a witness against himself, nor be deprived of life, liberty, or property, without due process of law; nor shall private property be taken for public use, without just compensation.

Amendment VIII (1791). Excessive bail shall not be required, nor excessive fines imposed, nor cruel and unusual punishments inflicted.

Amendment XIV (1868). Section 1. All persons born or naturalized in the United States, and subject to the jurisdiction thereof, are citizens of the United States and of the state wherein they reside. No state shall make or enforce any law which shall abridge the privileges or immunities of citizens of the United States; nor shall any state deprive any person of life, liberty, or property, without due process of law; nor deny to any person within its jurisdiction the equal protection of the laws.

Source: Certified by Superintendent of Documents, U.S. Government Printing Office. https://www.gpo.gov/fdsys/pkg/CDOC-110hdoc50/pdf/CDOC-110hdoc50.pdf (accessed July 11, 2016).

Callins v. Collins (1994)

This Texas case involved an appeal by Bruce Edwin Callins, a murderer awaiting execution for his 1980 killing of a man during a robbery. The Court denied his petition for a writ of certiorari without a written opinion. Nevertheless, Justice Blackmun, who had voted to uphold the death penalty in Gregg *and on other occasions earlier in his career, issued a dissenting opinion expressing his personal frustration with the death penalty itself and with attempts to devise rules to make capital punishment fair and constitutionally workable. Here, just two months before announcing his retirement, Blackmun concluded in no uncertain terms that the "death penalty experiment has failed." He announced that he would "no longer tinker with the machinery of death." Like Justices Brennan and Marshall (and, based on his 1991 interview, Powell) before him, Blackmun joined the ranks of those who regarded the death penalty as categorically prohibited by the Constitution. Justice Scalia took issue with Blackmun in a strongly worded opinion of his own. Excerpts from Scalia's concurring opinion appear first, followed by excerpts from Blackmun's dissent.*

The petition for a *writ of certiorari* is denied.

JUSTICE SCALIA, concurring.

. . . . The Fifth Amendment provides that "[n]o person shall be held to answer for a capital . . . crime, unless on a presentment or indictment of a Grand Jury . . . nor be deprived of life. . . without due process of law." This clearly permits the death penalty to be imposed, and establishes beyond doubt that the death penalty is not one of the "cruel and unusual punishments" prohibited by the Eighth Amendment.

. . . [H]owever, over the years since 1972 this Court has attached to the imposition of the death penalty two quite incompatible sets of commands: the sentencer's discretion to impose death must be closely confined, but the sentencer's discretion *not* to impose death (to extend mercy) must be unlimited. These commands were invented without benefit of any textual or historical support; they are the product of just such "intellectual, moral, and personal" perceptions as Justice Blackmun expresses today, some of which . . . have been made part of what is called "the Court's Eighth Amendment jurisprudence." . . .

Convictions in opposition to the death penalty are often passionate and deeply held. That would be no excuse for reading them into a Constitution that does not contain them, even if they represented the convictions of a majority of Americans. Much less is there any excuse for using that course to thrust a minority's views upon the people. Justice Blackmun begins his statement by describing with poignancy the death of a convicted murderer by lethal injection. He chooses, as the case in which to make that statement, one of the less brutal of the murders that regularly come before us—the murder of a man ripped by a bullet . . . and left to bleed to death on the floor of a tavern. The death by injection which Justice Blackmun describes looks pretty desirable next to that. It looks even better next to some of the other cases currently before us which Justice Blackmun did not select as the vehicle for his announcement that the death penalty is always unconstitutional—for example, the case of the 11-year old girl raped by four men and then killed by stuffing her panties down her throat. . . . How enviable a quiet death by lethal injection compared with that! If the people conclude that such more brutal deaths may be deterred by capital punishment; indeed, if they merely conclude that justice requires such brutal deaths to be avenged by capital punishment; the creation of false, untextual and unhistorical contradictions within "the Court's Eighth Amendment jurisprudence" should not prevent them.

JUSTICE BLACKMUN, dissenting.

On February 23, 1994, at approximately 1:00 a.m., Bruce Edwin Callins will be executed by the State of Texas. Intravenous tubes attached to his arms will carry the instrument of death, a toxic fluid designed specifically for the purpose of killing human beings. The witnesses, standing a few feet away, will behold Callins, no longer a defendant, an appellant, or a petitioner, but a man, strapped to a gurney, and seconds away from extinction.

Within days, or perhaps hours, the memory of Callins will begin to fade. The wheels of justice will churn again, and somewhere, another jury or another judge will have the unenviable task of determining whether some human being is to live or die. We hope, of course, that the defendant whose life is at risk will be represented by competent counsel. . . . [W]e hope that the prosecution, in urging the penalty of death, will have exercised its discretion wisely, free from bias, prejudice, or political motive, and will be humbled, rather than emboldened, by the awesome authority conferred by the State.

But even if we can feel confident that these actors will fulfill their roles to the best of their human ability, our collective conscience will remain uneasy. Twenty years have passed since this

Court declared that the death penalty must be imposed fairly, and with reasonable consistency, or not at all, and, despite the effort of the States and courts to devise legal formulas and procedural rules to meet this daunting challenge, the death penalty remains fraught with arbitrariness, discrimination, caprice, and mistake. . . .

From this day forward, I no longer shall tinker with the machinery of death. For more than 20 years I have endeavored—indeed, I have struggled—along with a majority of this Court, to develop procedural and substantive rules that would lend more than the mere appearance of fairness to the death penalty endeavor. Rather than continue to coddle the Court's delusion that the desired level of fairness has been achieved and the need for regulation eviscerated, I feel morally and intellectually obligated simply to concede that the death penalty experiment has failed. It is virtually self evident to me now that no combination of procedural rules or substantive regulations ever can save the death penalty from its inherent constitutional deficiencies. . . . The problem is that the inevitability of factual, legal, and moral error gives us a system that we know must wrongly kill some defendants, a system that fails to deliver the fair, consistent, and reliable sentences of death required by the Constitution. . . .

Perhaps one day this Court will develop procedural rules or verbal formulas that actually will provide consistency, fairness, and reliability in a capital sentencing scheme. I am not optimistic that such a day will come. I am more optimistic, though, that this Court eventually will conclude that the effort to eliminate arbitrariness while preserving fairness "in the infliction of [death] is so plainly doomed to failure that it—and the death penalty—must be abandoned altogether." I may not live to see that day, but I have faith that eventually it will arrive.

Callins was executed by lethal injection.

Source: *Callins v. Collins* 510 U.S. 1141 (1994).

United Nations Resolution on the Use of the Death Penalty (December 20, 2012)

The UN General Assembly approved a series of resolutions calling upon member nations to abolish the death penalty completely and to establish an immediate moratorium on executions in the meantime. The 2007 Resolution (adopted December 18, 2007), the 2008 Resolution (adopted December 18, 2008), and the 2010 Resolution (adopted December 21, 2010) were reaffirmed by the 2012 Resolution.

Moratorium on the Use of the Death Penalty

The General Assembly, Guided by the purposes and principles contained in the Charter of the United Nations, Reaffirming the Universal Declaration of Human Rights, the International Covenant on Civil and Political Rights and the Convention on the Rights of the Child, Reaffirming its resolutions 62/149 of 18 December 2007, 63/168 of 18 December 2008 and 65/206 of 21 December 2010 on the question of a moratorium on the use of the death penalty, in which the General Assembly called upon States that still maintain the death penalty to establish a moratorium on executions with a view to abolishing it, Welcoming Human Rights Council decision 18/117 of 28 September 2011, Mindful that any miscarriage or failure of justice in the implementation of the death penalty is irreversible and irreparable, Convinced that a moratorium on the use of the death penalty contributes to respect for human dignity and to the enhancement and progressive development of human rights, and considering that there is no conclusive evidence of the deterrent value of the death penalty, Noting ongoing local and national debates and regional initiatives on the death penalty, as well as the readiness of an increasing number of Member States to make available to the public information on the use of the death penalty, Noting also the technical cooperation among Member States in relation to moratoriums on the death penalty,

1. Expresses its deep concern about the continued application of the death penalty;

2. Welcomes the report of the Secretary-General on the implementation of resolution 65/2065 and the recommendations contained therein;

3. Also welcomes the steps taken by some Member States to reduce the number of offences for which the death penalty may be imposed and the decisions made by an increasing number of States, at all levels of government, to apply a moratorium on executions, followed in many cases by the abolition of the death penalty;

4. Calls upon all States: (a) To respect international standards that provide safeguards guaranteeing protection of the rights of those facing the death penalty. . . . (b) To make available relevant information with regard to their use of the death penalty, . . . the number of persons sentenced to death, the number of persons on death row and the number of executions carried out, which can contribute to possible informed and transparent national and international debates, including on the obligations of States pertaining to the use of the death penalty; (c) To progressively restrict the use of the death penalty and not to impose capital punishment for offences committed by persons below 18 years of age and on pregnant women; (d) To reduce the number of offences for which the death penalty may be imposed; (e) To establish a moratorium on executions with a view to abolishing the death penalty;

5. Calls upon States which have abolished the death penalty not to reintroduce it, and encourages them to share their experience in this regard;

6. Calls upon States that have not yet done so to consider acceding to or ratifying the Second Optional Protocol to

the International Covenant on Civil and Political Rights, aiming at the abolition of the death penalty.

60th plenary meeting
20 December 2012

Source: United Nations A/RES/67/176 (accessed July 11, 2016). Available online at http://www.un.org/en/ga/search/view_doc .asp?symbol=A/RES/67/176. © 2012 United Nations. Reprinted with permission of the United Nations.

Introduction

This chapter provides a selection of useful sources for additional study. The first section of this chapter presents background sources that we found useful in working on this project and several previous ones. These materials provide a general overview of the evolution of capital punishment and issues surrounding its use. The second section presents electronic resources and links to a wide variety of materials, including bibliographies prepared by others. Links to databases that are updated regularly are also provided. In this way, the reader will have access to the latest developments, facts, and figures on the capital-punishment front. The third section provides lists of organizations and advocacy groups that deal with the death penalty. Contact information is provided.

General Information and Background

The following list includes resources of general interest. Regard this section as a general introduction to and overview of capital punishment and related issues.

Anti–death penalty demonstrators protest outside San Quentin State Prison in San Quentin, California, during the execution of Stanley "Tookie" Williams, the founder of the Crips gang, on December 13, 2005. (AP Photo/ Marcio Jose Sanchez)

"ABA Calls for Moratorium on Executions until Death Penalty Fairness Assured." June 15, 2002. http://www.pbs.org/wgbh/pages /frontline/angel/procon/aba.html.

> At its February 1997 meeting, the American Bar Association (ABA) House of Delegates passed, 280 to 119, a resolution calling for a halt to executions until courts can ensure that such cases are administered "fairly and impartially" and with minimal risk of executing innocent people. The resolution specified that the ABA takes no position on the death penalty itself.

Adler, Mortimer, ed. 1976. *The Annals of America, 1493–1754*, vol. 1. Chicago: Encyclopedia Britannica.

> First of a multivolume collection of documents from American history.

Allen, Francis A. 1981. *The Decline of the Rehabilitative Ideal*. New Haven, CT: Yale University Press.

> Asserts that rehabilitative punishment is failing as a result of loss of social cohesion in the United States.

American Law Institute. 1980. *Model Penal Code and Commentaries, Part II*. 3 vols. Philadelphia: American Law Institute.

> As the title suggests, this is a proposed model penal code. The commentary on the death penalty in vol. 1 at 110–171 is valuable.

Amnesty International. 2011. *USA: An Embarrassment of Hitches. Reflections on the Death Penalty 35 Years after Gregg v. Georgia, as States Scramble for Lethal Injection Drugs*. London: Peter Benenson House.

> Arizona encountered problems with its three-drug lethal injection protocols in the execution of Donald Beaty. Such problems threaten to undermine the legitimacy of capital punishment.

Aviram, Hadar, and Ryan Newby. 2013. "Death Row Economics: The Rise of Fiscally Prudent Anti-Death Penalty Activism." *Criminal Justice* 28 (1) (Spring): 33–40.

Recent developments reveal a policy trend favoring life without parole rather than the death penalty for the most heinous crimes. This article explains the recent successes of anti–death penalty legislative efforts as reflective of a focus on cost-effectiveness and savings.

Aycock, A. C. 2014. "The Death Penalty in the United States: A Complete Guide to Federal and State Laws." *Choice* 51 (7) (03): 1192–1193.

This book provides a description of state and federal laws on capital punishment, including information on death penalty offenses, aggravating and mitigating circumstances, who may attend an execution, and even laws about corpse disposal.

Bailyn, Bernard. 1992 (Enlarged edition). *The Ideological Origins of the American Revolution*. Cambridge, MA: Belknap Press of the Harvard University Press.

First published in 1967, this is the Pulitzer Prize–winning explanation of how the Framers thought, and why.

Banner, Stuart. 2002. *The Death Penalty: An American History*. Cambridge, MA: Harvard University Press.

Good new treatment of how the present death penalty stalemate evolved in American history.

Bardes, Barbara A., and Robert W. Oldendick. 2012. *Public Opinion: Measuring the American Mind*. Lanham, MD: Rowman & Littlefield.

A comprehensive introduction to polling and public opinion on the death penalty and other issues.

Beckman, Linda. 1998. "Chemical Castration." *West Virginia Law Review* 100: 853.

The article examines California's chemical treatment statute. Other states are exploring methods of treating and deterring sexual offenders.

Bedau, Hugo A., ed. 1964. *The Death Penalty in America*. Chicago: Aldine Publishing.
  The influential collection of essays by the prolific death penalty scholar and opponent.

Bedau, Hugo A. 1973. "The Case against the Death Penalty." American Civil Liberties Union Freedom Network (February 12, 2002). http://www.aclu.org/liberty/case_against_death.html.
  A pamphlet prepared for the American Civil Liberties Union's Capital Punishment Project, presenting major arguments against the death penalty.

Bedau, Hugo A., ed. 1982. *The Death Penalty in America*. New York: Oxford University Press.
  Updated third edition of the original.

Bennett, James V. 1970. *I Choose Prison*. New York: Alfred Knopf.
  Personal account of life as director of the federal prison system by one of the 20th century's most influential prison administrators.

Berger, Raoul. 1977. *Government by Judiciary: The Transformation of the Fourteenth Amendment*. Cambridge, MA: Harvard University Press.
  The history of the incorporation doctrine from its most eminent historical critic.

Berman, Douglas A. 2013. "*Graham* and *Miller* and the Eighth Amendment's Uncertain Future." *Criminal Justice* 27 (4) (Winter): 19–25.
  In the Supreme Court's juvenile sentencing rulings in *Graham v. Florida* (2010) and *Miller v. Alabama* (2012), the Court announced new limits on when states can sentence juveniles to prison terms of life without the possibility of parole. But the lines drawn raise new questions. Clarity remains elusive.

Berry, Kate. 2015. *How Judicial Elections Impact Criminal Cases.* New York: Brennan Center for Justice.
> Reelection campaigns make judges more likely to impose longer sentences, affirm death sentences, and even override sentences of life imprisonment to impose the death penalty.

Bessler, John. 1996. "The Midnight Assassination Law and Minnesota's Anti-Death Penalty Movement, 1849–1911." *William Mitchell Law Review* 22: 577.
> Good survey of the history of the death penalty in a single state.

Best, Harry. 1930. *Crime and the Criminal Law in the United States.* New York: Macmillan Company.
> Standard textbook from the era of rehabilitative punishment.

Blackstone, William. 1979. *Commentaries on the Laws of England.* 4 vols. Chicago: University of Chicago Press.
> Facsimile of the first edition of 1765–1769.

Bleich, Jeff, Kelly Klaus, and Deborah Pearlstine. 2001. "The Clinton Court." *Oregon State Bar Bulletin* 61 (July): 9.
> Former Supreme Court clerks discuss President Clinton's influence on federal law.

Bradford, M. E. 1993. *Original Intentions: On the Making and Ratification of the United States Constitution.* Athens, GA: University of Georgia Press.
> Essays on the "conservative" history of the Constitution, including the Fourteenth Amendment.

Branham, Lynn S. 2001. "The Prison Litigation Reform Act's Enigmatic Exhaustion Requirement." *Cornell Law Review* 86 (March): 483.

History and interpretation of attempt to control prison inmate lawsuits.

Brant, Irving. 1965. *The Bill of Rights: Its Origin and Meaning.* Indianapolis, IN: Bobbs-Merrill Company.
Concentrates on the First Amendment, but is an excellent general guide to English antecedents of Bill of Rights.

Bright, Stephen B. 1996. "The Electric Chair and the Chain Gang: Choices and Challenges for America's Future." *Notre Dame Law Review* 71 (July): 845.
Scathing critique of American death penalty and incarceration practices, by the director of Southern Center for Human Rights.

Bright, Stephen B. 1999. "Death in Texas." *The Champion* 23 (July): 16.
Discusses inadequacies in judicial oversight of death penalty cases in Texas.

Broom, Jack. 1994. "Judge Says Rupe Is Too Heavy to Hang." *Seattle Times* (September 20). http://community.seattletimes.nw source.com/archive/?date=19940920&slug=1931704.
A federal judge found that 410-pound death-row inmate Mitchell Rupe was too heavy to hang.

Burton-Rose, Daniel, Dan Pens, and Paul Wright, eds. 1998. *The Celling of America.* Monroe, ME: Common Courage Press.
Essays about the modern American prison system, many from prisoners.

Cardozo, Benjamin N. 1921. *The Nature of the Judicial Process.* New Haven, CT: Yale University Press.
Lectures on judging by one of the 20th century's most influential judges, later appointed to the Supreme Court.

Carrington, Frank. 1978. *Neither Cruel nor Unusual.* New Rochelle, NY: Arlington House.

Appeals for death penalty by emphasizing the fates of the victims of crimes.

Christian, Karen. 2001. "Note: And the DNA Shall Set You Free." *Ohio State Law Journal* 62: 1195.
Case histories of DNA testing with proposal that access to testing be created by statute.

Clark, Phyllis E., and Robert Lehrman. 1980. *Doing Time: A Look at Crime and Prisons*. New York: Hastings House.
Readable exposition of the rehabilitative theory of punishment from the end of the era.

Closen, Michael L., and Robert J. Dzielak. 1996. "The History and Influence of the Law Review Institution." *Akron Law Review* 30 (Fall): 15.
Good introduction to the evolution of legal scholarship presented in law reviews.

Cogan, Neil H., ed. 1997. *The Complete Bill of Rights*. New York: Oxford University Press.
One-volume source for the congressional debates, revisions, and ratification debates of the Bill of Rights.

Cohen, Bernard L. 1970. *Law without Order: Capital Punishment and the Liberals*. New Rochelle, NY: Arlington House.
A popular and somewhat heated defense of the retributive theory of punishment.

Colyer, Timothy P., and Robert M. Bohm. 2012. "You're Killing Me: A Review of State and Federal Death Penalty Statutes." *Criminal Law Bulletin* 48 (6) (November): 1276.
This study examines similarities and differences in U.S. capital punishment statutes by analyzing each jurisdiction's capital punishment scheme. Topics include death penalty eligibility, aggravating and mitigating circumstances, and related matters.

Cooley, Thomas M. 1927. *A Treatise on the Constitutional Limitations Which Rest upon the Legislative Power of the States of the American Union*. 2 vols. Boston: Little, Brown, and Company.

Eighth edition, by Walter Carrington, of Cooley's treatise.

Cooperman, Alan, Cary Funk, Elizabeth Sciupac, and Erin O'Connell. 2014. "Shrinking Majority of Americans Support Death Penalty." Pew Research Center (March 28).

In a 2013 Pew Research Center survey, 55 percent of Americans said they favor the death penalty for persons convicted of murder. While a majority of U.S. adults still support the death penalty, public opinion in favor of capital punishment has seen a modest decline since November 2011, the last time Pew Research asked the question. In 2011, 62 percent favored the death penalty for murder convictions.

Corwin, Edward S. 1928. "The 'Higher Law' Background of American Constitutional Law," in *The Rights Retained by the People*, edited by Randy E. Barnett, 1989. Fairfax, VA: George Mason University Press.

Reprint of seminal essay on American constitutional theory.

Corwin, Edward S. 1958. *The Constitution and What It Means Today*. Princeton, NJ: Princeton University Press.

The mid-20th-century successor to Cooley's and Story's commentaries on the Constitution, first published in 1920.

Cover, Robert M., and T. Alexander Aleinikoff. 1977. "Dialectical Federalism: Habeas Corpus and the Court." *Yale Law Journal* 86: 1035.

Intensely technical account of the transformation of criminal law by the habeas corpus ruling in *Fay v. Noia*.

Cristman, Bill. 2001. "Chandler v. United States: Does the Defense Attorney Have an Obligation to Present Mitigation Evidence in

Eleventh Circuit Death Penalty Cases?" *Georgia State University Review* 18 (Winter): 563.

> Discusses effective assistance of counsel cases in federal court.

Curran, Nadine. 2000. "Note: Blue Hairs in the Big House." *New England Journal on Criminal and Civil Confinement* 26 (Summer): 225.

> Exposition of the rapid growth in geriatric issues confronting prison administration.

DeMaio, Jerry R. 2001. "If You Build It They Will Come: The Threat of Overclassification in Wisconsin's Supermax Prison." *Wisconsin Law Review* 2001: 207.

> Introduction to the concept of the supermaximum prison.

Doherty, Carroll, Robert Suls, and Rachel Weisel. 2015. "Less Support for Death Penalty, Especially among Democrats: Supporters, Opponents See Risk of Executing the Innocent." Pew Research Center (April).

> A majority of Americans favor the death penalty for those convicted of murder, but support for the death penalty is as low as it has been in the past 40 years.

Dow, David R. 1996. "The State, the Death Penalty, and Carl Johnson." *Boston College Law Review* 37 (July): 691.

> Problems of representing a capital defendant after the trial are presented by lawyer who represented an executed murderer.

Dubber, Markus D. 1998. "The Right to Be Punished: Autonomy and Its Demise in Modern Penal Thought." *Law and History Review* 16 (Spring): 113.

> Interesting analysis of the conflict between rehabilitative and punitive theories of criminal sentencing.

Dulles, Avery. 2001. "Catholicism and Capital Punishment." *First Things* 112 (April): 30.

Informative summary of orthodox Roman Catholic position on the death penalty by American cardinal and theologian.

Elliot, Jonathan, ed. 1937. *Debates in the Several State Conventions on the Adoption of the Federal Constitution.* 5 vols. Philadelphia: J.B. Lippincott Company.
Reprint of the 1836 compilation of the Constitutional ratification debates.

Fabian, John. 2001. "The Paradox of Elected Judges: Tension in the American Judicial System." *Georgetown Journal of Legal Ethics* 15 (Fall): 155.
The recent history of elections decided on the basis of the death penalty issue.

Fish, Peter G. 2002. *Federal Justice in the Mid-Atlantic South: United States Courts from Maryland to the Carolinas, 1789–1835.* Washington, DC: Administrative Office of the U.S. Courts.
Massively researched and fascinating account of federal court implementation of the new U.S. criminal and civil laws in the first generations after ratification of the Constitution.

Foley, Daniel J. 2001. "Death by Election?" *Tennessee Bar Journal* 37 (December): 12.
How the political vulnerability of judges perceived as soft on the death penalty has altered rulings by Tennessee's Supreme Court.

Frank, Jerome. 1947. "Words and Music." *Columbia Law Review* 47: 1259.
Reflections on methodologies of judging by member of Court of Appeals for the Second Circuit and influential scholar.

Friedman, Lawrence M. 1973. *A History of American Law.* New York: Touchstone Books, Simon & Schuster.

The best single survey of American law in the 18th and 19th centuries.

Garland, David, Michael Meranze, and Randall McGowen. 2011. *America's Death Penalty: between Past and Present.* New York: New York University Press.
Most of the countries whose legal systems are normally compared to the United States have abolished capital punishment, but the United States continues to employ this punishment. In this book, leading scholars use comparative and historical investigations of capital punishment in Europe and America.

Garofalo, Andrew F. 2000. "Brennan v. State: The Constitutionality of Executing Sixteen-Year-Old Offenders in Florida." *Nova Law Review* 24: 855.
The article discusses the history of the death penalty for juveniles in the U.S. Supreme Court and the Supreme Court of Florida.

Glaser, Daniel. 1969. *The Effectiveness of a Prison and Parole System.* Indianapolis, IN: Bobbs-Merrill Company.
Abridged edition of the 1964 study of rehabilitative effect of prison and parole on criminals.

Goldberg, Arthur J. 1986. "Memorandum to the Conference Re: Capital Punishment." *South Texas Law Review* 27: 493.
Reprint of Justice Goldberg's 1963 memorandum calling for the Supreme Court to hold that the death penalty is cruel and unusual punishment.

Gordon, John S., 2000. "Thomas Edison's Deadly Game." *American Heritage* 52 (October): 15.
Discussion of improvements of the methods to punish criminals including Thomas Edison's invention of the electric chair as an option to hanging.

Greenberg, Jack. 1986 "Against the American System of Capital Punishment." *Harvard Law Review* 99 (May): 1670.

An article by anti–death penalty advocate criticizing the American system of capital punishment as it actually operates.

Grossman, Mark. 1998. *Encyclopedia of Capital Punishment*. San Diego: ABC-CLIO.
Reference book providing an overview of capital punishment from the 17th century BCE through the present.

Hall, Daniel E. 1995. "When Caning Meets the Eighth Amendment: Whipping Offenders in the United States." *Widener Journal of Public Law* 4: 403.
Concludes, in wake of Michael Fay incident, that public whipping may still be constitutional in the United States.

Hamilton, Alexander, James Madison, and John Jay. 1966. *The Federalist Papers*, edited by Roy P. Fairfield. Garden City, NY: Anchor Books, Doubleday & Co.
Readable exposition of the rehabilitative theory of punishment from the end of the era.

Haskins, Charles Homer. 1960. *Norman Institutions*. New York: Frederick Ungar Publishing Co.
First published in 1918, a survey of the roots of the Anglo-American law in the government of the Duchy of Normandy.

Herman, Peter G., ed. 2001. *The American Prison System*. New York: H.W. Wilson.
Well-chosen collection of essays and news articles covering the spectrum of modern prison issues.

Hirsch, Alan, and Diane Sheehey. 1993. *The Bail Reform Act of 1984*. Washington, DC: Federal Judicial Center.
Analysis of the federal law of pretrial detention, for use by the federal judiciary.

Holmes, Oliver Wendell, Jr. 1881. *The Common Law*. Boston: Little, Brown and Company.

Lectures explaining Holmes's philosophy of law before his appointment to the Supreme Court.

Horwitz, Robert. 1987. "John Dewey," in *History of Political Philosophy*, edited by Leo Strauss and Joseph Cropsey. Chicago: University of Chicago Press.
An introduction to the thought of the foremost American philosopher of the 20th century.

Howard, Roscoe C. 1996. "The Defunding of the Post Conviction Defense Organizations as a Denial of the Right to Counsel." *West Virginia Law Review* 98 (Spring): 863.
An argument that Congress's 1996 elimination of funding for death penalty attorneys is unwise and ultimately more costly.

Hudson, Daniel. 2000. *Managing Death-Sentenced Inmates: A Survey of Practices*. Lanham, MD: American Correctional Association.
Useful basic survey of issues for death row corrections officials by a corrections professional.

Ignatieff, Michael. 1978. *A Just Measure of Pain: The Penitentiary in the Industrial Revolution 1750–1850*. New York: Pantheon Books.
First-rate history of the prison system and theories of punishment.

Jackson, Jesse. 1996. *Legal Lynching: Racism, Injustice and the Death Penalty*. New York: Marlowe & Company.
Popular treatment of argument that the death penalty is unjust and unevenly applied.

Johnson, Alan, and Jon Craig. 2002. "Tragic Timing: Alton Coleman's Many Victims Fell Prey to Fate, Circumstances." *Columbus Dispatch* (April 15).
Discussion of Alton Coleman who had death sentences from three different states: Indiana, Ohio, and Illinois. These sentences were the culmination of a 1984 Midwestern crime spree that included up to eight murders, seven rapes, three kidnappings, and fourteen armed robberies.

Joyce, James A. 1961. *Capital Punishment: A World View*. New York: Thomas Nelson & Sons.
    A call for a worldwide end to capital punishment by a committed rehabilitationist.

Kenyon, J. P. 1966. *The Stuart Constitution, 1603–1688: Documents and Commentary*. London: Cambridge University Press.
    Presents relevant materials from English law before the Bill of Rights.

Kirchmeier, Jeffrey L. 2000. "Let's Make a Deal: Waiving the Eighth Amendment by Selecting a Cruel and Unusual Punishment." *Connecticut Law Review* 32 (Winter): 615.
    Questions whether waiver of prohibition against cruel and unusual punishment should be waivable.

Kirchmeier, Jeffrey L. 2002. "Another Place beyond Here: The Death Penalty Moratorium Movement in the United States." *University of Colorado Law Review* 73 (Winter): 1.
    History and current support for moratorium on executions.

Kitto, H. D. F. 1991. *The Greeks*. London: Penguin Books.
    New edition of 1951 classic introduction to classical Greek culture.

Klarman, Michael J. 1998. "Race and the Court in the Progressive Era." *Vanderbilt Law Review* 51: 881.
    Enlightening article about a neglected period of Supreme Court history.

Koosed, Margery M. 2001. "Averting Mistaken Executions by Adopting the Model Penal Code's Exclusion of Death in the Presence of Lingering Doubt." *Northern Illinois University Law Review* 21(Spring): 41.
    Article pointing up the role of uncertainty in verdicts recommending the death penalty.

Kronenwetter, Michael. 1993. *Capital Punishment*. Santa Barbara, CA: ABC-CLIO.
> Comprehensive treatment of the death penalty: its history, court rulings, and arguments from supporters and opponents.

Laurence, John. 1960. *A History of Capital Punishment*. New York: Citadel Press.
> An informative book on famous executions and executioners throughout history.

Lawes, Lewis E. 1969. *Man's Judgment of Death*. Montclair, NJ: Patterson Smith.
> Reprint of anti–capital punishment tract by the warden of Sing Sing Prison.

Ledewitz, Bruce, and Scott Staples. 1993. "No Punishment without Cruelty." *George Mason University Civil Rights Law Journal* 4 (Winter): 41.
> Good distinction between revenge and retribution by two opponents of the death penalty and life without parole.

Lee, Robert W. 1990. "Deserving to Die." *The New American* (August 13).
> An article contending that capital punishment is the only appropriate way for society to respond to heinous crimes.

Lewis, C. S. 1954. *English Literature in the Sixteenth Century*. Oxford: Clarendon Press.
> A substantial work of literary scholarship. Lewis presents a portrait of Renaissance humanism with its changes in politics, religion, and science.

Liebman, James S., Jeffrey Fagan, Valerie West, and Jonathan Lloyd. 2000. "Capital Attrition: Error Rates in Capital Cases, 1973–1995." *Texas Law Review* 78 (June): 1839.
> Brief, statistics-packed article concluding that the high error rate in capital cases requires overhaul of the system.

Lifton, Robert J., and Greg Mitchell. 2000. *Who Owns Death?* New York: HarperCollins Publishers.
> Social and psychological treatment of the death penalty from abolitionist perspective.

Little, Rory K. 1999. "The Federal Death Penalty: History and Some Thoughts about the Department of Justice's Role." *Fordham Urban Law Journal* 26 (March): 347.
> Excellent history and insider's appraisal of the administration of the Federal Death Penalty Act of 1994.

Locke, John. 1924. *Two Treatises of Civil Government.* London: J.M. Dent & Sons Ltd.
> Everyman's Library edition of Locke's classic essays of 1690.

Locke, John. 1967. *Two Tracts on Government.* Cambridge: Cambridge University Press.
> Translation by Philip Abrams of Locke's little-known work of 1660.

Logan, Wayne A. 2000. "Opining on Death: Witness Sentence Recommendations in Capital Trials." *Boston College Law Review* 41 (May): 517.
> Discusses cases from *Booth v. Maryland* to *Payne v. Tennessee.*

Maitland, F. W. 1908. (H. A. L. Fisher, ed.). *The Constitutional History of England.* Cambridge: Cambridge University Press.
> The development of English constitutional law by its foremost 19th-century expositor.

Margulies, Joseph. 2002. "Memories of an Execution." *Law and Inequality: A Journal of Theory and Practice* 20 (Winter): 125.
> Perspective by counsel on Texas's execution of his client "The Black Widow" in 2000.

McCafferty, James A. 1972. *Capital Punishment.* Chicago: Aldine-Atherton.

Another collection of essays for and against the death penalty, including valuable contributions by Jacques Barzun and Jack Greenberg.

McClellan, Grant S., ed. 1961. *Capital Punishment.* New York: H.W. Wilson.
Collection of essays, worthwhile for statements by Ohio governor Michael DiSalle and California governor Edmund G. (Pat) Brown.

McCormick, John. 1998. "The Wrongly Condemned: How Many Capital Cases End in False Convictions?" *Newsweek* (November 9).
An article chronicling false convictions in capital cases.

McDonald, Forrest. 1985. *Novus Ordo Seclorum: The Intellectual Origins of the Constitution.* Lawrence, KS: University of Kansas Press.
Intelligent treatise on the sources of principles believed by the Framers.

McKelvey, Blake. 1977. *American Prisons: A History of Good Intentions.* Montclair, NJ: Patterson Smith.
Excellent narrative history of America's experiences with prisons.

McNulty, Paul. 1995. "Natural Born Killers?" *Policy Review* 71 (Winter): 84.
Asserts that there will be an explosion of teenage crime by 2010 and that the juvenile court system will be inadequate.

Melusky, Joseph. 2000. *The American Political System: An Owner's Manual.* Boston: McGraw-Hill.
A political science textbook providing background discussion on the framing, ratification, and interpretation of the U.S. Constitution.

Melusky, Joseph A., and Keith Alan Pesto. 2003. *Cruel and Unusual Punishment: Rights and Liberties under the Law.* Santa Barbara, CA: ABC-CLIO.

An overview of key events and cases in the history of cruel and unusual punishment in the United States.

Melusky, Joseph A., and Keith Alan Pesto. 2011. *Capital Punishment: Historical Guide to Controversial Issues in America.* Santa Barbara, CA: Greenwood.
An examination of the debate surrounding the death penalty combining an analysis of important issues with excerpts from important cases, documents, and empirical data.

Melusky, Joseph A., and Keith Alan Pesto. 2014. *The Death Penalty: Documents Decoded.* Santa Barbara, CA: ABC-CLIO.
A one-stop collection of excerpts from more than 30 important Supreme Court opinions on the death penalty with an analysis of issues raised.

Mencken, H. L. 1926. "The Penalty of Death," in *Elements of Argument*, edited by Annette T. Rottenberg. (394–396). 1985. New York: St. Martin's Press.
The master of American satire derides the retributive theory of capital punishment.

Mill, John Stuart. 2002. "Speech in Favor of Capital Punishment." *Ethics Updates* (February 19). http://ethics.acusd.edu/Mill.html.
A speech delivered before Parliament on April 21, 1868, in opposition to a bill banning capital punishment.

Nygaard, Richard L. 1988. "Crime, Pain, and Punishment: A Skeptic's View." *Dickinson Law Review* 102 (Winter): 355.
Judge of Court of Appeals for the Third Circuit explains why he questions the effectiveness of traditional applications of punishment for crime.

Owens, John B. 2000. "Book Review." *California Law Review* 88 (January): 233.
Humorous review of suspense fiction about the Court by a former law clerk sheds light on the Court's decision-making process.

Paduano, Anthony, and Clive A. S. Smith. 1991. "The Unconscionability of Sub-Minimum Wages Paid Appointed Counsel in Capital Cases." *Rutgers Law Review* 43 (Winter): 281.
> Argues that indigent capital defendants too often get the defense they pay for.

Parker, Frank J. 1975. *Caryl Chessman: The Red Light Bandit.* Chicago: Nelson-Hall, Inc.
> Summing up of one of 20th century's most controversial death penalty cases.

Pew Research Center for the People & the Press. 2012. *Continued Majority Support for Death Penalty: More Concern among Opponents about Wrongful Convictions.* Washington, DC: Pew Research Center for the People & the Press.
> There is far less support for the death penalty than there was in the mid-1990s.

Pope John Paul II. 1995. *Evangelium Vitae (The Gospel of Life).* Libreria Editrice Vaticana. http://w2.vatican.va/content/john-paul-ii/en/ency clicals/documents/hf_jp-ii_enc_25031995_evangelium-vitae.html.
> Papal encyclical stating that the death penalty is morally acceptable when it is necessary to defend society, but that in view of improvements to penal systems, such cases are extremely rare if not nonexistent.

Post, Albert. 1944. "Early Efforts to Abolish Capital Punishment in Pennsylvania." *The Pennsylvania Magazine of History and Biography* 68 (January): 38.
> Early survey of abolitionism in a single state.

Pound, Roscoe. 1957. *The Development of Constitutional Guarantees of Liberty.* New Haven, CT: Yale University Press.
> Sources of American freedoms presented by influential legal scholar and educator.

Pound, Roscoe. 1999. *The Spirit of the Common Law.* New Brunswick, NJ: Transaction Publishers.
> Reissue of Pound's 1921 lectures on legal philosophy.

Prejean, Sister Helen. 1993. *Dead Man Walking: An Eyewitness Account of the Death Penalty in the United States*. New York: Vintage Books/ Random House.
> Sister Helen Prejean's experiences as a spiritual advisor to death row prisoners in Louisiana's Angola State Prison, source of the hit 1995 film.

Prettyman, Barrett, Jr. 1961. *Death and the Supreme Court*. New York: Harcourt, Brace & World.
> Prize-winning examination of the stories behind six capital punishment cases at the Supreme Court by a former law clerk.

Rapaport, Elizabeth. 1991. "The Death Penalty and Gender Discrimination." *Law and Society Review* 25: 367.
> Examines the unwarranted assumption that women murderers are chivalrously spared death sentences. The reason that relatively few women are on death rows is that they infrequently commit crimes that society labels sufficiently reprehensible to merit capital punishment.

Rapaport, Elizabeth. 2001. "Staying Alive: Executive Clemency, Equal Protection, and the Politics of Gender in Women's Capital Cases." *Buffalo Criminal Law Review* 4: 967.
> A study of the politics and law surrounding governors' decisions to commute the sentences of female death row prisoners.

Robbins, Ira P. 1993. "The Prisoners' Mail Box and the Evolution of Federal Inmate Rights." *Federal Rules Decisions* 144: 127
> History of federal prisons in 20th century presented through the development of a grievance system.

Roleff, Tamara, ed. 1999. *Crime and Criminals: Opposing Viewpoints*. San Diego: Greenhaven Press.
> Collection of essays on the death penalty and other sentencing issues.

Romano, Sally Ann. 1996. "If the SHU Fits: Cruel and Unusual Punishment at California's Pelican Bay State Prison." *Emory Law Journal* 45 (Summer): 1089.
> History of prison systems, concluding that supermax facilities violate the Eighth Amendment.

Sarat, Austin, and Jurgen Martschukat. 1998. "Recapturing the Spirit of Furman: The American Bar Association and the New Abolitionist Politics." *Law and Contemporary Problems* 61 (Autumn): 5.
> Presents the view that the abolitionist movement is gaining political strength.

Sarat, Austin, and Jurgen Martschukat. 2011. *Is the Death Penalty Dying? European and American Perspectives*. Cambridge: Cambridge University Press.
> This book examines European experiences with capital punishment and assesses what the United States can learn from these experiences.

Schwartz, Bernard, ed. 1980. *The Roots of the Bill of Rights*. 5 vols. New York: Chelsea House.
> Source documents for the Bill of Rights, from Magna Carta to notes of state ratifying conventions, edited and introduced by noted New York University law professor.

Semeraro, Steven. 2002. "Responsibility in Capital Sentencing." *San Diego Law Review* 39 (Winter): 79.
> Charges that appellate review of death sentences is inadequate.

Serrano, Richard A. 2001. "Forgotten in Life, Jail, and Death." *Los Angeles Times* (January 22).
> Richard Hammer tied his prison cellmate to a bunk and strangled him. Serrano discusses this incident and expresses no sympathy for the murderer.

Skelton, Meghan S. 1997. "Lethal Injection in the Wake of *Fierro v. Gomez." Thomas Jefferson Law Review* 19 (Spring): 1.
> A history of methods of execution with a call for lethal injection to go the way of the electric chair and gas chamber.

Stephens, Matthew L. 1990. "Instrument of Justice or Tool of Vengeance?" *Christian Social Action* 3 (10) (November).
> An article written by a prison chaplain criticizing capital punishment on grounds that it is motivated by revenge and it is applied in an arbitrary and racist fashion.

Story, Joseph. 1987. *Commentaries on the Constitution of the United States.* Durham, NC: Carolina Academic Press.
> Reprint of Story's treatise with valuable introduction by Ronald D. Rotunda and John E. Nowak.

Stuntz, William J. 1998. "Race, Class, and Drugs." *Columbia Law Review* 98: 1795.
> Explains how even racially neutral law enforcement can be rationally perceived as discriminatory and why perception of fairness is important to successful drug laws.

Surrency, Erwin C. 1987. *History of the Federal Courts.* New York: Oceana Publications.
> Presents the evolution of the jurisdiction and procedures of federal courts.

Thompson, E. P. 1975. *Whigs and Hunters: The Origin of the Black Act.* New York: Pantheon Books/ Random House.
> In-depth look at one capital punishment statute and how it was applied in Georgian England.

"U.S. Catholic Bishops' Statement on Capital Punishment." 1980. http://www.pbs.org/wgbh/pages/frontline/angel/procon /bishopstate.html (February 13, 2002).
> A 1980 statement issued by U.S. Roman Catholic bishops explaining their opposition to capital punishment.

U.S. Department of Justice. 2000. *Survey of the Federal Death Penalty System 1988–2000.* Washington, DC: Department of Justice.
> Internal document reviewing the performance of the Department of Justice's Review Committee on Capital Cases.

van den Haag, Ernest. 1986. "The Ultimate Punishment: A Defense." *Harvard Law Review* 99 (May): 1662.
> Defends capital punishment against various criticisms.

Veall, Donald. 1970. *The Popular Movement for Law Reform 1640–1660.* Oxford: Clarendon Press.
> Changes in English criminal law and procedure are set in the history of the English Civil War.

Weinstein, Henry. 2002. "Death Penalty Foes Mark a Milestone." *Los Angeles Times* (April 10).
> Weinstein discusses the story of Ray Krone, the 100th person who had been sentenced to death but who was exonerated since executions resumed in the 1970s.

Wekesser, Carol, ed. 1991. *The Death Penalty: Opposing Viewpoints.* San Diego: Greenhaven Press.
> Collection of essays, including classics by Cesare Beccaria, John Stuart Mill, and Horace Greeley.

White, Ahmed A. 2001. "Rule of Law and the Limits of Sovereignty: The Private Prison in Jurisprudential Perspective." *American Criminal Law Review* 38 (May): 111.
> The modern phenomenon of private prisons is traced to its roots and found wanting.

Wiener, Scott. 1996. "Popular Justice: State Judicial Elections and Procedural Due Process." *Harvard Civil Rights–Civil Liberties Law Review* 31 (Winter): 187.
> Can elected judges decide death penalty cases impartially? The author argues that the answer is no.

Williams, Kenneth. 2000. "The Deregulation of the Death Penalty." *Santa Clara Law Review* 40: 677.

> Post-1976 limitations on appellate and habeas corpus relief from the death penalty are criticized.

Williams, Kenneth. 2012. *Most Deserving of Death? An Analysis of the Supreme Court's Death Penalty Jurisprudence.* Farnham, England: Ashgate.

> This book argues that inconsistent jurisprudence contributes to a lack of public confidence about the role of capital punishment in the United States. Case studies deal with jury selection, ineffective assistance of counsel, the role of race, and claims of innocence. Also problematic is the lack of impact that international treaties have on capital punishment in America.

For original source documents relevant to the Eighth Amendment, the Supreme Court and its role in constitutional law, see the following:

Beccaria, Cesare. 1963 [1764]. (Henry Paolucci, trans.). *On Crimes and Punishments.* Englewood Cliffs, NJ: Prentice Hall.

Blackstone, William. 1979 [1765–1769]. *Commentaries on the Laws of England.* 4 vols. Chicago: University of Chicago Press.

Ford, Paul L., ed. 1968. *Pamphlets on the Constitution of the United States.* New York: Da Capo Press.

Kenyon, J. P., ed. 1966. *The Stuart Constitution 1603–1688: Documents and Commentary.* London: Cambridge University Press.

For American constitutional law, the history of ideas, and the transformation of American legal thinking, see the following:

Abraham, Henry J. 1993. *The Judicial Process.* 6th ed. New York: Oxford University Press.

Bailyn, Bernard. 1992. *The Ideological Origins of the American Revolution*. Enlarged edition. Cambridge, MA: Belknap Press of the Harvard University Press.

Berkin, Carol. 2003. *A Brilliant Solution: Inventing the American Constitution*. Orlando, Harcourt, Inc.

Bork, Robert H. 1996. "Our Judicial Oligarchy." *First Things* 67 (November): 21.

Clinton, Robert. 1999. "How the Court Became Supreme." *First Things* 89 (January): 13.

Douglas, William O. 1961. *A Living Bill of Rights*. New York: Doubleday.

Fairman, Charles. 1949. "Does the Fourteenth Amendment Incorporate the Bill of Rights?" *Stanford Law Review* 2 (December): 5.

Frankfurter, Felix. 1958. The Supreme Court in the Mirror of Justices." *ABA Journal* 44:.723.

Gunther, Gerald. 1964. "The Subtle Vices of the 'Passive Virtues': A Comment on Principle and Expediency in Judicial Review." *Columbia Law Review* 64: 1.

Maine, Henry S. 1970 [1861]. *Ancient Law: Its Connection with the Early History of Society and Its Relation to Modern Ideas*. Gloucester, MA: Peter Smith.

O'Brien, David M. 2005. *Storm Center: The Supreme Court in American Politics*. 7th ed. New York: W.W. Norton & Company.

Posner, Richard A. 2008. *How Judges Think*. Cambridge, MA: Harvard University Press.

Rehnquist, William H. 2001. *The Supreme Court*. New York: Alfred A. Knopf.

Silverstein, Mark. 1994. *Judicious Choices: The New Politics of Supreme Court Nominations*. New York: W.W. Norton & Company.

Stannard, David E. 1977. *The Puritan Way of Death*. New York: Oxford University Press.

Sutherland, Arthur E. 1965. *Constitutionalism in America*. New York: Blaisdell Publishing Company.

Watson, Bradley C. S. 2009. *Living Constitution, Dying Faith: Progressivism and the New Science of Jurisprudence*. Wilmington, DE: ISI Books.

For treatment of the death penalty and the problem of crime and punishment in general, see the following:

Berns, Walter. 1979. *For Capital Punishment: Crime and the Morality of the Death Penalty*. New York: Basic Books.

Cohen, Bernard L. 1970. *Law without Order: Capital Punishment and the Liberals*. New Rochelle, NY: Arlington House.

Cohen, Morris R. 1940. "Moral Aspects of the Criminal Law." *Yale Law Journal* 49 (April): 987.

Coyne, Randall, and Lyn Entzeroth. 2006. *Capital Punishment and the Judicial Process*. 3rd ed. Durham, NC: Carolina Academic Press.

DeGrandis, Michael P. 2003. "*Atkins v. Virginia*: Nothing Left of the Independent Legislative Power to Punish and Define Crime." *George Mason Law Review* 11 (Summer): 805.

Demleitner, Nora V. 2005. "Is there a Future for Leniency in the U.S. Criminal Justice System?" *Michigan Law Review* 103 (May): 1231.

Dershowitz, Alan M. 2004. *America on Trial: Inside the Legal Battles That Transformed Our Nation*. New York: Warner Books.

Dezhbaksh, Hashem, Paul H. Rubin, and Joanna Shepherd. 2003. "Does Capital Punishment Have a Deterrent Effect? New Evidence from Postmoratorium Panel Data." *American Law and Economics Review* 5 (August): 344.

Donohue, John J., and Justin Wolfers. 2005. "Uses and Abuses of Empirical Evidence in the Death Penalty Debate." *Stanford Law Review* 58 (December): 791.

Douglas, Davison M. 2000. "God and the Executioner: The Influence of Western Religion on the Death Penalty." *William and Mary Bill of Rights Journal* 9 (December): 137.

Greenlee, Harry, and Shelia P. Greenlee. 2008. "Women and the Death Penalty: Racial Disparities and Differences." *William and Mary Journal of Women and the Law* 14 (Winter): 319.

Hoeflich, M. H. 1986. "Law and Geometry: Legal Science from Leibniz to Langdell." *American Journal of Legal History* 30 (April): 95.

Jackson, Bruce, and Diane Christian. 1980. *Death Row*. Boston: Beacon Press.

Katz, Lawrence, Steven D. Levitt, and Ellen Shustorovich. 2003. "Prison Conditions, Capital Punishment, and Deterrence." *American Law and Economics Review* 5 (August): 318.

Kearns, Timothy S. 2005. "The Chair, the Needle and the Damage Done: What the Electric Chair and the Rebirth of the Method-of-Execution Challenge Could Mean for the Future of the Eighth Amendment." *Cornell Journal of Law and Public Policy* 15 (Fall): 197.

Kozinski, Alex, and Sean Gallagher. 1995 "Death: The Ultimate Run-On Sentence." *Case Western Reserve Law Review* 46 (Fall): 1.

Lanier, Charles S., William Bowers, and James R. Acker, eds. 2008. *The Future of America's Death Penalty: An Agenda for the*

Next Generation of Capital Punishment Research. Durham, NC: Carolina Academic Press.

Laurence, John. 1960. *A History of Capital Punishment.* New York: Citadel Press.

Lindgren, James. 1996. "Why the Ancients May Not Have Needed a System of Criminal Law." *Boston University Law Review* 76 (February/April): 29.

Mocan, H. Naci, and R. Kaj Gittings. 2003. "Getting Off Death Row: Commuted Sentences and the Deterrent Effect of Capital Punishment." *Journal of Law and Economics* 46 (October): 453.

Packer, Herbert L. 1964. "Making the Punishment Fit the Crime." *Harvard Law Review* 77 (April): 1071.

Presser, Stephen B. 1982. *Studies in the History of the United States Courts of the Third Circuit* Washington, DC: Government Printing Office.

Radelet, Michael, and Marian T. Borg. 2000. "The Changing Nature of the Death Penalty Debates." *Annual Review of Sociology* 26: 43.

Sellin, Thorsten. 1959. *The Death Penalty.* Philadelphia: Lippincott.

Sellin, Thorsten, ed. 1967. *Capital Punishment.* New York: Harper & Row.

Shapiro, Barbara J. 1969. "Law and Science in Seventeenth-Century England." *Stanford Law Review* 21 (April): 727.

Smith, Bruce P. 2005. "The History of Wrongful Execution." *Hastings Law Journal* 56 (June): 1185.

Stack, Steven. 1987. "Publicized Executions and Homicide." *American Sociological Review* 52 (August): 532.

Standen, Jeffrey. 2005. The New Importance of Maximum Penalties." *Drake Law Review* 53 (Spring): 575.

Stephenson, D. Grier. 1994. "Justice Blackmun's Eighth Amendment Pilgrimage." *BYU Journal of Public Law* 8: 271.

Stinneford, John F. 2008. "The Original Meaning of 'Unusual': The Eighth Amendment as Bar to Cruel Innovation." *Northwestern University Law Review* 102 (Fall): 1739.

Stras, David R. 2007. "The Supreme Court's Gatekeepers: The Role of Law Clerks in the Certiorari Process." *Texas Law Review* 85 (March): 947.

Student Note. 1910. "What Is Cruel and Unusual Punishment." *Harvard Law Review* 24: 54.

Student Note. 1966. "The Cruel and Unusual Punishment Clause and the Substantive Criminal Law." *Harvard Law Review* 79: 635.

van den Haag, Ernest, and John P. Conrad. 1983. *The Death Penalty: A Debate*. New York: Plenum Press.

Zimmerman, Paul R. 2006. "Estimates of the Deterrent Effect of Alternative Execution Methods in the United States: 1978–2000." *American Journal of Economics and Sociology* 65 (October): 909.

For personal accounts, see the following:

Bessler, John D. 2003. *Kiss of Death: America's Love Affair with the Death Penalty*. Boston: Northeastern University Press.

Greenhouse, Linda. 2005. *Becoming Justice Blackmun: Harry Blackmun's Supreme Court Journey*. New York: Times Books.

Hawke, David F. 1971. *Benjamin Rush: Revolutionary Gadfly*. Indianapolis, IN: Bobbs-Merrill Co.

Williams, Daniel E. 1993. *Pillars of Salt: An Anthology of Early American Criminal Narratives.* Madison, WI: Madison House Publishers, Inc.

Electronic Resources

Several of the following websites serve as "gateways," including extensive links to print and electronic resources. The following list is intended to be suggestive rather than comprehensive.

The American Bar Association Death Penalty Moratorium Implementation Project
http://www.abanet.org/moratorium/home.html
> Contains news updates and the text of studies commissioned by legislatures of several states that have changed or are studying changes in death penalty legislation, including California, Illinois, Maryland, and New Jersey. Most assessments contain well-chosen bibliographies of news articles and law journal essays in opposition to the death penalty.

Amnesty International
http://www.amnestyusa.org/our-work/campaigns/abolish-the-death-penalty/death-penalty-campaign-resources
> This site includes fact sheets, background materials, and other information compiled by Amnesty International.

Bureau of Justice Statistics
http://bjs.gov/
> This site provides statistics about crime and victims, drugs and crime, criminal offenders, the justice system in the United States, law enforcement, prosecution, courts, and related matters.

Chronicling America
http://chroniclingamerica.loc.gov/
> An archive of daily newspapers from 1789 to 1922. It includes accounts of executions, notable trials, editorials, and related commentaries.

The Death Penalty Information Center
http://www.deathpenaltyinfo.org/
> Includes updated fact sheets, regularly updated statistics, information about upcoming executions, an execution database, state-by-state comparisons, podcasts, and lists or relevant resources.

Death Penalty Links, Clark County (IN) Prosecutors Office
http://www.clarkprosecutor.org/html/links/dplinks.htm
> This site includes a wealth of information on timelines, methods of execution, public opinion polls, and so on. The list of links to other resources is very comprehensive. See "1000+ Death Penalty Links."

Department of Justice, Bureau of Justice Statistics
http://www.ojp.usdoj.gov/bjs/
> Keeps current statistics on crime in general and capital punishment in particular, including the manual used by the U.S. attorneys to decide when and how to seek the death penalty: *United State Attorneys' Manual*, Chapter 9.10.00–190.

Fascinating Facts about the Constitution
http://www.constitutionfacts.com
> This site provides an assortment of facts about the Constitution. The site includes famous quotes, crossword puzzles, glossary of terms, Declaration of Independence, Articles of Confederation, Bill of Rights, state constitutions, foreign constitutions, dates, the Founding Fathers, and information about the Supreme Court.

Federal Death Penalty Resource Counsel
http://www.capdefnet.org/fdprc/fdprc_gateway.htm
> This site is maintained by a working group of the federal public defenders, and contains a bibliography of news articles and scholarly essays opposed to the death penalty.

The Federal Judicial Center
http://www.fjc.gov/
> Contains many useful documents written specifically for federal judges, most notably *Resource Guide for Managing Capital Cases Volume I: Federal Death Penalty Trials* (2004) and *Resources for Managing Capital Cases Volume II: Habeas Corpus Review of Capital Convictions* (2004). This site is a useful place to explore the nuts and bolts of death penalty procedures.

The Federalist Papers
http://federalist.freeservers.com/papers.html
> This is a website for the *Federalist Papers*. Madison's, *Federalist* Number 51 and Hamilton's *Federalist* Numbers 78 and 84 are most directly relevant to the federal judiciary.

Free Legal Research Resources: Harvard Law School Library Guide
http://guides.library.harvard.edu/free
> Provides selected free online legal research resources.

Human Rights: Death Penalty
http://www.derechos.org/dp/
> This site provides international perspectives on the death penalty.

Kruglick's Death Penalty Links
http://www.bioforensics.com/kruglaw/dp_links.htm
> The Kruglick's Forensic Resource and Criminal Law Search Site provides a wide variety of relevant links. The site is sponsored by Forensic Bioinformatics, offering evaluations of DNA evidence and consulting services.

Learn More about the Death Penalty: An Annotated Bibliography
http://www.ihmsisters.org/www/media/justice_peace_and_ sustainability_autogen/death.penalty.bib.pdf
> This site of the IHM Sisters provides a Catholic perspective.

The Legal Information Institute
http://www.law.cornell.edu/
>   This website provides access to historical and recent Supreme Court decisions.

The National Constitution Center
http://www.constitutioncenter.org.
>   This is the website for the National Constitution Center.

The National Death Penalty Archive
http://library.albany.edu/archive/ndpa
>   The State University of New York at Albany's School of Criminal Justice website includes unpublished works of historical interest, such as the originals of clemency petitions. The archive also contains the original papers of the Espy File, as well as the papers of two of the United States' most prominent writers about the death penalty, Hugo Bedau (against) and Ernest van den Haag (for).

Oyez: U.S. Supreme Court Multimedia
http://www.oyez.org
>   This website provides links to cases, upcoming arguments, and other information concerning the U.S. Supreme Court.

PACER (Public Access to Electronic Court Records)
http://www.uscourts.gov/
>   Provides access (for a fee) to decisions of lower federal courts.

Report of the Advisory Committee on Wrongful Convictions, September 2011, John T. Rago, Esq. (Chair)
http://jsg.legis.state.pa.us/resources/documents/ftp/documents/9-15-11%20rpt%20-%20Wrongful%20Convictions.pdf
>   This report for the Pennsylvania General Assembly's Joint State Government Commission chronicled wrongful convictions and reasons including mistaken eyewitness identification, false confessions, incriminating admissions,

interrogation practices, postconviction relief, adequacy of legal representation, and prosecutorial misconduct. The report discussed "best practices" and included reform suggestions and redress for wrongful convictions.

Supreme Court of the United States
http://www.supremecourt.gov
This is the official website for the Supreme Court of the United States.

Top Ten Pros and Cons: Should the Death Penalty Be Allowed?
http://deathpenalty.procon.org/view.resource.php?resourceID=002000
ProCon.org is an independent, nonpartisan, nonprofit public charity. This site is a useful introduction to the capital punishment debate.

Web Guide to U.S. Supreme Court Research
http://www.llrx.com/features/supremectwebguide.htm
Gail Partin, associate law librarian at Dickinson School of Law, prepared this web guide to Supreme Court research.

Organizations

The overwhelming majority of the organizations devoted to or active on the capital punishment issue are abolitionist.

Selected Organizations Based in the United States

American Civil Liberties Union—Death Penalty Project
Executive Director
122 Maryland Avenue NE
Washington, DC 20002
http://www.aclu.org/death-penalty/
(212) 549-2500

This division of the ACLU concentrates on efforts to end the death penalty through public education and legislative action.

It has been particularly active in attempting to influence federal legislation on the subject. ACLU publications and information about the organization's activities in general are available from the national headquarters.

For those wishing to become active in local efforts of the ACLU, there are affiliate offices in every state and the District of Columbia. Some states have more than one. Addresses and telephone numbers can be found in the appropriate local telephone directories, at http://www.aclu .org/, or by calling or writing to the national office in Washington, D.C. Other cities with offices include the following, listed by state:

Alabama (Montgomery)

Alaska (Anchorage)

Arizona (Phoenix)

Arkansas (Little Rock)

California (Los Angeles, San Diego, San Francisco)

Colorado (Denver)

Connecticut (Hartford)

Delaware (Wilmington)

District of Columbia (Washington)

Florida (Miami)

Georgia (Atlanta)

Hawaii (Honolulu)

Idaho (Boise)

Illinois (Chicago)

Indiana (Indianapolis)

Iowa (Des Moines)

Kansas (Kansas City)

Kentucky (Louisville)

Louisiana (New Orleans)

Maine (Portland)

Maryland (Baltimore)

Massachusetts (Boston)

Michigan (Detroit)

Minnesota (Minneapolis)

Mississippi (Jackson)

Missouri (St. Louis, Kansas City)

Montana (Billings)

Nebraska (Lincoln)

Nevada (Las Vegas)

New Hampshire (Concord)

New Jersey (Newark)

New Mexico (Albuquerque)

New York (New York)

North Carolina (Raleigh)

Ohio (Cleveland)

Oklahoma (Oklahoma City)

Oregon (Portland)

Pennsylvania (Philadelphia, Pittsburgh)

Rhode Island (Providence)

South Carolina (Columbia)

South Dakota (Sioux Falls)

Tennessee (Nashville)

Texas (Austin, Dallas, Houston)

Utah (Salt Lake City)

Vermont (Montpelier)

Virginia (Richmond)

Washington (Seattle)

West Virginia (Charleston)

Wisconsin (Milwaukee)

Wyoming (Laramie)

American Friends Service Committee
1501 Cherry Street
Philadelphia, PA 19102
(215) 241-7000
http://www.afsc.org/

One of the most active of religious organizations in the United States opposing the death penalty and all other forms of violence, whether committed by individuals or by governments.

Amnesty International USA Program to Abolish the Death Penalty
322 Eighth Avenue
New York, NY 10001
(212) 807-8400
http://amnesty-usa.org/abolish/

Amnesty International USA (Regional Headquarters)
AIUSA Mid-Atlantic Regional Office
608 Pennsylvania Avenue NE
Fifth Floor
Washington, DC 20003
(202) 544-0200

AIUSA Midwest Regional Office
53 W. Jackson, Suite #731
Chicago, IL 60604
(312) 427-2060

AIUSA Northeast Regional Office
58 Day Street, Davis Square
Somerville, MA 02144
(617) 623-0202

AIUSA South Regional Office
131 Ponce De Leon NE, #200
Atlanta, GA 30308
(404) 876-5661

AIUSA Western Regional Office
9000 W. Washington Bl., 2nd Floor
Culver City, CA 90232
(310) 815-0450

Winner of the Nobel Peace Prize, Amnesty International collects and disseminates information about human rights abuses around the world, including the United States. "Amnesty International opposes the death penalty in all cases, believing it to be the ultimate cruel, inhuman and degrading treatment and a violation of the right to life as proclaimed in the Universal Declaration of Human Rights and other international human rights instruments." For general information, you may get in touch with any of the regional offices listed above. For information about publications, write or phone the national office in New York.

Campaign to End the Death Penalty
National Office
P.O. Box 25730
Chicago, IL 60625
(773) 955-4841
http://www.nodeathpenalty.org/

Founded in 1995, the Campaign to End the Death Penalty now has many chapters across the country. Stresses "grassroots organizing" to win support for prisoners currently on death row. Publishes the online newsletter *The New Abolitionist.*

Catholics against Capital Punishment
P.O. Box 5706
Bethesda, MD 20824
(301) 652-1125
http://www.igc.org/cacp/

A Roman Catholic abolitionist group, which communicates Catholic teaching concerning the death penalty to federal and state legislators, encourages the clergy to speak out against the death penalty, and mobilizes Catholic laity opposition to it.

Citizens United for Alternatives to the Death Penalty
PMB 297
177 U.S. Hwy #1
Tequesta, FL 33469
(800) 973-6548
E-mail: cuadp@cuadp.org
http://www.cuadp.org/

CUAAD works to end the death penalty in the United States through "invigorated education about viable alternatives" and "strategic and tactical grassroots activism."

Clergy Coalition to End Executions
Suite 450 Gables One Tower
1320 So. Dixie Highway
Miami, FL 33146
(305) 794-3088
http://www.ClergyCoalition.org/
   An "international interfaith coalition which supports alternatives to the death penalty."

Death Penalty Information Center
1320 18th Street NW
5th Floor
Washington, DC 20036
(202) 293-2531
http://www.deathpenaltyinfo.org/

Death Penalty Worldwide
Cornell Law School
Myron Taylor Hall
Ithaca, New York 14853-4901

This first-of-its-kind center focuses on research, advocacy, and litigation of death penalty issues around the world.

Established to "serve the media and the larger community as a clearinghouse for data and resources on the myriad issues surrounding capital punishment," including "polls, academic studies, and newspaper coverage." Although it clearly opposes the death penalty, the Death Penalty Information Center attempts to provide objective information on the subject. It has several publications available, as well as a speakers' bureau of "informed sources on capital punishment, including unexpected voices [opposing the death penalty] from the law enforcement community and families of victims."

Defense for Children International USA
21 South 13th Street
Philadelphia, PA 19107
(215) 569-3996

This advocacy group for the protection of children has information on juveniles and the death penalty.

Hands Off Cain
P.O. Box 6966
New York, NY 10128
http://www.handsoffcain.org

A "citizen's and parliamentarians' league for the abolition of the death penalty worldwide."

Innocence Project Northwest
University of Washington School of Law
1100 NE Campus Parkway
Seattle, WA 98105-6617
http://www.law.washington.edu/ipnw/

Dedicated to proving the innocence of the wrongfully convicted. Also provides links to other universities with similar projects

International Centre for Criminal Law & Human Rights (US)
110 East D Street, Suite A
Benicia, CA 94530
(707) 745-1362

An international organization that specializes in human rights laws.

Justice for All
P.O. Box 55159
Houston, TX 77255
(713) 935-9300
http://www.jfa.net/

A pro–death penalty criminal justice reform organization.

Loyola Death Penalty Resource Center
636 Baronne Street
New Orleans, LA 70113
(504) 522-0578

Collects information related to death penalty issues.

Mennonite Central Committee, U.S. Office
P.O. Box 500
215 12th Street
Akron, PA 17501
(888) 563-4646

Provides abolitionist literature and other educational materials.

Murder Victims' Families for Reconciliation
Director
2161 Massachusetts Avenue
Cambridge, MA 02140
(617) 868-0007
http://www.mvfr.org/

The director is William Pelke, the grandson of an elderly woman murdered by four teenage girls in Gary, Indiana. One of the girls was sentenced to death at the age of 16.

NAACP Legal Defense & Educational Fund
99 Hudson Street, 16th Floor
New York, NY 10013
(800) 221-7822

Once headed by Thurgood Marshall, the NAACP Legal Defense & Educational Fund (LDF) was founded by the NAACP in the 1940s. It is still allied with the NAACP, but it is no longer a part of it. Among its other activities, LDF helps to defend black defendants charged with, or convicted of, capital crimes. It opposes the imposition of the death penalty on others as well, including juveniles and mentally retarded people.

National Bar Association
Executive Director
1225 11th Street NW
Washington, DC 20001-4217
(202) 842-3900
http://nationalbar.org/

The national professional association for attorneys can provide information on legal questions surrounding the death penalty.

National Coalition to Abolish the Death Penalty
1436 U Street NW
Suite 104
Washington, DC 20009
(888) 286-2237
http://www.ncadp.org/

The most inclusive of the national groups working to end capital punishment, the NCADP helps consolidate the efforts of a broad range of national and local organizations and institutions active in the abolitionist cause.

National Criminal Justice Reference Service

P.O. Box 6000
Rockville, MD 20849-6000
(800) 851-3420
http://www.ncjrs.org/

A subdivision of the U.S. Department of Justice that provides information on all aspects of the U.S. criminal justice system, including the death penalty.

National Legal Aid and Defender Association
Death Penalty Litigation Section

1625 K Street NW
Eighth Floor
Washington, DC 20006
(202) 452-0620
http://www.nlada.org/

Devoted to the needs and interests of those actively engaged in defending people liable to receive the death penalty. Publishes a newsletter, the *Indigent Defense*.

Northern California Coalition to Abolish the Death Penalty

1611 Telegraph Avenue
Suite 1501
Oakland, CA 94612
(510) 836-3013

An active branch of the National Coalition, which works to educate the public on death penalty issues by various means, including pamphlets and forums in high schools. Along with its other activities, the group participates in demonstrations against the death penalty; it was especially active in organizing the demonstrations outside San Quentin Prison in the weeks leading up to the execution of Robert Alton Harris.

Religious Action Center of Reform Judaism
2027 Massachusetts Avenue
Washington, DC 20036
(202) 387-2800

Affiliated with the Union American Hebrew Congregations, which represents the nation's reform congregations, the Religious Action Center actively opposes capital punishment.

Washington Legal Foundation
2009 Massachusetts Avenue
Washington, DC 20036
http://www.wlf.org/

A "nonpartisan public interest law institution organized to engage in litigation and the administrative process in matters affecting the broad public interest," the foundation supports the retention of death penalty. In addition to its efforts on behalf of capital punishment, it is active in promoting the "defense on individual rights," aiding crime victims, supporting a strong defense, and "challenging regulations which impede a free market economy." Publishes studies on matters of public policy, including the death penalty.

Selected Organizations Based Abroad

Amnesty International
International Secretariat
1 Easton Street
London WC1X 0DJ
United Kingdom
(44) 020-7413-5507
http://www.amnesty.org/

The largest and best-known international nongovernmental organization dedicated to human rights.

Australian Coalition against the Death Penalty
P.O. Box 577
Endeavour Hills VIC 3802
Australia
(61) 0411-538950
http://acadp.com/

A nonprofit activist organization for human rights, opposed to the death penalty.

ECADP International (European Coalition to Abolish the Death Penalty)
Head Office
Postfach 1326
46363 Bocholt
Germany
(49) 2871-260515
http://www.ecadp.org/

ECADP Belgium (Country Representative)
E-mail: board@bel.ecadp.org (English, Dutch, and French)

ECADP Denmark (Country Representative)
(45) 97-40-76-28 (Danish, English, and German)
E-mail: board@den.ecadp.org

ECADP France (Country Representative)
(33) 4-90-75-94-75 (French, English, Italian, and German)
E-mail: board@fra.ecadp.org

ECADP Germany (Country Representative)
(49) 2871-26-05-15 (German and English)
E-mail: board@ger.ecadp.org
Press office: (49) 221-76-69-18 (German and English)
E-mail: press@ger.ecadp.org

ECADP Norway (Country Representative)
(47) 63-90-87-36 (English and Norwegian)
E-mail: board@nor.ecadp.org

ECADP Switzerland (Country Representative)
E-mail: board@sui.ecadp.org (German, English, Italian, and French)

ECADP The Netherlands (Country Representative)
(31) 75-621-96-15 (Dutch, English, and German)
E-mail: board@ned.ecadp.org

An international nonprofit organization, open to all who oppose the death penalty worldwide. Although international in scope, its primary focus is on the United States, presumably because, of the world's chief practitioners of capital punishment, it is the one most likely to be affected by international opinion.

Hands Off Cain—Brussels
Rue Belliard 97 (European Parliament)
113 Mon 229 B 1047
Brussels, Belgium
See **Hands Off Cain—New York**

Hands Off Cain—Rome
Via di Torre Argentina 76-00186
Rome, Italy
See **Hands Off Cain—New York**

Human Writes
27 Old Gloucester Street
London WC1N 3XX
United Kingdom
http://www.humanwrites.org/

Organizes letter writing to condemned inmates.

Inside-Outside
Postbus 1599
9701 BN Groningen
Netherlands
http://home.planet.nl/~inside-outside/

A Dutch group that organizes letter writing to condemned inmates.

International Centre for Criminal Law & Human Rights
Helmstraat 16C
Suite D2NL–6211
TA Maastricht, Netherlands
(31) 43-350-0074

See **International Centre for Criminal Law & Human Rights (US)**

LifeLines—Ireland
4 Chapel Manor
Chapelizod
Dublin 20
Ireland
http://homepage.eircom.net/~lifelines/Lifelines.htm

Organizes letter writing to condemned inmates.

LifeLines—United Kingdom
The Well House
Furneux Pelham
HERTS
SG9 0LN
(12) 79-777083
http://www.lifelines.org/

Organizes letter writing campaigns to condemned inmates.

Office of the High Commissioner for Human Rights
OHCHR-UNOG
8–14 Avenue de la Paix
1211 Geneva 10, Switzerland
(41-22) 917-9000
http://www.un.org/rights/index.html

The UN Commission on Human Rights, to which 53 states belong, examines, monitors, and publicly reports on "major phenomena of human rights violations worldwide," as well as human rights situations in specific countries or territories.

Introduction

The death penalty has been used for many years, from Ancient China through modern times. Early methods of execution were truly barbaric, including dismemberment, disembowelment, boiling alive, breaking on the wheel, burning at the stake, and other gruesome practices in which torture was added to the actual death sentence. In the United States, capital punishment is evaluated with an eye toward evolving standards of decency. In the interest of making executions swift and humane, lethal injection is now the preferred method in states that have the death penalty. This chapter provides a brief chronology of notable developments and mileposts in the history of the death penalty.

7th through 5th centuries BCE   Mediterranean civilizations

In Athens, Draco's Code (ca. 621 BCE) makes death the penalty for virtually all offenses. The Book of Exodus imposes the death penalty for intentional homicides and requires compensation for accidental homicides and the death of slaves. In Rome, the Twelve Tables (ca. 450 BCE) prescribe death penalty for libel and nonpayment of debts.

A staff member adjusts paintings by death row inmate Robert Butts on display at Amnesty International in London, England, on October 10, 2016. The paintings formed part of an exhibition of artwork by prisoners held on death rows across the United States. (Carl Court/Getty Images)

1st through 15th centuries CE Roman and Byzantine Empire The Roman Empire uses the death penalty to enforce public order. Constantine becomes emperor (313 CE) and decriminalizes Christianity. In the Western Roman Empire, migrating Germanic tribes replace Roman rule in the fifth through eighth centuries; they use trial by ordeal and trial by battle. Payment of compensation (weregild) is a widely accepted alternative to death penalty.

ca. 890 England King Alfred the Great adapts customary law and the biblical books of Exodus and Leviticus into criminal code, prescribing the death penalty and alternative monetary penalties for crimes that break the king's peace.

1066 William of Normandy becomes king of England and halts the use of death penalty by local feudal lords.

12th through 15th centuries Monarchical governments develop in England and Western Europe, displacing local feudal control of criminal procedure with a common law. Trial by ordeal is abandoned after 1215, but trial by battle lingers for several centuries. The common law of crime and punishment is developed by royal judges; offenses punished by death include treason, murder, manslaughter, mayhem, robbery, rape, sodomy, arson, burglary, and larceny. Lesser offenses (misdemeanors) are punished as judges direct. The defense of "benefit of clergy" (a claim of exemption from secular courts) is used to avoid death penalty for some crimes.

16th and 17th centuries England and the colonies King Henry VIII (reigned 1509–1547) declares the monarch to be the head of an English national church (ca. 1535), confiscating property belonging to monastical orders. His successors (Queen Mary I, a Catholic, and Queen Elizabeth I, an Anglican) move to subject churches to government control by the widespread use of capital punishment to enforce uniform religious observance. Beginning in the 1600s, the American colonies are settled in part by refugees from religious conflict. The last heretic is burnt in England under King James I, in 1612.

1610 The failing colony at Jamestown, Virginia, is placed under the Lawes Divine, Morall and Martiall, imposing death for offenses such as unauthorized trading with the Indians and blasphemy.

1636 The Massachusetts Bay Colony lists 13 crimes punishable by death, including idolatry and witchcraft.

1640s Civil War in England leads to the beheading of King Charles I (1649) and to some legal reforms. The use of torture by courts is forbidden. Attempts to reduce number of capital offenses are defeated. In Massachusetts, the Body of Liberties (1641) forbids "cruel and inhuman" punishments, but permits limited use of torture as an investigative technique.

1665 The Duke of York's laws for New York prescribe death for murder, manslaughter, and kidnapping, but also for atheism and for smiting one's natural father or mother.

1682 William Penn's Great Law for Pennsylvania permits the death penalty only for murder and treason.

1685 King James II's judges' excessive use of capital punishment after attempted coup by the Duke of Monmouth is denounced as the "Bloody Assizes."

1688 A bloodless coup ("The Glorious Revolution") replaces King James II with William III (William of Orange) and Mary II as joint monarchs of England.

1689 Parliament passes a Bill of Rights including provision forbidding cruel and unusual punishments.

18th century The relative mildness of English criminal practice is used by French writers like Montesquieu and Voltaire to criticize the French monarchy.

1718 Parliament passes an act authorizing "transporting" some convicted criminals to the American colonies as indentured servants. Transportation and pardons save most capital defendants from execution for crimes like larceny.

1723 Concerned over vagrancy and poaching, Parliament enacts the Waltham Black Act, adding new capital offenses without the protection of benefit of clergy.

1745–1746   The suppression of the Jacobite Rebellion in Scotland is accompanied by the use of capital punishment.

1764   Cesare Beccaria publishes *Essay on Crime and Punishment*, advocating abolition of torture and capital punishment. Responding, European countries abolish torture and restrict death penalty. Beccaria is read by English and American lawyers, including Thomas Jefferson and John Adams.

1775–1791 United States of America   In 1775, the Revolutionary War begins. As American states declare independence, most adopt Bills of Rights modeled on the English Bill of Rights, outlawing but not defining *cruel and unusual punishments*. The Articles of Confederation (1781) leaves criminal laws to state governments. The Northwest Ordinance (1787) outlaws cruel or unusual punishments. A new constitution is proposed (1787) and ratified (1789). In 1790, the first Congress enacts a federal crime bill with mandatory death penalty for treason, murder, and rape on federal property; counterfeiting; and piracy on the high seas. The Bill of Rights is ratified (1791). The Fifth Amendment forbids denial of life, liberty, or property without due process; the Eighth Amendment forbids but does not define *excessive bail, excessive fines*, and *cruel and unusual punishments*. In 1787, Dr Benjamin Rush delivers a speech on prison reform at the home of Benjamin Franklin, *An Enquiry into the Effects of Public Punishments upon Criminals and upon Society*, making the first American argument for total abolition of the death penalty as inhumane. In 1793, Pennsylvania jurist (later U.S. attorney general) William Bradford argues that capital punishment should be abolished for lesser crimes because juries hesitate to convict even the guilty when death is a possible penalty.

19th century   States pass laws ending public executions—Connecticut (1830), Rhode Island (1833), Pennsylvania (1834), and New York, New Jersey, and Massachusetts (1835)—usually providing that hangings take place in a state prison with a few official witnesses. Public hangings remain popular spectacles, however.

1846   Michigan is the first state to abolish the death penalty.

1859   Abolitionist John Brown, tried by Virginia for treason, conspiracy, and murder for the raid on the federal armory at Harper's Ferry, is hanged.

1865   Mary Surratt, convicted by a federal military tribunal of allegedly conspiring to assassinate President Lincoln, is hanged.

1878   *Wilkerson v. Utah* upholds execution by firing squad.

1889   Federal law allows, for the first time, an appeal from a death sentence imposed in federal trial court. The Supreme Court later holds, in *McKane v. Durston* (1894), that the Constitution does not require a state to allow appeals from criminal verdicts.

1890   *In re Kemmler* upholds execution by electrocution. William Kemmler is the first person executed in the electric chair. *Holden v. Minnesota* holds that Minnesota's switch from public hanging to hanging in prison (and forbidding newspaper accounts of the execution) does "not infringe any right secured by the constitution of the United States."

1891   The Evarts Act creates federal appeals courts below the Supreme Court.

1897   Federal law reduces the offenses eligible for the death penalty to treason, murder, and rape. Mandatory federal death penalty is abolished in favor of jury discretion to choose capital punishment or life imprisonment.

20th century   The Supreme Court begins incorporating portions of the Bill of Rights into the Fourteenth Amendment's Due Process Clause, making them applicable to actions by state and local governments.

State governments begin experimenting with rehabilitation, using separate juvenile courts and indeterminate sentences with eligibility for parole instead of mandatory sentences.

A short-lived abolition movement before World War I leads to the repeal of capital punishment statutes by Kansas, Minnesota, Washington, Oregon, North Dakota, South Dakota,

Tennessee, Arizona, and Missouri. Eventually all except Minnesota reinstate some death penalty provisions.

1915 *Malloy v. South Carolina* upholds South Carolina's switch from execution by hanging to execution in the electric chair. By this time, 12 states have adopted electrocution as a method of execution: New York (1888), Ohio (1896), Massachusetts (1898), New Jersey (1907), Virginia (1908), North Carolina (1909), Kentucky (1910), South Carolina (1912), and Arkansas, Indiana, Pennsylvania, and Nebraska (1913).

1923 In *State v. Gee Jon*, Nevada's supreme court upholds Nevada's executions by the gas chamber.

1924 In Chicago, attorney Clarence Darrow pleads Richard Loeb and Nathan Leopold Jr. guilty to the kidnapping and murder of Leopold's 14-year-old cousin. Darrow claims that his clients were mentally disturbed as a result of their privileged social environment. His clients receive life sentences. Loeb is later murdered in prison; Leopold is paroled after 33 years.

1927 Nicola Sacco and Bartolomeo Vanzetti, Italian immigrants with anarchist sympathies, are electrocuted on August 27 by Massachusetts for two murders in 1920. Harvard Law professor Felix Frankfurter, later a Supreme Court justice, writes *The Case of Sacco and Vanzetti*, claiming that they were innocent.

1930s The federal government begins organized collection of crime statistics. Executions reach an all-time peak in the United States, averaging 167 a year.

1936 A crowd estimated at between 10,000 and 20,000 watches the hanging of Rainey Bethea in Owensboro, Kentucky. Kentucky abolishes public executions in 1938.

1937 A crowd estimated at 1,500 watches the last known public execution in the United States, the hanging of Roscoe Jackson in Galena, Missouri. Missouri switches to use of a gas chamber in 1938.

1947 *Louisiana ex rel. Francis v. Resweber* holds that the Due Process Clause does not make the Eighth Amendment binding on states.

1948 The UN General Assembly adopts the Universal Declaration of Human Rights by a vote of 48–0 (with 8 abstentions). Article 5 provides, "No one shall be subject to torture or to cruel, inhuman, or degrading treatment or punishment." Although the United States ratified the UN treaty and voted for the Universal Declaration, the Universal Declaration has no legal force in federal law.

1949 West Virginia becomes the last state to switch to electrocution as its method of execution.

1953 Julius and Ethel Rosenberg are electrocuted by the federal government for espionage.

1957 Alaska, Hawaii, and Delaware abolish the death penalty.

1958 *Trop v. Dulles* rules that loss of citizenship as a punishment for military desertion violates the Eighth Amendment. Four justices comment that there are weighty arguments against capital punishment too.

1959 Sociologist Thorsten Sellin publishes *The Death Penalty,* asserting that statistical comparisons of states with and without the death penalty show that the death penalty does not deter homicide. Sellin publishes additional studies showing that the death penalty for murdering police officers does not deter police murders, and the death penalty for life prisoners who murder does not deter prison murders.

1960 California executes Caryl Chessman, the "Red Light Bandit," for kidnapping and sexual assaulting (but not murder) women he stopped while impersonating a police officer. Chessman spent a then-record of 11 years on death row, with eight stays of execution and seven trips to the Supreme Court.

1961 Delaware readopts the death penalty.

1962   *Robinson v. California* holds that the Fourteenth Amendment makes the Eighth Amendment binding on states.

1963   In the last federal execution for 38 years, Victor Feguer is executed for interstate kidnapping and murder. Justice Arthur Goldberg urges abolition of the death penalty. Lee Harvey Oswald assassinates President Kennedy on November 23. Jack Ruby murders Oswald on November 24. A Texas jury finds Ruby guilty of murder and recommends the death penalty, but Ruby dies in prison in 1967.

1964   Oregon abolishes the death penalty.

1965   Iowa and West Virginia abolish the death penalty. Great Britain abolishes the death penalty.

1966   James French is electrocuted in Oklahoma. He reputedly tells newspaper reporters to run the headline, "French Fries."

1967   California executes Aaron Mitchell and Colorado executes Luis Jose Monge in their gas chambers. An unofficial moratorium on executions begins as class actions challenging the death penalty are litigated nationwide. Canada sharply restricts the death penalty.

1968   *United States v. Jackson* invalidates the federal death penalty for kidnapping.

1969   Jurors who have objections to the death penalty but who could nevertheless follow the judge's instructions cannot be excluded for cause from jury service (*Witherspoon v. Illinois*). *Boykin v. Alabama* rejects a death sentence for a defendant who pleaded guilty to five armed robberies because the guilty plea was not made voluntarily and with understanding of the potential penalty.

1970   *Maxwell v. Bishop* concludes that an Arkansas death sentence for rape was invalid because jurors opposed to the death penalty had been excluded, in violation of *Witherspoon v. Illinois*.

1971   *McGautha v. California* upholds a California law giving the jury complete discretion over the decision to return a death sentence or lesser punishment and an Ohio law allowing imposition of the death penalty without a separate penalty phase.

1972   California's supreme court finds California's death penalty is both cruel and unusual (*People v. Anderson*); 104 inmates are taken off California's death row, including Charles Manson and Sirhan Sirhan. *Furman v. Georgia* holds that the death penalty is cruel and unusual punishment because juries impose sentences arbitrarily. The decision overturns all existing death penalty laws and death sentences.

1975   Economist Isaac Ehrlich publishes *The Deterrent Effects of Capital Punishment: A Matter of Life and Death*, asserting that statistical studies show that each death penalty execution saves approximately eight lives.

1976   Solicitor General Robert Bork, citing Ehrlich's study, argues to the Supreme Court that re-enacted death penalty statutes are constitutional. *Gregg v. Georgia* holds that Georgia's two-stage process—a trial on guilt followed by a penalty hearing—does not violate the Eighth Amendment. *Woodson v. North Carolina* and *Roberts v. Louisiana* find that mandatory death sentences are unconstitutional. Canada, which last executed anyone in 1962, abolishes the death penalty.

1977   Utah executes Gary Gilmore by firing squad. He is the first person executed in the United States in almost 10 years. Oklahoma is the first state to adopt lethal injection as its method of execution.

1979   The American Bar Association calls for improvements in the level of competency of counsel in capital cases.

1982   Texas executes Charles Brooks by lethal injection. He is the first person executed by this method in the United States.

1984   Six Virginia death row inmates escape from prison, triggering a massive manhunt. All six are recaptured within three weeks.

1986   Roger "Animal" DeGarmo claims that he auctioned two witness seats to his execution for $1,500 bids. Texas Department of Correction officials refuse to allow the sales. *Ford v. Wainwright* holds that the Eighth Amendment forbids the execution of persons who are insane. Chief Justice Rose Bird and Justices Joseph Grodin and Cruz Reynoso are removed in a California retention election. It is widely believed that voters responded to the justices' well-known opposition to the death penalty.

1988   *The Miami Herald* reports that Florida spent an average of $3.2 million per execution carried out from 1973 to 1988.

1989   *Penry v. Lynaugh* holds that the Eighth Amendment permits the execution of mentally retarded persons. *Stanford v. Kentucky* holds that the Eighth Amendment permits the death penalty for 16-year-old murderers. In 2003, Governor Paul Patton of Kentucky commutes Stanford's sentence to life imprisonment.

1992   After an all-night exchange of faxes in which the Supreme Court repeatedly overruled stays of execution by the Ninth Circuit Court of Appeals, California executes Robert Alton Harris in the gas chamber on April 21 for the murder of two teenagers in 1978. Virginia executes Roger Keith Coleman for a 1981 rape and murder. *Coleman v. Thompson* (1991) held that Coleman had no constitutional right to a competent attorney in a habeas corpus appeal, which was dismissed for being filed three days late. Despite media claims that Virginia possibly executed an innocent man, DNA testing in 2006 confirms that Coleman was in fact guilty. The *Dallas Morning Herald* reports that Texas spends an average of $2.3 million per death penalty prosecution.

1993   Kirk Bloodsworth becomes the first person exonerated by DNA evidence. After nine years in prison (two of them on death row) for the 1984 murder of a nine-year-old girl, Bloodsworth is set free by a judge and later pardoned by Maryland's governor. In 2004, Kimberly Ruffner pleaded guilty to that murder and received a life sentence. Washington executes Westley Dodd by hanging. Helen Prejean, C.S.J., writes *Dead Man Walking: An Eyewitness Account of the Death Penalty in the United States*. It is made into a hit movie in 1995, changing the method of execution used from electrocution to lethal injection.

1994   President Clinton signs the Federal Death Penalty Act of 1994, making dozens of federal crimes subject to death penalty "if death results" in the course of the crime. Illinois executes John Wayne Gacy for 33 murders committed before 1980, mostly of young boys whose bodies were buried under the crawl space beneath Gacy's residence. A federal judge holds that Washington may not execute Mitchell Edward Rupe by hanging because Rupe had gained so much weight in prison that he likely would be decapitated during a hanging. Rupe dies in prison, in 2006, of natural causes. Kansas reinstates the death penalty for murder. In *Callins v. Collins*, Justice Blackmun declares his opposition to any use of the death penalty.

1995   New York reinstates the death penalty for murder after George Pataki, who campaigned in favor of capital punishment, is elected. Justice John Paul Stevens speculates that excessive time on death row may violate the Eighth Amendment. Later, Justice Stephen Breyer agrees with Stevens, and Justice Clarence Thomas criticizes both, arguing that excessive delays are the result of the Supreme Court's "Byzantine death penalty jurisprudence."

1996   The Antiterrorism and Effective Death Penalty Amendments Act (AEDPA) becomes effective, limiting state prisoners in most cases to one federal habeas corpus petition and requiring federal courts to defer to state court rulings unless they are so unreasonably wrong that the error was beyond any possibility for fair-minded disagreement. In *Felker v. Turpin*, the

Supreme Court holds AEDPA constitutional. Delaware executes Billy Bailey by hanging after he declines the option of lethal injection. Utah executes John A. Taylor by firing squad. The Ninth Circuit Court of Appeals holds that California's method of execution by lethal gas is cruel and unusual punishment. California changes its default method of execution to lethal injection, but permits a condemned inmate to request the gas chamber.

1997   In February, the American Bar Association calls for moratorium on executions until death penalty fairness is assured. Timothy McVeigh is convicted and sentenced to death for the bombing of the Oklahoma City federal building in 1995.

1998   On Thanksgiving Day, seven Texas death row inmates escape their cells and one, Martin Gurule, makes it over the fence, triggering a massive manhunt. Gurule's body is found in a nearby river a week later.

1999   Journalism students at Northwestern University report on many cases in Illinois of innocent defendants being convicted and sentenced to death. Anthony Porter is freed from death row as a result. Federal government finishes work on a new federal death row at the United States Penitentiary in Terra Haute, Indiana. Arizona executes Karl LaGrand by lethal injection and his brother, Walter LaGrand, in the gas chamber. Russia abolishes the death penalty. President Boris Yeltsin commutes approximately 700 death sentences to terms of imprisonment.

2000   Columbia University professor James Liebman's study asserts that more than two-thirds of more than 4,500 death penalty cases between 1973 and 1995 were overturned at least once for serious trial error. Frank Lee Smith dies of cancer after 14 years on Florida's death row. Postmortem DNA testing exonerates him of participation in the 1985 rape and murder of an eight-year-old girl. Governor George Ryan declares a moratorium on executions in Illinois. Governor Jeanne Shaheen vetoes legislation that would have repealed the death penalty in New Hampshire. The move is symbolic only: New Hampshire's last execution was in 1939. Governor Frank O'Bannon orders a study of Indiana's death penalty system to ensure innocent persons are not executed.

2001   On his last day in office, President Clinton commutes the federal death sentence of drug kingpin Ronnie Chandler to life imprisonment. On June 11, Timothy McVeigh becomes the first person executed under the federal death penalty since 1963. Eight days later, Juan Raul Garza becomes the second.

2002   Ray Krone leaves an Arizona prison after DNA testing establishes probable guilt of another person. Krone, the 100th death-row prisoner to be freed as innocent, and Kirk Bloodsworth (see 1993) are invited to testify before a Senate committee. *Atkins v. Virginia* holds that the Eighth Amendment forbids execution of mentally retarded murderers. Governor Parris Glendenning declares a moratorium on executions in Maryland. Ohio executes Alton Coleman by lethal injection. Coleman had been on the death row of three states for a three-month spree in 1984, during which he committed robberies, rapes, and seven murders in Illinois, Indiana, and Ohio. A federal trial judge in New York City declares the Federal Death Penalty Act of 1994 unconstitutional because of the risk of executing innocent defendants. The Second Circuit Court of Appeals reverses his ruling five months later.

2003   On his last day in office, Governor George Ryan commutes to life imprisonment the death sentences of all 167 inmates on Illinois's death row. On his first day in office, Governor Robert Ehrlich rescinds the moratorium on executions in Maryland. A Virginia jury decides John Allen Muhammed should die for the first-degree murder of 10 persons killed in sniper attacks during 2002. A separate jury convicts his teenage accomplice, Lee Malvo, but declines to recommend the death penalty. Economists Lawrence Katz, Steven Levitt, and Ellen Shustorovich's *Prison Conditions, Capital Punishment,* *and Deterrence* offers statistics showing that the risk of death in prison from inmate violence and poor health care deters crime, while the death penalty is carried out so rarely that it has no additional deterrent effect. Economists H. Naci Mocan and R. Kaj Gittings's *Getting Off Death Row: Commuted Sentences and the Deterrent Effect of Capital Punishment* offers statistics showing that each execution deters approximately five murders, while each commutation of a death sentence causes about five murders. Economists Hashem Dezbaksh, Paul Rubin, and Joanna Shepherd's *Does Capital Punishment Have a Deterrent Effect? New Evidence from Postmoratorium Panel Data* provides statistics showing that execution deters approximately 18 murders.

2004 Maryland executes Steven Oken for rape and murder. A California jury convicts Scott Peterson for the first-degree murder of his pregnant wife. Peterson joins the nation's largest death row population in a state where more than 670 death sentences have been imposed but only 13 executions have been carried out since *Gregg v. Georgia* (1976). New York's Court of Appeals decides, in *People v. LaValle*, that New York's death penalty statute violates the state constitution and that death penalty cases can be brought only as noncapital cases until the legislature enacts a different sentencing statute. The death penalty is effectively ended in New York.

2005 President George W. Bush's State of the Union address announces an expansion of federal efforts to use DNA evidence to prevent wrongful convictions. *Roper v. Simmons* holds that the Eighth Amendment forbids the death penalty for murderers who commit their crimes before age 18. The *Stanford Law Review* devotes an entire issue to the discussion of modern studies addressing whether the death penalty deters crime. Law professor John Donohue and economist Justin Wolfers publish *Uses and Abuses of Empirical Evidence in the Death Penalty Debate*, asserting that after almost 40 years Sellin's 1967 study is close to state of the art. The only clear conclusion is that too few executions are carried out to determine the effect of the death penalty on the homicide rate.

2006 Richard Moore, age 76, dies of old age after 26 years on Indiana's death row for the shotgun murders of his ex-wife, father-in-law, and a police officer responding to the crime. Governor Richard Codey imposes moratorium on executions in New Jersey. The Ninth Circuit Court of Appeals (*Morales v. Hickman*) affirms a ruling that California can execute Michael Angelo Morales for the rape and murder of a 17-year-old girl if an anesthesiologist is present to make sure California's lethal injection protocol does not result in Morales regaining consciousness and suffering pain during the execution. No anesthesiologist is found who will take part. Morales remains on death row. Economist Paul Zimmerman's *Estimates of the Deterrent Effect of Alternative Execution Methods in the United States: 1978–2000* offers statistics showing that while electrocution deters murder, other methods such as lethal injection do not.

2007 In South Dakota's first execution in 60 years, Elijah Page is executed by lethal injection. The UN General Assembly approves a nonbinding recommendation for a moratorium on the death penalty. New Jersey repeals its death penalty statute, the first state to do so since *Gregg v. Georgia* (1976).

In *People v. John Taylor*, A New York court applies an anti–death penalty ruling to vacate the sentence of the state's last death-row inmate.

2008 Nebraska's supreme court decides, in *State v. Mata*, that use of the electric chair violates the state constitution, but affirms Raymond Mata's death sentence if the legislature passes a constitutional method of execution. *Baze v. Rees* holds that the Eighth Amendment permits the use of the three-drug method of lethal injection. *Kennedy v. Louisiana* holds that the Eighth Amendment forbids the death penalty for rape of a child not resulting in death. Texas executes Jose Ernesto Medellin for his part in the gang rape and murder of two teenage girls in 1993. Medellin, a Mexican national living in Texas since childhood, draws international attention after a ruling by the International Court of Justice that Mexican citizens should be allowed to raise the claim that they had been denied information under the Vienna Convention about their right to contact the Mexican consulate. The Supreme Court holds in *Medellin v. Texas* that although the United States ratified the Vienna Convention, Texas is not required to obey the decision of the International Court of Justice, or even President George W. Bush's memorandum that Texas courts should hear Medellin's claim. Law professor Jon Gould and attorney Lisa Greenman publish a study for the Judicial Conference of the United States, examining the costs of defending federal death penalty cases in 119 cases between 1998 and 2004 in which the federal death penalty was authorized. *Report on the Cost Quality and Availability of Defense Representation in Federal Death Penalty Cases* concludes that the median cost of defense in such cases is approximately $353,000, seven times the median cost when the death penalty is not sought.

2009 New Mexico repeals the death penalty, the second state to do so since *Gregg v. Georgia*. Washington State's supreme court stays executions pending a hearing on whether its lethal injection method inflicts cruel and unusual punishment. In *In re Davis*, the Supreme Court orders a hearing to determine whether evidence discovered after trial established that Troy Davis was innocent of the 1989 murder of a police officer. After proceedings conclude, Georgia executes Troy Davis.

2010 Utah executes Ronnie Lee Gardner by firing squad for a 1985 murder he committed during an escape attempt.

2011 Governor John Kitzhaber imposes a moratorium on executions in Oregon. Illinois repeals the death penalty.

2012 The *Salt Lake Tribune* reports that a study commissioned by the Utah legislature estimates the cost of a capital case in Utah to be $1.6 million more than one seeking life without parole. Connecticut repeals the death penalty.

2013 Maryland repeals the death penalty.

2014 A federal trial judge declares California's death penalty unconstitutional. The Ninth Circuit Court of Appeals reverses his ruling 16 months later.

2015 Nebraska repeals the death penalty, pending voter referendum in November 2016. Governor Tom Wolf imposes a moratorium on executions in Pennsylvania. Dissenting in *Glossip v. Gross*, Justice Stephen Breyer urges the Court, "rather than try to patch up the death penalty's legal wounds one at a time," to consider whether the death penalty violates the Constitution. Justice Antonin Scalia responds, "Welcome to Groundhog Day."

2016 In *Kansas v. Carr*, the Supreme Court holds that individualized capital sentencing procedures are not required where multiple defendants took part in the same capital murder because separate juries would increase the risk of inconsistent results. In *Hurst v. Florida*, the Supreme Court invalidates Florida's capital sentencing procedure that permits a judge to impose a death sentence, with a jury playing only an advisory role, because the "Sixth Amendment requires a jury, not a judge, to find each fact necessary to impose a sentence of death." In *White v. Wheeler*, the Supreme Court unanimously scolds the Sixth Circuit Court of Appeals for repeatedly using habeas corpus to overturn death sentences without following AEDPA's requirement of deference to state court findings. The Delaware Supreme Court strikes down the state's death penalty law.

2017 Arkansas Governor Asa Hutchinson announced plans to execute eight men in 11 days starting April 17 before the State's supply of midazolam, the anesthetic used in the lethal injection cocktail, expired at the end of the month. No state executed this many people in such a compressed time span since capital punishment was reinstated in 1976. Court orders stayed the executions of four of these inmates: Bruce Ward, Don Davis, Stacey Johnson, and Jason McGehee. Four of the executions were carried out: Ledell Lee (on April 20), Jack Jones and Marcel Williams (both on April 24), and Kenneth Williams (on April 27). Ledell Lee's final plea for a stay of execution was rejected by the U.S. Supreme Court by a 5–4 vote with newly appointed Justice Neil Gorsuch, in his first recorded vote, providing the fifth vote allowing the execution to proceed. Justices Stephen Breyer and Sonia Sotomayor wrote separate dissents. Breyer repeated his view that the randomness and arbitrariness with which executions are carried out contravenes the purpose of a rule of law. Sotomayor reiterated her concerns about the dangers of midazalom.

2017   Eric Matthew Frein was sentenced to death on April 26 for killing a Pennsylvania state trooper and seriously wounding another in a 2014 ambush. Governor Tom Wolf put all Pennsylvania executions on hold in 2015 while waiting for a legislative commission to issue a report on capital punishment. The last execution in the Commonwealth was performed in 1999.

2017   After a U.S. District Court found Ohio's lethal injection procedures unconstitutional, Governor John Kasich postponed the execution dates for several inmates pending full review from the U.S. Sixth Circuit Court of Appeals. Nine executions were delayed.

When a term has several meanings, only the one relevant to the subject of capital punishment is included.

abolitionist   A person who opposes the death penalty in all circumstances and wants capital punishment abolished.

actual innocence   A claim that a defendant as a matter of fact did not commit a crime, as distinguished from a claim that a defendant is not guilty because of lack of proof or because of a legal error.

AEDPA (Antiterrorism and Effective Death Penalty Act of 1996)   Congress's only significant law regarding **habeas corpus**, it imposes a one-year statute of limitations on filing federal petitions and forbids federal courts from freeing state prisoners unless the state court's rulings were not only wrong but so unreasonable that no fair-minded judge could agree with them. The Supreme Court upheld AEDPA in *Felker v. Turpin* (1996) and repeated in *Harrington v. Richter* (2011) that habeas corpus was for the correction of "extreme malfunctions" only, not of all errors.

appeal   A request to a higher court to overturn a lower-court decision. The Supreme Court and the highest court of many states can decline to hear an appeal (discretionary review); in many states, the highest court must accept death penalty appeals (mandatory review).

bill of rights The first 10 amendments to the Constitution, ratified in 1791. Originally a limit on the power of the federal government, the Bill of Rights now also prevents state and local governments from violating individual rights.

capital punishment Inflicting death as the legal punishment for a crime.

commutation A legal action by the president or a governor reducing the severity of a criminal sentence, especially by reducing a death sentence to a sentence of life imprisonment; also called a *pardon*, especially when it results in release from imprisonment.

Constitution of the United States The fundamental law of the United States, drafted by the Constitutional Convention in Philadelphia in 1787, ratified in 1789, and amended 27 times since. Article VI requires all federal and state officials to swear or affirm their support for the Constitution as "the supreme Law of the Land . . . any Thing in the Constitution or Laws of any State to the Contrary notwithstanding."

court A government body presided over by a judge (sometimes with a jury) that makes decisions about legal rights. A *trial court* hears evidence and makes findings of fact. In the federal system, *district courts* are trial courts; there are 94 federal districts, 1 or more in each state. *Appeals courts* review judgments of the trial court but they do not conduct their own trials; there are 13 federal courts of appeals, 12 of which are defined by geographic region (or *circuit*). The *Supreme Court* is the highest federal appeals court.

court-appointed counsel A lawyer assigned by a judge to represent a defendant, usually because the defendant cannot afford one. The Sixth Amendment guarantees a right to counsel but is silent about court-appointed counsel. Federal and state statutes guarantee court-appointed counsel in capital cases. Because court-appointed counsel are paid by state and local governments at lower rates than retained attorneys, there are complaints that they may lack experience or have insufficient resources to mount effective defenses. Some states have prescribed minimum qualifications for court-appointed counsel in capital cases.

crime An act forbidden by the laws of a particular state or the federal government. The same act may be both a state and a federal crime. A murder during a carjacking would be a crime under state law and also a federal crime under Congress's power to regulate interstate commerce. Prosecution by both federal and state authorities does not violate the Fifth Amendment's Double Jeopardy Clause.

death-qualified jury In a capital case, each juror has sworn that she or he is willing to sentence a guilty defendant to death should the evidence warrant it. A person who cannot put personal reservations aside can be excluded from jury service in a capital case.

death row The section of a prison in which condemned prisoners are held awaiting execution.

Eighth Amendment "Excessive bail shall not be required, nor excessive fines imposed, nor cruel and unusual punishments inflicted."

federal Pertaining to the United States as a whole or to the national government.

habeas corpus Latin for "you have the body." It is used to determine the legality of a person's detention.

judge A public official who presides over trials and makes legal rulings. In the federal system, judges are appointed by the president, confirmed by the Senate, and serve for life unless impeached. State selection processes vary.

judicial review The power of a court to decide whether a law or government action is consistent with a state or federal constitution. The Supreme Court is the final arbiter of whether federal or state laws or government actions are constitutional.

jury nullification   The jury's refusal to convict a defendant they believe to be guilty under the law because they consider the law to be wrong or the punishment too harsh.

life without parole (LWOP)   A sentence requiring that the person never be released from imprisonment. A convict can be released by commutation, pardon, or change in the law.

murder   Unlawful, intentional killing. Capital punishment can be inflicted only for the most serious murders (*murder* or *first-degree murder*) in which the defendant specifically intended to cause death and aggravating circumstances are present. State laws may define aggravating circumstances differently.

opinion   The written explanation for a court's decision. A *majority opinion* of the Supreme Court has the support of five or more justices. A *plurality opinion* receives fewer than five votes but more than any other opinion. A *concurring opinion* agrees with the result but offers additional reasoning. A *dissenting opinion* disagrees with the decision.

penalty or sentencing phase   The second part of a capital murder trial, held after the defendant's guilt has been established (*guilt phase*), to determine whether the sentence will be death or some lesser penalty.

recidivist   A repeat offender. Recidivist murder is an aggravating circumstance (see **murder**) under most state's laws.

retentionist   One who wants the death penalty retained for murder.

state court   Part of the judicial system of a particular state. A state court can interpret its state's constitution to afford *more* protection to persons than the U.S. Constitution gives them.

writ of certiorari   Latin for "to certify." It is an order by the Supreme Court to a court of appeals or to the highest court of a state accepting a federal question for discretionary review. It takes the votes of four justices to "grant cert."

About the Authors

Joseph A. Melusky serves as professor of political science, director of the Center for the Study of Government and Law, coordinator of Public Administration/Government Service, and director of the Pre-Law Program at Saint Francis University. He has been a full-time member of the teaching faculty at Saint Francis since 1980. He has received a number of teaching awards including the Swatsworth Award, the Honor Society Outstanding Faculty Award, the Alumni Association's Distinguished Faculty Award, and the Dr. John F. Coleman Award for Outstanding Teaching and Research. He has served as interim vice president for Academic Affairs, chair of the Department of History and Political Science, chair of the Education Department, and dean of General Education. He is a former president and vice president of the Pennsylvania Political Science Association, former executive director, president, and vice president of the Northeastern Political Science Association (NPSA), and former member of the Executive Council of the Pennsylvania Humanities Council. He is director of Employment Services of the NPSA. He has served as a judge of elections in Blair County, Pennsylvania, since 1997. He has published numerous papers and several books including, *The Death Penalty: Documents Decoded* (2014), *Capital Punishment* (2011), *Cruel and Unusual Punishment: Rights and Liberties under the Law* (2003; all with Keith A. Pesto), *The Contemporary Constitution: Modern Interpretations* (2006), *The American Political System: An Owner's Manual* (2000), *The Bill of Rights: Our Written Legacy* (1993; with Whitman Ridgway), *To Preserve These Rights: The*

Bill of Rights 1791–1991 (1991), and *The Constitution: Our Written Legacy* (1991). He earned his M.A. and Ph.D. in political science from the University of Delaware and has done postgraduate work at the Universities of Delaware and Michigan and Carnegie-Mellon University.

Keith A. Pesto is the U.S. Magistrate Judge for the Johnstown Division of the U.S. District Court for the Western District of Pennsylvania, a post he has held since 1994. He has also been a lecturer at Saint Francis University, Loretto, Pennsylvania, and Juniata College, Huntingdon, Pennsylvania. With Joseph Melusky, he is coauthor of *The Death Penalty: Documents Decoded* (2014), *Capital Punishment* (2011), and *Cruel and Unusual Punishment: Rights and Liberties under the Law* (2003). He earned his BA in political economy from Johns Hopkins University in 1980 and his J.D. from the University of Pennsylvania in 1983.